AMAZON LEARNING CONSUMER BEHAVIOR STRATEGY

JOHN LOK

Contents

Preface

Introduction

Nowadays, many businesses had begun to apply internet to operate their online businesses. So, online business model will be very popular to let global online buyers can apply internet channel to buy any kinds of products, they are living far away from themselves countries. It implies that future e-commerce market competition will be very serious. However, some businessmen still feel shops and online-stores both sale mode may be attractive sale channels to let consumers to choose their products to buy. On another side, some businessmen only feel online-stores sale channel is the best sale mode or another side, some businessmen only feel visiting shop method is only the traditional best sale mode.

In my this book, I shall indicate the most famous Amazon e-commerce organization will face what kinds of marketing competitive challenges, how Amazon ought implement its management and marketing both strategies to solve Amazon future possible competitive challenges. Does Amazon need facility management department? What function of benefits will bring when Amazon sets up one facility management department? Why Amazon need to learn human behavior If the Amazon lacked one facility management department, what the disadvantage it will bring to influence the Amazon organization's operation? Have they relationship between raising efficiency or improving performance and facility management to Amazon ecommerce department? I believe that Amazon is global the best famous and successful e-commerce organization. It needs to solve how to persuade online buyers to prefer to click its web-stores to choose to buy any kinds of brands products as well as how to persuade its any kinds of brands of sellers to choose to apply its online purchase channels to instead themselves online purchase channels. I hope my readers can have more clear understanding whether future what challenges that Amazon may face and how it can implement strategies to solve its future competitive challenges.

Prologue

Table of content

ONE

AMAZON KNOWLEDGE INNOVATION STRATEGY

There are both kinds of knowledge innovation influences to Amazon ecommerce organization develops in success, one is e-commerce technological knowlegge as well as another is social innovation knowledge. I shall explain the reasons why these both knowledge may cause Amazon e-commerce organization grows in success as below:

E-commerce technological knowledge innovation

What does knowledge innovation mean? Why and how does Amazon ecommerce organization need to continue to innovate its online shopping knowledge sale channel? Can knowledge innovation impact positive online shoppers number grow to Amazon? Why does Amazon ecommerce organization apply knowledge innovation strategy to grow itself organization to achieve global online buyers number in success? In fact, when we can prepare to innovate our knowledge to be perfect. Consequently, it can help our social development more success, e.g. non manual driving vehicle, e-commerce, construction houses on water skill, hospital new robotic surgeon equipment, manufacturing robotic technology , even space tourism leisure development etc. different kinds of technology innovation, they are depended on how human can attempt to learn to innovate or improve ourselves traditional old knowledge to be changed to any kinds of new or not discovered unique knowledge. So, human ought need to continue to learn how to innovate our old traditional knowledge to be more perfect. The question concerns how human can continue to change our old knowledge to innovate in succeed. I shall attempt to indicate how Amazon ecommerce organization can apply knowledge management innovation strategy to improve itself online pucrhase and sale platform to attract global many online buyers number choose its any kinds of product online purchase channel in preference as below:

What does knowledge innovation mean? The role of knowledge innovation means that knowledge management assists in building competencies required in the innovation process. Though knowledge accessibility and knowledge flow to organization, staff members are able to increase their skills levels and knowledge both formally and informally. An increase in skills can improve the quality of innovation as well as in society. When the country have many people can attempt to learn how to change and knowledge old knowledge to new knowledge, then they my bring their societies to develop more rapidly. So, it seems that knowledge innovation may help society, organization and individual to bring new knowledge to attribute to our future societies easily. It will be a very important factor influence human future development in success.

However, knowledge innovation concept is not just represented by introducing or implementing new ideas or methods. The definition of meaning of innovation can be defined as a process, but involves multiple activities to uncover new ways to do things. Innovating helps developing original concepts and is to driver of optimizing operations. The purpose of innovation is to come up with new ideas and technologies that increase productivity and generate greater

output with the same input on organizational aspect.
So, knowledge innovation may be applied on organization aspect, such as Amazon ecommerce organization, even individual and social aspects. On Amazon ecommerce organizational knowledge innovation aspect, innovation secures tomorrow's revenue, lowers costs and differentiates companies from the market. However, a good business model that only provides a brief market advantage and disappears after a year is not the right approach. Hence, organizational knowledge innovation aims to help the organization to raise competitive effort in long term.
Does knowledge provide innovation in Amazon ecommerce organization? Knowledge management creates a culture conductive to tacit knowledge creation, sharing ideas in the organization, which plays an important role in the innovation process. Is knowledge management necessary for innovation? Beside the financial basis knowledge is the most important resource for innovations, in order to lead a company successfully, systematic handling of " knowledge", becomes more important. Today, the increase in value develops from the productivity and the innovation in business society.
What is the role of knowledge for individual? Knowledge is important for personal growth and development, knowledge sharpens our skills like reasoning and problem solving. A strong base of knowledge helps brains function more smoothly and effectively. We become smarter with the power of knowledge and solve problems more easily. Hence, innovation is about knowledge creating new possibilities through combining different knowledge sets. These can be in the form of knowledge about what is technically possible or not particular configuration of this world meet an articulated or latent need.
For Amazon knowledge innovation can bring the positive effects of technology improvement example, there are just a few of the ways in which technology may positively affect our physical and mental health. Health apps to track chronic illnesses and communicate vital information to doctors , health apps that anyone tracks diet,

any kinds of sport exercise and mental health information . Hence, technology innovation had been applied to health apps smart phone product to help we to track our health from ourselves smart phone apps equipment easily any time.

What impact did this innovation have on daily life? It increased the regional differences among various groups of people across the country, it become a major method of long distance communication to many years. It allowed people to sign documents from across the country. So, innovation can be applied to administer tasks aspect. Also, it can increase productivity and brings citizens new and better goods and services that improves our overall standard of living.

The benefits of innovation are sometimes slow to materialize. They often fell broadly across the entire population. According to Krathwohl (2002), he indicated that knowledge can be categorized into four types: (1) factual knowledge (2) conceptual knowledge (3) procedural knowledge and (4) metacognitive knowledge. So, if human hopes to implement knowledge innovation in success, we need to know how to learn these 4 types of knowledge innovation elements. For organizational knowledge management components example, the best four components are people, process, content/ IT and strategy.

Regardless of the industry size or knowledge needs of Amazon ecommerce organizations, organizations always need people to lead, sponsor, and support knowledge sharing. Sharing knowledge innovation how influences social development. Social innovation includes social processes of innovation, such as open source methods and techniques and also the innovation which have a social purpose, like activism , virtual volunteering, or distance learning. Social innovation may include the social processes of innovation. However, social innovation is important because it can provide a unique opportunity to step back from a narrow way of thinking about social enterprise, business engagement and to recognize instead the interconnectedness of various factors and stakeholders. For science and technological social innovation example, science and technology can help a nation's process and development science and technology innovation are connected with development because they have historical record of bringing advances that have led to healthier, longer, and more productive lives and they are key ingredients to solutions to the most serious poverty and economic development challenges.

Social knowledge innovation

So, social innovation may bring human benefits, such as providing food and lifestyle products world wide with focus on environmental and social innovation , giving every child in the world the chance to learn code and helping the visually impaired interact with their surroundings. Hence, social innovation means new solutions (products, services, models, markets, processes etc.) that stimultaneously meet a social need (more effectively than existing solutions) and lead to new or improved capabilities and relationships and better use of assets and resources. However, a social innovation process consists of a sequence of activities that seals to find solutions to a special challenge. The process itself brings a new approach that has social impact in its means (process) and ends (solution).

There are 6 keys characteristics of a social innovation, as told by Colombian social enterprises, they include: Addresses real needs of people in a community, requires a deep understanding of the problem, localizes and humanizes the problem, builds trust and collaborates with the community in need, is sustainable and scalable and adapts constantly. Hence, every one may attempt to learn in social innovation. You will learn what social innovations are and understand how they are help solve societal problems. You will get an overview of important literature and debates on social innovation. You will also learn and apply methods to develop , implement and scale social innovations.

How can social innovation be improved to apply to Amazon ecommerce organization case? Major cross business/cross functional projects should also have social innovation objectives include: leadership programs that include volunteering activities may help employees develop their skills and lead to greater innovations during their daily work in any organizations. How does the idea of social innovation connect with social needs? We define social innovations as new approaches to addressing social needs. They are social in their means and in their ends. They engage and mobilize the beneficiaries and help the transform social relations by improving beneficiaries' access to power and resources.

For social innovation on education aspect, teaching technological literacy, critical thinking and problem, solving through science education gives students the skills and knowledge, they need to succeed in school and beyond. The essence of how science and technology contributes to society in the creation of new knowledge , and then utilization of that knowledge to boost the prosperity of human lives, and to solve the various issues facing society. Hence, when many consumers believe online shopping channel is one kind of convenient visa card payment and safe purchase , rapid goods transport to different countries, many different kinds of products choice channel. Consequently, global societies will be influenced to accept online shopping method / mode to replace traditional shops visting purchase mode. This kind of social online purchase knowledge innovation may influence Amazon ecommerce organization develops in success in long future days.

Amazon ecommerce organization warehouse products transport process and workplace innovation

How Amazon needs to consider warehouse goods delivery service tasks ?

Why does Amazon need to innovate its warehouse products transport process to raise rapid products delivery service to different countries consumers as well as let buyers can view any products photos to feel their good quality, good design shape to attract customers consideration from its websites/ web stores in short time? What advantages will be bought to Amazon after Amazon warehouse delivery products had been innovated in success? Can products innovation help the product to improve its market image to Amazon? Can product innovation raise Amazon growth? I shall attempt to indicate reasons to explain above questions?

In our business societies, any products ought need to be concerned how to innovate them to be good quality. The key practical benefits of innovation may include: Improved productivity, reduced cots, increased competitiveness, improved brand recognition and value, building new business partners relationship, helping the business to increase turnover and improved profitability.

So, it seems that product innovation may bring positive impact more than negative impact to any businesses. In fact, after the buy innovates itself products, innovation ought may help the business to charge higher prices for new products before competitors products come on the market. Being innovative good for the firm's reputation, even people naturally interested in its future products, if they have been first in the past as well as innovations in processes can add value to existing products/ services.

So, the meant is by product innovation, it means that a product innovation is the introduction of a good or service that is new or significantly improved with respect to its characteristics of intended uses. Mainly, these reasons can explain why innovation is important: Innovation grows business, increasing profit, innovation helps any businesses stay ahead of the competition, innovation helps businesses take advantage of new technologies, such as Amazon ought need to innovate its warehouse products delivery service to let global buyers feel Amazon can provide rapid products delivery service to themselves homes after they paid visa card to buy any Amazon products from its web stores rapidly. On organizational benefit aspect to Amazon warehouse products delivery service innovation, innovation may help Amazon organization differentiates its 3 rd parties sellers themselves products when they decide to display their products photos on Amazon web stores, e.g. if your organization is using innovation on its processes, its because doing so will save your time, money, or other resources, and give your organization a competitive advantage over other companies stuck in their system.

In common, innovation may include four types. Incremental,

disruptive , archihectural and radical, they help illustrate the various ways that companies can innovate. For technological innovative advantages, it increases productivity and brings citizens new and better goods and services that improve their goods and service that improve their overall standard of living.

The benefits of innovation are sometimes slow to materialize. They often broadly across the entire population. Hence, the advantage of product innovation may include: Growth, expansion and gaining a competitive advantage. A business that is capable of differentiating their product from other businesses in the same industry to large extent will be able to reap profit. Examples of product innovation in improved products involves introducing beter or more functionality to existing products, e.g. electric and gas lawn mower, GPs in car , battery car, non-manual driving auto car etc. So, product innovation is the creation, development and implementation, a new product, process and service, with the aim of improving efficiency, effectiveness or competitive advantages. Such as Amazon case, it needs to make products AI warehouse delivery service innovation, e.g. chaning to artificial intelligent products delivery service from workers delivery service in order to raise its goods can delivered to different countries buyers homes in the shortest time rapidly every day.

How does innovation help Amazon ecommerce organization grows its online buyers number? In fact, one of the major benefits of innovation is its contribution to economic growth. Simply put, innovation can lead to higher productivity, meaning that the same input generates a greater output. As productivity rises, more goods and services are produced. In other words, Amazon online buyers number grows.

Instead of innovation on product aspect, innovation is also important in the workplace, it can help staffs to raise efficiency. Innovation is vital in the workplace, because it gives companies an edge in penetrating markets faster and provides a better connection to developing markets, which can lead to bigger opportunities, especially in rich countries or developed countries.

However, when an organization decides to implement innovation before it implements , it needs to concern these possible risks of innovation. Operational risk, e.g. failing to meet your quality, cost or scheduling requirements, commercial risk, e.g. failing to attract enough customers, financial risk,, e.g. investing in unsuccessful innovation projects. But, when the organization decides to implement any innovation, it may hope innovation how contribute to success. Especially as customers become more demanding. Entrepreneurs need an innovation to survive to boost your business productivity, growth and profitability more easily.

IN simple, innovation may improve sales and customer relationship, reduce waste and costs boost your market position, improve employee relations. What does the right time to organizations make decisions to innovate ? When the firm discovers its customers use the product and they field praise and complaints. And they probably have ideas, however, that can be refined into a better product. Innovative companies make it clear they want ideas, that the door is open and there is always a friendly ear for changes, then they will start to come it. It may be right innovation time, when customers have any unique idea to concern the product after they use.

What is required to introduce innovation in an organization, such as Amazon ecommerce organization? To successfully implement innovation, you need to know exactly what makes an innovative organization as well as how it contributes to its growth. Our organizaitons also need to require an innovative culture where everyone is able to think independently . So, these reasons can explain why our organizations ought need to innovate, being bold in taking on the innovation challenge build people's readiness and receptivity to change, assisting people to resolve their unconscious biases and resistance to it, developing both customer intimacy and customer empathy. However, although innovation can bring positive impact in a business, but it is so difficult to implement because new ideas and initiative depend on the people who work for the organizations. It is a lot harder to achieve desired results.

Innovation is not about optimizing gross margins , but about attempt how finding new ways to create more value for yourselves profit image to attract more customers consideration.

Innovation is difficult to implement, because no system, process, or industry knows how to change, more innovations are worth exploring for many. Technology for example, can be re-purposed into new innovative solutions provide your customers with new value. The challenge is that when it comes to disruptive innovation, it almost always involves " higher risk" compared to incremental changes and thus can not be managed the same way as regular business projects are managed.

Hence, maintaining quality and product improvement and process development often involves standardization, whereas innovation can rarely be standardized . Also, new innovationds can not be measured using the same metrics and value drivers as the existing products and services . To overcome this major barrier to innovation, companies should approach disruptive innovation differently compared to how they are used to approaching regular projects. This, any organizations need to understand that they may fail to innovate. In the beginning, innovation and most specifically disruptive kind, is inferior to the existing products and services on the market. Because product improvement takes a lot of time and requires multiple iterations, the value for the customer at this point is minimal , when distuptive innovation initally caters only to a small and not so profitable customer base, established organizations are focused on serving more demanding, high and customers using their existing value channels. This is where it typically has higher profit margins, which is why established companies with rational decision-making processes usually choose not to invest in disruptive initiatives in the early stages. The problem occurs when incumbents attempt to apply new technologies to their existing value networks or refuse moving into new markets because they are seen as too small to drive growth goals or are simply perceived to have too low margins. So, for organizations that prioritize reaching scale through operational efficiency, it makes more sense to focus on growing the business through incremental means, such as invest in risky and uncertain innovations.

On conclusion, in reality, however, Amazon ecommerce organization needs to do both simultaneously improve the core business and exploit new business opportunities . Hence, when Amazon organization decides to innovate its 3 rd party sellers their product, on warehouse goods AI delivery processing or AI workplace safe working environment . Amazon needs to find a balance between different types of innovations to choose which is the most effective goods delivery and warehouse workplace safe and efficient goods delivery innovation, which is a lot more sustainable may be stay in the Amazon e-business growth in the long term to in order to implement Amazon AI warehouse goods delivery service and warehouse working environment efficient and safe workplace innovation in order to let its all warehouse workers to feel comfortable and safe feeling and raise their goods delivery tasks efficiently.

AI creates Amazon efficient service growth

How does (AI) technological development will influence Amazon develops in success ?

(AI) robotic automation technology can bring Amazon warehouse goods delivery service task more efficient

Future, (AI) robotic automation technology can be applied to Amazon warehouse goods delivery tasks in order to help it to shorten goods transport time to be delivered to overseas different countries buyers homes in the shortest time rapidly every day. For example, nowadays, UK computer and space explore technology had reached the mature stage. It means that UK government ought not need to continue spend much resource to research these two kind technologies. Otherwise, the (AI)robotic automatic manufacturing technology, e.g. human intelligence new product. It has need to develop because human intelligence machines will bring beneficial to satisfy human everyday life need, e.g. hospital patients' activities need, if the patent who can not walk easily, but the human intelligence machine can assist the patient walk to anywhere conveniently. So, he/she does not need to sit on wheel chair and apply the human intelligence machine man to help him/her to drive on the intelligence automatic driving vehicle to go to anywhere conveniently.

Otherwise, increased automation in low wage countries, e.g. China, Korea, Africa, Hong Kong etc. which have traditionally manufacturing firms, could use automatic technological manufacturing to bring lose cost advantage and potentially lose their ability of achieving rapid economy growth by shifting workers to factory jobs. So, UK government and businessmen needs to consider automation technology development, i.e. 3D printing manufacturing industry will encourage UK companies to move manufacturing process, closer to gain the biggest advantage from this 3D automation technology development.

A growing concern of premature de-industrialization in energy and developing countries could require new models and a need un-skillful the UK workforce. In the future, the best way toward for UK cities will reduce their exposure to automation is to boost their technological dynamic and attract more UK skilled workers. Automation technology progress can give UK manufacturers' employee benefits, such as long term healthy productivity improvement, raising productivity efficiency and product quality, macroeconomic and microeconomic effects of automation technological change, it's change will be beneficial to UK society, i.e. automation active labor market policies, which could help UK job seekers find jobs from training to incentive to support self-employment to create high technological job employment chance in UK society. So, raising science, technology, engineering and math subjects update skills level are needed to UK any universities, which can be increasingly important in UK society, these factors could complicate the ability of UK high automation technology education to adopt to the UK automation manufacturing technological change. A talent mismatch already exists in UK, with many well UK educated workers can find employment in lower-skilled jobs.

To combat this, greater coordination will be needed between the education, training and employment sectors in UK society.
Why are high automatic technology product development models needed to improve to Amazon warehouse goods delivery improvement service ? UK government and manufacturers need to consider how to achieve high technology product development models. According to Hauser et al. (2006) indicated the high technology (high tech.) development process, is influenced by the innovative process, bringing products on exception value which stimulate product market demand. Innovation provides products the specific basis for which world economies compete with each other on the global market. Able to find new solutions, innovations generate significant changes in existing markets, destroy them, or create new marketing (Hauser et al. 2006). So, UK manufacturers need to concern on any manufacturing high technology product development process because which can influence any new products development to manufacture to sell to any overseas or domestic both markets successfully.
What does high tech. product warehouse goods delivery transport service improvement mean? Mohr et al. (2010) argues that there are two reasons why it is important to clarify and specific high technology : (1) due to the impact of technologies on the economy, attempts are made to classify economic production and incomes ; (2) due to the impact of high tech. on the environment. Standard marketing strategies are being modified and adopted , therefore, it is necessary to know the products to focus on. Why does Amazon need to consider warehouse high technological product delivery transportation process? Nowadays, high tech. products are complex, advanced, requiring specific technical knowledge, which is technologically not discontinued and being produced at the companies which have twice as many technical personnel and invest twice as many in scientific research and development than other companies. Moreover, these products are time-sensitive as scientists are continuously searching for new approaches for invention of more advanced technologies which make all preceding

ones lower-ranking. The most important, nowadays global consumers will adopt the particular technology. It means that Amazon needs to improve high technological goods delivery service process to avoid the delay when global any online shoppers choose to buy any kinds of high technological products from Amazon web stores.

Anyway, nowadays customer individual needs in high tech. environments are characterized by sudden changes related to unpredictable fashion. Even, consumers concern about how to preserve new product' competitive technological standard is completely incompatible with technological uncertainty. The most important factor is the prevalence rate of any new products development process, which is influenced by slower than of traditional products. In many cases high-tech. automatic product market are being materialized slower than which are expected. The technological uncertainty challenges will exist in development process, such as uncertainty related to the timetable for development of the question whether the new product will be function as promised. In automatic high-tech. industries, the time requires for product development is difficult to predict as , commonly, it takes longer than expected , uncertainty related to unanticipated consequences and uncertainty about the product life cycle related to competition products. In conclusion, these factors will influence future Amazon any kinds of new automatic technological product warehouse delivery process to avoid to delay to deliver to different countries buyers themselves homes rapidly every day.

Future economists predict automatic technology how to influence future ecommerce goods efficient delivery service

Before, all over the world presented picture of demonstrate in London on the occasion of the meeting of the G20. Some economists indicated disastrous economy consequences will occur to any one of Western country , such as UK, so if any one of Western country did not consider automatic technology development to itself country. They indicated one example, such as material incentives to produce disappeared throughout Russia and, when Society leadership called off the experiment, the country faced industrial output reduced to 10% of what had been registered in 1914 and agricultural output reduced to such low levels as to cause widespread famine.

Why would UK encounter disastrous economy consequences if UK government did not encourage manufacturers spend money to invest to innovate automatic technology industry, such as Amazon online goods global delivery service case? According to a variety of anthropological studies, a collectivity is unable to operate efficiently with everybody giving talent workers have chance to devote whose best effort to manufacture any high technological products, e.g. human intelligence vehicle or airplane. Hence, economic incentives are needed to manufacturers to invest high technological automatic industry development. Because the economists predict future ecommerce organizations will have many talent worker numbers, their number will be more than a certain number of normal effort workers, due to technological education level is very excellent to provide to train many young technological manufacturing students to find this kind of high technological manufacturing job. So, the high technological manufacturing job seekers need to future ecommerce market in order to raise ecommerce any organizational development.

Assuming that future UK ecommerce market will have high technological automatic manufacturing workers who would desire only to introduce changes in the workings of the international e-commerce economic order and policies of countries participating in the present economic order rather than change the order itself, what will be UK manufacturers their specific economic preferences in the future? It implies that either concentrate on spending more investment to automatic high technological development, e.g. human intelligence automatic high technological products or still concentrate on spending more investment to common traditional technological products to future UK ecommerce market.

However, UK was a developed Western country which had had

strong automatic high technological development effort very long time. Otherwise, it compared to some developing countries, such as Asian China, Hong Kong, Korea etc. Asian countries their future economic growth rate will show un- surprising , different patterns, so the Asian countries has weak effort to invest high automatic technological product development, such as human intelligence technological development. The catching-up process suggests low economic growth rate in the high automatic technological product development to the Asian developing countries in the future.

Hence, the future economists predict that it views as probable successors of the Western world economic leadership if any Western country , such as UK manufacturers who prefer to invest to any high automatic technological products development , e.g. developing on human intelligence automatic technological products more than traditional common technological products development. On the one side, but it seems important to stress that two very poor countries among the challengers-China and India-are examples of countries that changed their institutions and economic policies from no or little economic freedom to more economic freedom. Because there two countries whose governments prefer to lend loans to encourage their country manufacturers prefer to invest high automatic technological products manufacturing. On the other side, attitudes toward foreign direct investment (FDI) have undergone change since the 1960 s and a large majority of less developed countries, e.g. China and India are now competing strongly among themselves and with developed market economies for direct investment from multinational companies. So, UK will face China and India high automatic technological product competitors in the future. And in fact, all countries that joined Western developed economies did that without much (if any) external inflow of public resources. It is right time that UK government needs to lend loans to encourage domestic manufacturers to invest high automatic technological products to raise whose international high technological products sale effort to win its future competitors. So, machine resources will be increased demand to o UK manufacturers if who chose to spend machine resources to innovate to manufacture any new and high technological automatic products to raise human daily life needs in the future. It means that it is right time UK manufacturers need buy much machines to prepare to manufacture many future high technological automatic products when these machine prices are low. Because the future global machine prices will possible be raised if many China and India manufacturers will also buy many machines in the future. For example, USA government had provided much financial support to assist sugar cane producers to develop their businesses. And they are dependent to a much larger extent than sugar cane producers and sugar processors in the USA on government. Without very high subsidies to renewable energy generation, they would not have survived at all. So, USA government had been the first country which could lent much financial assistance to encourage domestic renewable energy generation manufacturers to develop high technological energy manufacturing business. So, UK government needs follow USA to lend financial assistance to encourage domestic high technological automatic industry development.

Future economists also predict China and India will be competitors for future leadership in the global e-commerce economy, special high technological products. China has been the media and analyst's favorite for quite some time. Quantitative projections have seemingly supported such expectation. Such as China and India had manufactured many high technological new space rockets products, ocean war large ships etc. Moreover, China has become one of the major world trade players in the early twenty-first century.

Many long-term forecasts, assuming similarly high economic growth rates in the decades ahead, predict that China will surpass the USA in terms of aggregate GDP somewhere between 2020 and 2030 or later, say between 2030 and 2050 year. The future economists conclude on the basis of these predictions that China will not only pass the USA in aggregate product (GDP), but its economy and economic policies will influence the rest of the world to a similar extent that the USA does at present.

I stressed a very important point to future global ecommerce organization growth, namely that the UK future high technological automatic product competitor China and India, namely that economies not only grow, but in the process change their structure. China and India have been industry very rapidly (the first transition) and building the physical infrastructure that accompanies industrialization changes to technology in the future. However, at a certain per capita GNP level the two countries, such as China and India will face another structural shift when which technological development will reach the mature stage in the future. China and India had been primarily historical pattern of economic development because the shift in the role of engine of growth from industry to services is to a much greater extent a qualitative shift. Both higher and different skills are required. And, even more importantly, interactions generating ideas driving the highly human-capital-intensive service economy require a much freer environment, not only in the economic area. Chinese exports have been heavily labor-intensive. This being the case, they contributed to the expansion of industrial employment, offering for the first time in the history of China a taste of (very modest) prosperity to more than 100 million new industrial workers and their families. This is the major component of the success accomplished by Chinese economic growth. Richer trade partners create room for more trade, so the Chinese should hope that intra-South trade, that is, trade between the emerging economies of Asia, the Middle East, Africa and Latin America, will open up new and growing opportunities. I presume that if Western economy , such as UK did not developed high technological automatic industry to stable their social welfare, so thoroughly slowed down their economic growth.

Will it allow China to accomplish the transition to a mature, innovation, service-sector-based ecommerce market economy? It has allowed the economy to industrialize much more successfully, even if the labor shift from agriculture to industry has not yet been completed. But it is a long way off the next major test: the second high technological industry transition of the economic structure to China. Bear in mind that Russia attempted it twice and failed at both attempts.

But even, assuming that China at some point in the future does succeed in accomplishing the second transition, will it be able to supersede the USA, for example, as the main global high automatic technological innovation center if it wants to become the No.1 global high technological industry ecommerce economy? Given the nature of the centralized state and its stability to collect financial resources , China's ability to increase research and development expenditure to high automatic technological products and to hire a mass of researchers, engineers, technicians and other specialists should not be doubted. This process in already taking place.

But , again, Soviet Russia already exceed the USA in the R&D/GDP ratio in the 1970s, long before the communist collapse, with no effects on its innovativeness. Inputs matter less than outputs, quantity in the innovation process mean much less than quality. The latter characteristics depends importantly on economic, civic and even political institutions. Otherwise, independent India had three options open to it in 1946s. It could pursue spontaneous economic development, with some state intervention to be sure, along the lines of basically free market capitalism; it could turn the clock back and try to recreate the rural-agricultural and handicraft based. The dominant way of thinking was Society -style priority to industrialization and , within industralization , priority to heavy industry. In other words, not textiles and clothing, which has been developing well in India since the mid- nine teen century, but production of sewing machines and , even better, production of machines the produce sewing machines.

The results were only to be expected. The heavy stress on the expansion of capital-intensive heavy industries in a very poor country quickly strained the ability of the Indian economy to generate adequate savings. Moreover, some of these industries were above the level of industrial competence of an underdeveloped economy. Thus, the amount of required resources (capital, skilled labor) was usually larger per unit of output than in the same industries in more mature, richer industries economies. In another view point, India will develop light industries, just as any other poor country with a great deal of unskilled labor, had a comparative advantage and no less importantly, an economy in which, due to their low capital/labor ratio, light industries could employ many more people, spreading prosperity more widely in a poor country. So, it explain that why China will have more effort to develop heavy high technological industry in the future. Thus, India got less economic efficiency, less employment than in a spontaneously developing economy, less ability to compete internationally in light industries suitable for an underdeveloped economy and finally got heavy industry unable to compete even on the domestic market and, therefore requiring no less heavy a dose of protection. Overall India got an underperforming economy, in particular in its relations with the rest of the world.

To conclude by comparing the performance of the traditional sectors of the Indian economy and the performance of its modern, human -capital-intensive subsector of manufacturing and skill intensive service sector. The latter both employ workers with high- and medium -high skillful level (in branches ranging from computer software and biotechnology and pharmaceutical high technological light industry). India is ahead of China in terms of the output and export of such products and services. Thus, it implies that Amazon ecommerce organization ought concentrate on developing high automatic heavy high technological warehouse goods delivery service industry, e.g. human intelligence technological warehouse delivery products because these industry is not better development to other many countries' strong effort , such China and India large population countries, they still have weakness to develop warehouse AI delivery service skills in themselves ecommerce organizations.

TWO

AMAZON SUCCESS LEADERSHIP MANAGEMENT BEHAVIOR

How Amazon leader be one successful CEO?
If it is not, what are the unique personal characteristics between one general CEO and one successful CEO ? Instead of personal characteristics, which kinds of skills to any successful CEOs, they will need? Why do some CEOs encounter fail to manage themselves companies? Why do some CEOs feel difficulties to manage themselves companies? This book can indicate some evidences to explain what factors can influence the person can be successful CEO to let readers to understand. Readers can learn whether what personal factors can help general CEO to become excellent CEO in any organizations.

The different characteristics between common CEO and successful CEO
The characteristics of common CEO
What are the common characteristics to general CEO? IN general,

CEO person specification includes: High level of self-motivation, creativeness high level of self confidence. So, In general, qualities and traits of a chief executive officer, he /she may have courage, passion , but an excellent CEO is draw to change and effective action. Also CEO needs have resillence and drive ability. It means threat the CEOs, leaders ought know that taking risks and making large-scale changes can lead to organizational growth or can fall dramatically.

A CEO must posses certain traits to be an effective leader, e.g. ability to learn from the past experience, strong communication skills, building relationship, realistic optimism, easily understanding, listening people and adapting to necessary management styles.

What makes a good CEO leader? At a leader, a common CEO needs to posses strong communication skills. From motivating your employees to meeting set deadlines. You should have the ability to communicate your needs, when you hope to become a common CEO. If you want to be a good CEO, you must be consistently clear in your communication. But, some successful executives may have these 7 personality traits, such as visioning, in-depth problem solving and analysis, attapting change, driving for results, influencing and persuading, managing others, organizational resources allocation.

Hence, it seems that it is not all people these 7 successful CEO. In fact, many companies own common CEOs more than successful CEOs in human resource view. In general, an organizational leader (CEO) , he /she does not need special management train, he /she depends on his/her past working experiences training to climb up to become the company's leader. SO, taking risks and acceptance fail or acceptance attempt, they may be general CEO personal characteristics . All of these personal characteristics, it is not difficult to own to general CEOs in any organizations. But if the organization hopes to help the business owner to manage himself/ herself overall organizational different departmental operation more effectively and efficiently. The CEO must own unique personal characteristics and excellent managing ability in order to help his/

her boss to manage whole organization excellently. Hence, one successful CEO must own unique personal skills or abilities and personal judgment characteristics to compare common or general CEOs in any organizations.

For example, when one organization has seriour financial resource allocation to provide different departments challenges, it is the best chance to examine the CEO how to apply shortage financial resource to provide to different departments in order to still keep efficient operation aim. If the CEO can know how to arrange shortage financial resource to provide to salespeople salaries expenditure , shop or office rent, water , electricitiy , telephone fee etc. operational expenditure, factory workers salaries and factory machines productive energy expenditure, product manufacturing processing material expenditure etc. resource management expenditure allocation effectively. Consequently, the overall organizational performance can still keep positive growth, or profit can still raise. Then, I believe that this organization leader may be one successful CEO , he/she does not ne one common CEO or failure CEO role to this organization.

The characteristics of successful CEO

What factors cause the CEO can be one successful leader to his/her organization? What are this CEO personal unique characteristics own? I believe that any successful CEOs must oen unique personal characteristics that common CEOs must not own, I shall explain as below:

Usually , any successful CEO must need time from common CEO to become. Every successful CEO must communicate with their employees using concise, easy-to-understand language, open-mindedness, approachability, growth mindset, ethics, decisiveness. All these characteristics may need to any successful CEO. A chief executive officer (CEO) is the highest-ranking executive in a company , whose primary responsibilities include: making major corporate decisions, managing the overall operations and resources of a company, acting as the main point of communication between the board of directors (the board) and these corporate .

Hence, a successful CEO needs have these 5 key managerial skills: Technical skills, conception skills, interpersonal and communication skills, decision-making skills. The roles that a manager plays in the organization require having some skills. Hence, one successful CEO must need to know how to supervise and manage staffs for his / her overall organization. A successful CEO also needs to understand every part and function of the business: accounting, finance, HR, marketing , legal , operation supply chain, sales and information technology. Also, one successful CEO also needs to consider organizational cultural fit, industry understanding , building good soft communication skills between staffs and him/her or between customers and its sale service staffs. Moreover, a successful leader with a CEO mindset has a clear direction for the future, and is not afraid to share it. Do not be scared to set yourself, when you are the organizational CEO and your team, ambitious and exciting goals, sure that you have smaller, achievable steps in these as well. So you can maintain motivation.

For next example, if you are your firm's CEO, you can help your firm shareholders grew in power and their demand for booming stock prices led to booming pay. It means that you 's CEO salaries increase or decrease, it depends on share price driven salaries, when your organization's share price can often keep high price position to compare similar competitors ' share prices. Then, you 's CEO salary may keep increase, because your can manage firm's share price often keeps on high price position in share market. However, one successful CEO must need to own there managerial skills in order to help his/her organization can grow rapidly. The managerial skills may include as below:

Technical skill, it means that the abilities, knowledge, or expertise required to perform specific, job-related tasks. Technical skills are related to jobs in science, engineering, technological, manufacturing or finance. They are learnt through on-the-job experience or structured learning, e.g. data analysis, project management, technical writing, software proficiency, programming languages, artificial intelligence, machine learning, data engineering, visualization, network and information security, cloud computing.

The next is conceptual skill, a successful CEO also needs have conceptual skill, it is the ability to analyze and evaluate whether a company is achieving its goals and its business plan. Conceptual skills are skills that enable individuals to identify , conceptualize and solve problems. It is important in the workplace because it allows professionals to think and with though abstract ideas and come up with multiple solutions to complex issues. Hence, conceptual skills include the ability to view the organization as a whole, understand how the various parts are interdepend end, and assess how the organization relates to its external environment. These skills allow managers to evaluate situations and develop alternative courses of actions. Conceptual skills may include: abstract thinking, analytical skills, congnitive skills, communication, contextualizing, creative thinking, critical thinking, decision making. Hence, one successful CEO may be a conceptual person, who is one conceptual thinker, he /she has an understanding of why something is being done. The conceptual thinker can think at an abstract level and easily apply the CEO himself/herself insights to the situation. So, any common CEO may attempt to improve conceptual thought processing and increase work performance by these methods:

Observe leadership. using challenges as case studies, seeking outside knowledge, staying up-to-date on the industry, applying new practices, discussing concepts with colleagues, finding a mentor, learning about the organization. So, one successful CEO needs to own critical thingking skills: Analysis, interpretation, inference, explanation, self-regulation, open-mindedness and problem solving, strategic thinking includes careful and deliberate anticipation of threats to guard against and opportunities to pursue. Ultimately strategic thinking and analysis can help CEO to lead to a clear set of goals, plans, and new ideas have abstract thinking and feeling, it is the ability to understand concepts that are real, such as freedom. So, analytical skills refer to the ability to collect and analyze information , problem solve and make decisions. Successful CEO can know how to use analytical skills when detecting patterns, brainstorming, observing , interpreting data and making decisions based on the multiple tailors and options available to you, such as the organizational CEO, e.g. creative thinking visual art, communication skills and open-mindedness to any one successful CEO, he /she ought own.

Finally, successful CEO needs have excellent interpersonal communication and decision making skill. Why is decision making and communication an important skill? It can help any CEo to raise the ability to make a decision of good leadership skills. Decision making is an on-going process in every organization, large or small. Having critical thinking skills allow the CEO to ascertain the problem and come up with a solution that is benefical to the company and its employees. So, one successful CEO needs to own soft and hard skils both.

For making decision for the organization, the successful CEO must have decision making skill to find the best solution to the challenge in process. He /she can define the problem, challenge or opportunity clearly, generate of possible solutions or responses, evaluates the costs and benefits or pros and associated with each option, selects a solution or response and knows how to implement the option chosen clearly.

Any CEO can learn how to improve decision making in workplace, such as following these steps: starting with the desired outcome, or goals, rely on data and insights to spot patterns, use S.W.O.T analysis, simulate the outcomes, trust your instincts and identify your cognitive biases. Identifying critical factors which will affect the outcome of a decision, evaluate options accurately and establish priorities, anticipate outcomes and see logical consequences, navigate risk and uncertainty,, reason well in requiring quantitative analysis. On conclusion any one CEO must need time to improve his/her hard and soft skills in order to become one successful CEO to his /her organization.

What skills to one successful CEO owns

We can learn that it is difference between one common CEO and unique successful CEO personal characteristics. Then, it beings this question: What are the skills that one successful CEO ought own? I believe that one successful CEO ought own these skills that one common CEO he /she won't own.

Building excellent communication skill:

Top performing CEO, ough know that strong communication skills are the secret to influence final success. Successful CEOs understand that influence is required if they are to inspire people to willingly act upon what they have to say. Highly influential CEOs deliver on these communication skills daily as below:

Successful CEOs understand the importance of clear, concise communication. They recognize that in the absence of simplicity comes confusion. For example, one organizational CEO sent an email to his employees listing only three objectives he wished for the company to focus on : " customers, team and execution". Instead of providing a dozen areas of opportunity . This CEO also maintained a short list of objectives that were clear. He kept employee goals concise, guiding them to focus to perform excellent services to let customers feel satisfactory. Such as this case, it explains that where one CEO focuses on concise and clear communication, he makes it easier for others to follow. This level of influence ensures that others remember what was said and are inspired to act accordingly.

Top CEOs are known for their sharp minds, and business acumen. They know that frequent communication between employees and senior leadership to be very important in their ability to stay engaged. For conference discussion case, when a successful CEo discusses ongoing company objectives and action items. he begins each all by sharing status updates of previous discussions, including what the executive staff is doing to secure the company's future. Each call concludes with a 30 minute open question forum, where all employees have the chance to ask questions and on ideas the executives discussed. Allowing employees to collaborate and share ideas creates a sense of ownership . It permits insight into the company's goals and encourage employees to engage in its success with ideas of their own.

By creating an atmosphere, successful CEOs encourage employees to share ideas. As a result, CEOs build stronger relationships and deepen trust in leadership . For example, when one CEO maintains an open-door policy and is known for frequently visiting employees on the floor, no matter the department or position. As a result, the CEO builds personal relationships that foster trust and candidacy that only comes with real influence. So , the difference between the successful CEO's communication skill and common CEO's communication skill is that a common CEO has influence based solely on his /her title may intimidate employees to act on direction, but successful CEO is a leader who influences others to act willingly has establish the trust and credibility necessary for lasting success. Unfortunately, too may leaders fail to share this level of detail with their staffs leading employees to question their intention. They neglect communication weaknesses that need improvement . As a result, the entire organization will benefit from improved performance and communication . When leaders admit they are not perfect and are willing to improve, employees follow suit.

What makes a CEO successful? Findings from a database of 17,000 c-suite assessments reveal that successful CEOs demonstrate four specific behaviors that prove critical to their performance. They are decisive, they engage for impact, they adapt proactively, and they deliver reliably. So, as a leader, you need to posses strong communication skills. From motivating your employees to meeting set deadlines, you should have the ability to communicate your needs and even show your employees how things are down. If you want to be a good CEO, you must be consistently clear in your communication.

What is the most important skill to a CEO? In short, the single important role of a CEO is to make absolutely certain that the right CEO is running the company and then do what is necessary to encourage that CEO's effectiveness, strategy, vision, culture shareholder value, all crucial and all within the scopr of the CEO's role. Hence, successful CEO needs to know whether what he/ she actually does. A chief executive officer (CEO) is the highest ranking executive in a company, whose primary responsibilities include making major corporate decisions, managing the overall operations and resources of a company, acting as the main point of communication between the board of directors. Hence, CEO needs to report to the board of directors, with most CEOs being members and sometimes chair of the board, president, they report to the CEO and the board of directors and sometimes they are board members. Hence, a CEO needs to understand every part and function of the business: accounting, finance, HR, marketing, legal , operations, supply chain , sales , information technology . In business speak, the CEO's job is to define the mission (purpose), strategy (direction), and metric (pace and performance). These three elements provide the essential elements that a growing company needs to be able to perform. So, a successful CEO must need to find the effective strategy to help his/her company to solve any challenges in ay time. When the chairman technically has higher level power, the CEO is indeed the boss of a company. The CEO does by the law answer to their board of directors, which is ultimately headed by the chairman. In general., the CEO job starts when the organization reaches about 20 employees, prior to 20 employees, the job resembles more of a product management role. CEOs at this stage are trying to develop a visable product and generate some revenue. In general, successful chief executives tend to demonstrate four specific behaviors that prove critical to their performance. For example, holding people accountable and the ability to motivate a team, high-performing (CEO) do not necessarily stand our for making great decisions all the time, rather they stand our for being more decisive. They make decisions earlier, faster, and with greater conviction. Also, they do so consistently, even with incomplete information, and in unfamiliar domains . Interestingly, the highest IQ executives , they are intellectual complexity, when the quality of their decisions is often good, because of their pursuit of the perfect answer, they can take tool ong to make choices or set clear priorities and their teams pay a high price. These smart but slow decision makers, their teams either grow frustrated , which can lead to the attrition of valuable talent ot become overcautious themselves.

Moreover, high-performing CEOs understand that a wrong decision is often better than no decision at all. It means that a bad decision was better than a lack of direction. Most decisions can be undone, but a successful CEO has learnt to move with the right amount of speed. To that end, successful CEOs also knows when not to decide, whether a decision should actually be more lower down in the organization and if delaying, it is a week or a month time, would allow important information without causing harm.

Hence, strong performers balance keen insight into their stakeholders' priorities with focus on delivering business results. They start by developing an understand of their stakeholders' needs and motivations and get many people on board by driving for performance. So, CEO needs to bring others along plan and execute disciplined communications and influencing strategies. Indeed, the skilled CEO gains the support of their colleagues by confidence that they will lead the team to success, even if that means taking uncomfortable or unpopular moves. These CEOs do not shy away from conflict in the pursuit of business goals. The ability to handle different viewpoints significantly faster than average.

Factors Influence CEO Success Or Fail

In fact, any CEOs will be influenced to succeed or how to manage their organizations by personal psychology and personal skills or knowledge and external environment factors. However, CEO is such leader role to any organizations. Can owning high level leadership skillful CEOs manage their organizations more easily to compare owning low level leadership skillful CEOs? May leadership skill be main factor to influence any one CEO's person success or fail? I shall attempt to explain as below?

In fact, I feel any CEo must need have these kinds of leadership skills. They ma y include: First, recognizing strengths, everybody with an organization has their strengths, and it is essential that you are able to identify the strengths of individuals, and recognizing weaknesses, second, reacting to employee needs, third, clarity and fourth, willingness to make tough decisions and conflict management skill. Why does every CEO need have leadership skill? Effective leaders have the ability to communicate well, motivate their team, handle and delegate responsibilities, listen to feedback and have the flexibility to solve problems in an ever changing workplace. Hence , in CEO personal psychological view, an excellent CEO is drawn to change and effective action, courage , passion and resilence and drive attitude . A good leader knows that taking risks and making large-scale changes can lead to organizational growth or can fall dramatically.

Why is CEO leadership important to the performance of a firm? Research evidence provides overall support for the positive relationship between leadership and firm performance (Lowe et al, 1996). CEOs with transactional leadership can successfully manage goal accomplishment and contribute to the enhancement of the firm performance. So, it seems that CEO's leadership has indirect or direct relationship to influence his / her whole organizational performance whether it can grow up rapidly or slowly, even fall down rapidly or slowly, because if the firm's CEO can not manage different department teams cooperate efficiently. Then, the firm's leader personal leadership effort may influence whole organization different department teams to cooperate smoothly. Although, CEO must not need to contact all department staffs every day, but he /she needs to contact any department managers in order to know whether their departments have any challenges , when managers feel difficulties to solve. If the CEO had low level leadership ability, he /she won't discuss with any department managers to conclude the best opinions to solve the challenges more easily. For example, when financial budget department manager discovered that his organization had deficit challenge recently. If he can not solve lack of cash available problem. Then, his organization's deficit will be increased easily. Consequently, it will influence staffs salaries can not pay on time, it won' t have cash to buy enough manufacturing material to prepare to be supplied to manufacture to provide products to provide to market to sell, factory can not have enough money to buy new productive machines to replace old productive machines etc. different kinds of organizational operational needs.

However, if the CEO owning high level leadership skills, he may know hoe to lead this financial budget manager to solve " deficit" challenge. Although, deficit seems to be simple matter, but if this financial budget manager can not know how to manage cash available in order to allocate to different departments operations, e.g. allocating the limiting amount of cash to urgent departments to use in prior. Then, deficit challenge will increase cash shortage number more seriously. So, high leadership skill mist need to any one organizational CEO in order to help his/her organization can solve any challenges more efficiently and easily. Otherwise, low leadership effort owning CEO only influences his/her organization can not grow up more rapidly, even it can fall down rapidly. Consequently, the organization will only liquidate or it will be sold out rapidly.

What does excellent leadership skill need to CEO? Many psychologists indicate excellent leadership may include these essential elements: Integrity, ability to delegate, communication, self - awareness, gratitude, learning agility, influence effort, empathy.In common, characteristics of a good leader, he / she can help staffs and makes the essential large-sacle decisions that keep the organization can operate efficiently and reduce challenges occur. Integrity is especially important for top-level executives who are charting the organization's actions and making countless other significant decisions. Ability to delegate , delegating is one of the core responsibilities of a leader, the goal enables the CEO's direct reports, facilitate teamwork, provide autonomy, lead to better decision making and help the CEO's direct reports grow. Effective leadership and effective communication are intertwined.

So, any CEOs need to be able to communicate in a variety of ways, from transmitting information to coaching your staffs (managers).

Any CEO must be able to listen to , and communicate with, a wide range of staffs across roles, social identities and more. The quality and effectiveness of communication across the CEO's organization directly affect trhe success of the CEO's business strategy. So, better communication skill can actually improve the CEO's organizational culture. Self-awareness is focuses skills for leadership. The better leadership skill to the CEO , he / she can understand himself / herself managing ability, the more effective , he /she can do. Do you know how other people view you or how you show up at work?

Gratitude can lead to higher self-esteem, reduced depression and anxiety, learning agility is the ability to know what to do when you do not know what to do. So, great leaders are great learners, with strong learning agility to get started , when you are one organization's CEO in beginning, you must need to learn how to influence your whole organizational staffs behaviors to be the perfect.

" Influence" may be through locial , emotional or cooperative appeals, is a component of being an effective leader, influence is quite different from manipulation, and it needs to be done and it requires emotional intelligence and trust. Empathy is correlated with job performance and is a critical part of emotional intelligence and leadership effectiveness. A successful leadership CEO needs have empathetic behaviors towards his / her direct reports, empathy can be for improving workplace conditions. Courage is such that when the CEO wants to voice a new idea, provides feedback to a direct report or flag a concern for someone above him / her. That is part of the reason courage is a key skill for good leaders. Rather than avoiding problems or allowing conflicts to faster, courage enables leaders to step up and move things in the direct direction. A workplace with high levels of psychological safety and a strong coaching culture will further support truth and courage. Finally CEO needs to know how to treat people with respect on a daily basis is one of the most important things . A leader can do that it will ease tensions and conflict, create trust, and improve effectiveness.

On conclusion, when the CEO can know how to build these psychological and emotion feeling, then the CEO can be trained to improve leadership skill in order to know hoew to manage his / her organization efficiently and effectively.

Can training provision raise CEO leadership

Any organizational CEO is the top level managerial position. So, it is one job to anyone. Any organizational positions may have training provision in order to improve the staff personal job skills, e.g. organizations can provide internal accounting training to accounting clerk, even accounting manager training in order to let they can learn company's accounting policy in order to improve their accounting tasks more proficient, or a law firm can provide legal draft training to general law clerks in order to improve their legal draft writing skils, or one company's data processing department can provide data processing training to improve data processor typing speed to learn more proficient to type its documents, or property agent firm can provide property sale speaking training to its property sale agents to improve their property sales presentation skill or insurance agent firms can provide insurance sale speaking training to its insurance sale agents to improve their insurance sales skills.

Hence, it seems that any organizational positions may apply training methods to improve any staff individual performance in any organizations. So, it brings this question: Can organizations provide training to improve CEO performance to achieve more proficient? To answer this question, we need to suppose same kinds of business CEO positions , they ought be trained to improve their performance. If it is true, whether what kinds of businesses CEO positions, they may be applied training method to improve their managerial skills? How and why to these kinds of business CEO positions, they can be trained to improve their proficiency? I shall attempt to answer as below:

In fact, general CEO typically have a bachelor's or master's degree in business administration or a fiels related to their industry. Some CEO positions require that candidates have a master's or even depending on the industry , education, for instance. So, one university CEO or president, he /she needs have education psychology master or doctorate level to any kinds of degree. They need have high educational level to do university leader. Hence, CEO, training can focus on learning or educational aspect, e.g. certified CEO program is general education certification course designed for business leaders globally (CEO senior managers) and aspiring business leaders who are looking to build upon existing qualifications and business experience.

What does CEO coach training method mean?

However, every CEO needs a coach in organization , because a coach suports the CEO to manage conflict effectively often decisoin of the CEO please one group and displease another. The CEO needs a partner who the CEO can be open with, one who is going to be sensitive, and objective, honest and respectful. Hence in any organizations, a coash can teach the CEO these managing skills to manage their organizations more easily, e.g. flexibility, value driven decision making, delegating, leadership, clear vision implementation.

Hence, in general, coach training needs usually take 2 to 3 years to complete. The organizational CEO will does on the-job-training and spend time with a training provider. Employers will set their own entry requirements. So, in popular, many CEOs use a CEO coach over the course of their career. No athlete would be embarrassed they use a coach. Yet, CEOs believe they do not need a coach of their own. However, any organization is the final decision making person, when the organization feels that the CEO's managerial effort is poor, it can attempt to provide a proficient managing experience coach to train this CEO's management skill in order to achieve this organization's CEO ability requirement within 2 to 3 years. For example, a CEO peer group training, interchangably called CEO peer groups or networks, these organizations generally arrange reqular meetings in confidential environments where CEOs can share ideas, best practices, experiences and advice together to attempt how to improve their managerial skills.

So, executives look for in a coach, a good executive coach does not need to have the exact background or experience as the CEO , but a familiarity will help him or her better understand the CEO thinking and needs. More importantly, the CEO coach needs skills, the CEO either does not have and wants to attain, or ones that can help strength the CEO opportunity areas.

In general, what leaders want from coaching. Coaching empowers leaders to do expectional work. Coaches establish and advantageous relationship that uncovers hidden strengths and weaknesses within the leader. Goals will be created to enable leaders to indicate their weaknesses and track their progress. What is better up coaching? Coaching training can address the CEO must pervasive organizational challenges with the organizational unique combination of coaching to achieve a growth approach to mental fitness and organizational health more effectively.

Have a CEO coach is similar to the executive or leadership coach , but with the added responsibility of working with the CEO who is working in the firm. So, coach can attempt to help the CEO potentially make the most significant difference in the company's success and lives and careers of those who work for the company. Hence, any organizations can provide executive or leadership coach to improve the CEO's leadership skills by these 5 caoching styles, such as below:

Democratic coaching, this method gives the term freedom and accountability, with the coach stepping in only when meeded to keep the process going, or authoritarian coaching, holistic coaching, authcratic coaching and vision coaching training methods, for example, entrepreneur coach can help new and existing business owners with any number of tacks to foster their entrepreneurship. In fact, entrepreneurship is not about having a business, but about having an entrepreneurship mind. So, CEOs can be trained from any style of coach in order to improve their management and leadership skills to more proficient in their organizations. So, it means that coaching training is one kind of effective training method to improve CEO's performance in any organizations.

On conclusion, I believe that it is only one kind of training method to train any organizational CEOs to become proficient CEO, it is coaching training method, instead of providing general educational level to the CEO for leadership knowledge, because coach training is one kind of organizational leadership practice training, it can satisfy any CEOs to raise leadership effort effectively to help the CEO to manage his/her organization easily.

Amazon leader / founder owns new business foundation strategies mind

Any new business founders, they ought hope their new businesses can run long time. The question concerns that how they can help their new businesses run long time, e.g. at least above 5 years . I shall attempt to apply behavioral economic theory to solve this common challenge as below.

Keeping a new business is in difficult economic time is challenging. Every new business is different and each carries its own risks and rewards in behavioral economy view. These sifferences cause some new business founders attempt to copy another similar new business founder strategy. Still, these are save general strategies business owners can follow to help themselves new businesses to copy another similar new business strategy succeeds in possible.

However, some of these copying another new business founder strategy's owner still feels their sopying another new business founder strategy may help them to succeed. So, they still have risk or they may encounter failure, if the another similar new business founder strategy can not be suitable to be adopted to themselves new business similiarly. So, it explains that why some new business founder can not keep their new businesses can run long time, because they feel the other similar new business founders their strategies can help to develop their new businesses succeed together. But in fact, there are may new business founders their copying strategy decisions are wrong. They feel their copying another new business founder's strategy can help them to develop in success. So, their new business strategies ought also help their new businesses to develop or grow long time. However, there are many new businesses can not run above 5 years, due to there new business founders choose the wrong copying strategies from another similar new business or old business competitors.

New business founder needs to look at the big picture, it means that long term customer behavior change picture. Because consumer behaviors must often change suddenly in any time. So, any new business founder ought attempt to discover whether what their product buyers behaviors will change after 5 years, even 10 years in predicting. People have a tendency to attack the most obvious immediate prodblems without hesitation. That's understandable and might make good business sense in some suitations. However, it is also advisable to step back and look at the big picture to see what is still working and what might need changing.

Its an opportunity to better comprehend the size and the scope of exciting problem and further understand your new firm's decision model, determining how its strengths and weaknesses come into play. What is a business model? The term business model refers to a firm's plan making a profit. It identified target market, e.g. which is age customer group, where is the geographical sale place, and anticipated expenses. However, business models are improtant for both new and established businesses. They help new developing companies attract investment, recruit talent, and motivate management and staff. Establishing businesses should reguarly update their business plans or they will fail to anticipate trends and channelgens. So, business models both levers are pricing and costs. It is a high -level plan for profitably , a business in a specific marketplace. A primary component of the business model is the value proposition. This is a description of the goods or services that a new business offers and why they are desirable to customers, ideally stated in a may that differentiates the products or services from its competitors.

A new business enterprise's business model should also cover projected startup costs and financing sources, the target customer base for the new business, marketing strat egy , a review of the competition, and projections of revenue ans expenses. It may also define opportunities in which the new business can partner with other established companies, e.g. the new business model for an advertising business may identify benefits from an arrangement for referrals to and from a printing company. So, successful new businesses need have good business models that allow them to fulfill client needs at a competitive price and a sustainable cost. Over time, many new businesses revise their business models from time to time to reflect changing business environments and market demands. However, the business model may not tell new business founder everything about a company's prospects, but the investor who underatands the business model can make better sense of the financial data.

New business founder also needs to consider organizational internal matter, e.g. suppose a new business founder discovers that two employees are making mistakes with inventory that cause certain supplies to be overstocked or understocked. When a initial reaction might be to fine those employees. It might be wiser to examine whether the manager who hires and supervises them properly trained time. If the manager is to blame, that person could be fired, but this might not be the best solution. If the manager's relationship with client have a history of bringing in repeat business and substantial revenue. They are likely someone, you would want to keep. However, retraining might be a better alternative than termination.

Infact, by thoroughly reviewing the strengths and weaknesses of the employees, the owner is looking at the issue from a top-down perspective, reducing or eliminating the chance that the problem will occur when avoiding a change that could adversely impact future sales. Hence, a similar kind on analysing how youe new products or services fit into the marketplace in your new business beginning stage, how the economic crisis has affected your customers and suppliers and all the other key aspects of your new business. You need to know how well your new business model fits the current environment and forecast what various alternative scenarios of the future mighr mean for it.

For one interesting new business behavioral economic view to recuriting new employees view example, any new business owners or large corporational founders tend to be either wise or follish when they hire the least expensive workers sometimes, the productivitiy of these workers may be suspect. Hiring one worker who costs 20% more than the average workers, but works 40% more effectively make of crisis. By seeking resumes and interviews from new applicants. New business founders can make change to new staff when needed to increase efficiency. So, how to choose any department new staff recruitment , it is very important to influence the new business furher develops for long time. Don't sacrifice quickly, keeping a handle on costs is crucial in tough times. Owners need to stay on the offensive and get employees on board with changes that are being made. However, any one new business founders need have good sense to predict when their new products or new services need to be changed in order to adopt customer behavioral changing environment.

ON conclusion, so any new business founders hipe to keep themselves new businesses can run long time, they must need to know " consumer behavioral psychology" how and why to cause their change in order to implement the most effective new business strategy to improve their sale methods to achieve the most satisfactory level to their potential clients' purchase needs or service needs in long time. Consequently , their new businesses ought keep long running time in this old and new product / service competitor market.

Avoiding new business low value method

Internet marketing promotion strategy

Any new business founders do not hope their new business market worth falls rapidly or share price falls rapidly. What facors may cause new business share price or market value falls rapidly? What methods to help new businesses keep the same share price is stable long time or market value can be kept in the stable worth, even share price can be influenced the rise or market value can be influenced to rise? I shall attempt to explain some useful methods, they may influence new business market value to avoid falls down, or share price can rise more easily.

TO avoid new business low value, these ways may be used in developing new business. They may include: Knowing what your client individual actual need, e.g. rice cooker product, cooking rice function must need , but avoiding to spend long time or short time to cook rice rapidly, big rice cooker size to cook more rice, long time keeping rice warm function. All these factors may influence rice cook buyers individual choices. Some housewives also need the kind of rice cooker has above all these functions, before they make rice cooker purchase decision. So, knowing what your clients real needs, they are essential to product manufacturers, offering great customer service, e.g. repair sevice, after sale enquiry (following up equiry to the client, nurture existing customers and look for new sale need opportunities, use social media attending networking events, give back to your community, measure what works and refine your approach as you go. So, if the business founder can manage sale and customer, service both teams to achieve the best service performance to let clients feel , then they may persuade many clients continue choose to continue to buy their products more easily. So, salespeople and customer service staffs training method may be one main influential factor to help the organization to raise market share value. If the organization can design useful training course to raise its salespeople sale skills or customer service staff service performance.

Which businesses can be started with less investment? For India country example, these low investment business wil be helped the new business founder to earn the most profitable, e.g. dropshipping is one of the most successful business in India, because in India, even global there are many tall offices need dropshipping equipment to transport window cleaners to clean tall office windows. So, dropshipping cleaners'window ability may influence India deopshipping firm share price changes to rise up or fall down. Because India dropshiping companies window clean workers window cleaning performance can bring property management company clients to make dropshipping window cleaning service provider choice.

I mean that India dropshipping office window or global dropshipping office windoe clean service providers, their new business market value or high stable shar e price value, their value is depended on whether their dropshipping window cleaners clearning window skills or window clean priperty management clients‘ window clean needs. So, for dropshipping office cleaning service provider case example, how to improve dropshipping office window cleaning workers' windows clean ability, it is only one influential method to influence dropshipping office window cleaning firm service providers their shares prices whether they can keep stable market position, even share price can be risen easily. How to improve dropshipping office cleaning workers‘ office windows cleaning skill is very important to influence dropshipping office window service providers' shares prices are at the stable high price level. For courier company example, how to improve courier service performance, e.g. shorten the document / goods delivery time between the document or goods sender countey and the document or goods country receiver, when the document or goods can not bt delayed to send to the overseas receiver whose home from the another country sender, e.g. From US sends the document to China in common general couriers need 5 days , but the US courier company can send the documents to China, it only needs 2 days delivery time. Then, it may attract many China goods or documents receiving clients to choose the US courier service providers. So, how to keep the US new courier servier providers, or market value or share price value, it depends on whether it may help its overseas documents or goods receiving clients to reduce how long time to let they can receive the documents or goods from US. So, the avoiding delivery time delay is the import factor to influence courier goods / documents delivery service provider new business market value.

Moreover, any one new business founder may promote themselves new business in a low budger. These methods may include: posting amazing content on your new firm's blog, creating a google my new business account, building a free or cheap email list, contributing an article to an industry magazine, attending local networking events, co-sponsor a contest. So, internet channel may help any new business to build a rapid promotion network to let many people to know that this kind of new business exist, it aims to let potential clients number increases in short time in possible. So, internet may be a kind of new promotion tool to help any new business market share value rises in short time, the internet strategies for effective promotion of new business, e.g. creating a website, geting listed on google, advertise on facebook, email customers, and potential customers use google Adwords, paid media advertising , social networks and viral marketing, internet marketing, email marketing, direct selling, point-of-purchase marketing, co-branding, cause marketing , conversational marketing .

All of these internet promotion methods may help new businesses to rise market growth value or share price in short time. Hence, internet promotion method is preferable to choose to compare general TV, advertising , newspaper, advertising, magazine advertising, radio adverting, sales promotion, general selling, publicity promotion methods because internet promotion marketing is one kind method, it may bring the new product or new service providing message to let many potential clients to know from the new firm's email ot website in short time rapidly. It is one kind of new global promotion method for any kinds of new busienss development in beginnning.

So, any new business founder may prefer to choose internet promotion method in orde to let many potential cients to know their new products ot services are existence. So, attracting new customers method may use social media optimizing the new business founder's social media account, improves website and engage with loyal customers, give branded gifts , referral discounts, social media contects, and giveways, sending email to survey customers, researching your competitors and finding out who their customers are, target email advertisement, smart social media, responding to every email, tweet , facebook comment, e-publish user reviews from internet media channel. All of these new internet promotion strategies may help any kinds of new businesses to promote their products or services to let clients to know in short time rapidly from internet media promotion channel. The internet promotion marketing strategy is one kind of low cost promotion strategy, low cost marketing stragtegy for startups, cheapest new businesses to start and focused low cost strategy company.

Why internet promoting strategy can help new business to avoid low market value? The reason is simple, because when the new firm sends one email message to let any one country's email user to know. This new product or new service email message can let global any one emaill user to know that this new product or new service business is existence in market. When the email user receives the new business' semail message, it may keep in itself email box. So, the email user won't lose the one email message and it can often remember this new product, or new service provider is existence in market. So, any one email user when he/she receives new product or service provider 's email, this email is such as the private advertisment between the new business founder and the email receiver. So, email advertising is different general product magazine, TV, newspaper , radio advertisment. It is public promotion advertisement.

Hence, the feeling of private advertisment, it is the most influential factor to persuade potential consumers to choose to buy the new product or use the new service from this provider, because when the potiential client receives the email promotion from the new product/ new service provider, he /she may feel surpise to raise interest to click the advertismeent email to see whether what benefits can be given ti him/her if he /she chooses to buy the new product or use the new service. If one say, the new product / new service provider can send about 1,000 promotion email to let global 1,000 different countries possible potential clients to know its new product/new service is existence in market. Consequently, this email network promotion method can help this new business founder to advertise his / her new product /new service to let global 1,000 email users to know in one day. When, its potential clients number increases, it implies that its new product or new service market existence value will be possible to influence to rise up. Hence, emial promotion method may influence any kinds of new businesses to rise market value in short time in possible, because when may email receivers become to the new business potential clients. Consequently, the new business's share price may be influenced to riase up then its market value may also be follow to influence to rise up. So, it seems that email promotion method may be nowadays a kind of the most effective promotion method to help any new businesses to raise up share price or raise market value in short time.

Becoming talent human how influences social changes

Nowadays we tend to think about social and digital technology more from a personal or consumer perspective than their business or professional applications, but as the Digital Era continues to progress, many of technology's most profound impacts are likely to be in the world of work. In addition to changes in product and business development, knowledge management, data analysis, and other operational processes, transforming talent management will be a key priority for organizations striving to be employers of choice.

- Digital technology encourages to create talent human

Why does digitial technology encourage to create talent human or excite human to learn new things ? The human capital implications of social and digital technologies impact virtually everyone, regardless of the type of organization they work for, their profession, their functional area, or their career stage. That means that the talent management functions in all organizations, as well as the professionals who staff and lead them, have a critical role to play in ensuring the efficient and effective transition and transformation from Industrial Era models and processes to their Digital Era upgrades.

It's no surprise that talent management has already become more "high tech." Many employment related activities have been digitized, and there has been a corresponding increase in employee self-service. It's important to remember, however, that digitization is not the same thing as digital engagement, and that the rise of "high tech" solutions doesn't necessitate the loss of a "high touch" approach to managing an organization's human assets. Transforming talent management requires digitization, to be sure, but it also involves leveraging social and digital technologies in ways that promote and enhance communication, collaboration, and engagement - not just between an employee and the organization, but between and among employees themselves.

Talent Acquisition

The logical place to start when talking about the impact of social and digital technologies on talent management is talent acquisition, where the greatest advances have been made. Anyone who has searched and applied for jobs in the past 10 years is very familiar with how technology has transformed the application process, which in most organizations (and virtually all large ones) is now almost completely digitized and automated. However, there are other ways in which social and digital technologies are impacting talent acquisition that may not be as well-known or commonly understood. Social media sites in particular (such as Facebook, YouTube, and Pinterest) are a great way to promote an employer's brand and offer realistic previews of work life, people and culture in organizations. Online games and simulations can also be used to get a sense of what working for an organization would be like, and give organizations themselves an opportunity to determine if a prospective candidate would be a good cultural fit and potentially successful.

On organizational working environment aspect, some employers are recognizing the value of digital alumni networks or communities to maintain strong relationships with former employees. One of the primary motivations for doing this is that the employees may return one day and/or make referrals to or from their personal and professional networks. Similarly, talent networks enable organizations to establish and maintain relationships with professionals in key areas like IT and engineering, even when there isn't a current opportunity to have those folks be a part of the organization. Moreover, social media can bring positive influence to impact organizations to encourge employees to attempt or feel needs to learning new things for their tasks needs. Due to social media has actually transformed every stage of the recruiting process in significant ways - so much so that the traditional recruiting funnel can be recast in "social" terms. At the top of the funnel are activities like social advertising (i.e., placing job ads on social networks like Facebook), social sourcing (i.e., searching for candidates who meet certain criteria on networks like LinkedIn), and social referrals (i.e., having current employees share position openings with their online personal and professional networks). And at the bottom of the funnel is social screening (i.e., reviewing a candidate's public activity in social networks to identify potential hiring risks).

- Learning management is needed to feel needs to any organizations

Learning management is probably the another most advanced area when it comes to adopting and adapting to new technologies. As with recruiting and other processes, the initial advances are in the area of digitization, with social software applications evolving next. One of the obvious digital impacts is the increased use of elearning and online learning platforms with self-paced study. There are also countless instructional videos on the web, both free and fee-based, that address a virtually unlimited range of topics. And we can't forget MOOCs - massive, open, online courses - which have proliferated in the past couple of years. Finally, many organizations have also started to leverage tablets and other mobile devices for learning, as well as using simulations and games to help employees develop specific skills. In addition to offering training through a variety of multimedia channels, organizations are increasingly using a range of digital tools for assessing employees' skills. They're also allowing employees to play an enhanced role in identifying their key skill sets and training needs, and can even have them create their own learning and development plans. Allowing employees to take a more active role in their own learning and skills management enables organizations to develop and maintain a more complete and accurate knowledge and skills database, which in turn enables them to maximize the value of the workforce in which they've already invested.

1. Formal learning management systems and platforms are also beginning to incorporate social technologies in a variety of ways. Promoting connections and interactions among participants, as well as with the instructor, can enhance the learning experience both during and after a course. Creating course-based cohorts that allow people to continue to interact with each other via a digital community - even when their shared learning experience is face-to-face - can promote both knowledge transfer and retention, in addition to increasing commitment and engagement through interpersonal connections.

2. Informal learning - which is now also referred to as social learning - is greatly enhanced by social technologies as well. In fact, this is probably the greatest opportunity and area of growth for organizations of all types and sizes. Through private social networks, intranets and other internal platforms that have incorporated social technology elements, organizations are better able to facilitate employee learning as they perform their job duties and complete work activities. Along with the networks themselves, features like advanced search, identified subject matter experts, digital communities of practice, wikis and more enable employees to access and learn from colleagues who are not just next door or down the hall, but even in another city, state or country!

As organizations move forward with leveraging technology to enhance learning initiatives, it will become increasingly important for them to address issues related to digital literacy and digital competencies. For the past several decades we've generally taken what I refer to as an LIY, or Learn It Yourself, approach to digital knowledge and skills. Although organizations may invest in teaching someone how to use a specific application related to their job, they make virtually no investment in helping individuals learn how to use general digital tools like Microsoft Office and even email. Left to their own devices, most people - and I include myself in this group- are much less efficient and effective at using these tools than they could or should be. As our tools get even more sophisticated, we need the foundational knowledge and skills to be able to use them well - and this foundation should probably be provided via more formal training. In other words, many people need to be "taught how to learn" in the Digital Era. If organizations aren't going to provide the formal training workers need to do that, it's probably in an individual's best interests to pursue those kinds of development opportunities on their own.

- What are social influences on human behavior when talent human number increases?

Social Influences on Human Behavior Because human beings are social and learn from observation rather than depending entirely on instinct, almost all aspects of human psychology and behavior are socially influenced. Languages, modes of dress, gender roles and avoided taboos are all agreed upon at a group level and form the basis of culture. What are the characteristics of social change? Small-scale and short-term changes are characteristic of human societies, because customs and norms change, new techniques and technologies are invented, environmental changes spur new adaptations, and conflicts result in redistributions of power. This universal human potential for social change has a biological basis.

This universal human potential for social change has a biological basis. It is rooted in the flexibility and adaptability of the human species—the near absence of biologically fixed action patterns (instincts) on the one hand and the enormous capacity for learning, symbolizing, and creating on the other hand. Because human beings are social and learn from observation rather than depending entirely on instinct, almost all aspects of human psychology and behavior are socially influenced. Languages, modes of dress, gender roles and avoided taboos are all agreed upon at a group level and form the basis of culture.

On conclusion, when one country can create many talent human, e.g. students, workers. Then they can bring more positive attribution to help or assist themselve country to develop rapidly. Consequently, the country's economic growth speed will be rapid. So, I believe that it has close relationship between economy growth and talent human number to any countries in nowadays societies.

Amazon ecommerce founder successful factors

Nowadays, we are encountering digital age period. Many customers choose to apply websites and mobile apps to buy their products. So,many merchants also choose online e-commerce channel to build online purchase platform to raise its competitive ability in online e-commerce market.

So, customers can apply mobile apps or merchants themselves websites to buy any products in any time and any places conveniently.

However, in electronic (ecommerce) industry, Amazon is the global largest online retail delivery provider. It sells different kinds of products from internet, e.g. books, electronic products, music, movie Cd, DVD, magazine, garden and homw useful tools, children toys, computer,

software, even, cars from online channel to global online shoppers. So, there ate many online buyers choose to buy any products from Amazon web services middle channel. In fact, its products prices can be low, a wide selection, ease website use and convenience to meet all of its customers' needs in one virtual store. So, it can still own the high share market in online retail delivery service industry. I shall indicate that Amazon successful factors as below:

It has a clear aim or mission. It's mission is to be Earth's most customer-centric company , where people can find and discover anything , they want to buy online. So, it will gather data ro analyze whether why and how customers will select to buy the kinds of products from internet. Why do its customers forget to choose to buy any products from shops and they choose Amazon to buy their preferable products from online? I believe that it has these characteristics to attract them such as:

It can provide return after sale services within the reasonable time when the customer feels that he does not need to use the product or feels unsatisfactory to the product, then he can return the product to Amazon and Amazon must refund money to him as well as it can provide free charge of grocery delivery service to every customer home. Instead of these attractive service, it also began to enter publishing market. In July 2002, Amazon started offering services to website developers, marketings its kindle
product, aimed at capturing the publishing market for digital books, then it can sell paper books from online channel. It aims to let readers can choose to either download to read ebooks from its website or borrow ebooks to read from its electronic library or paid visa to print paper books to deliver their paper books to their homes conveniently. So, readers feel that they can enter Amazon publish website to choose any interesting books to buy or borrow to read , they do not need to go to book stores or libraries.It is Amazon's competitive and attractive and unique strengths to build its customers on this online retail market.

On its organization mamagement aspect, it has one effective and efficient management strategy. It has a good CEO manages his e-commerce business. Bezos has been chairman of the board of Amazon , since he founded the compnay in 1994. Amazon has a limitless stock on hand at all time, it enables Amazon to collect high margins when providing low prices, and lets customers to feel consideration every second. So, when the customers feel any enquiries, his customer service team members can apply its intra website email message channel to send email to answer his enquiries when they enter Amazon intra-website email message channel to send email to ask them any enquiries and they can reponse their enquiries immediately in any time or they can phone to Amazon customer service hotline to enquiry them directly. So, its customer service staffs can answer their enquiries either by phone or email communication in short time rapidly. They won't delay to response their enquiries to avoid they feel worry or unhappy or complain. So, efficient customer service performance can help it to satisy its customer service needs and build good customer service relationship and repeat purchase chance will increase also.

However, global online retail marketplace is expanding rapidly. So, Amazon will have many new or potential online retail competitors, if it neglected to improve its strategy to adapt every online customer individual need or purchase taste, due to customers' purchase need will often change, such as price demand, product delivery time demand, customer service demand etc. spects. So, Amazon needs have different market strategies in different time in order to attract customers' choices in different economic environment, if it hoped to keep online retail leader position.

For example, how to encourage or raise customers' online purchase desires when economy is poor environment. When many people loss jobs, due to many businesses liquidate and loss many clients. So, they need to dismiss many staffs. Then, in society, many families will reduce their consumption desires because their parents loss jobs. So, Amazon needs improve its strategies on above different aspects in order to attract or persuade them to spend much time on internet shopping activities.

Instead of organization management aspect and customer service aspect, the other critical success factors for developing an e-business strategy to Amazon, they may include: How to apply network technology to keep long term close relationship between Amazon its e-commerce organization, online customers, partners, stakeholders and product suppliers. It is very important to influence Amazon's success, because Amazon , such as the e-business delivery service provider will loss the kinds of product sale chance, if the product providers dislike its sale delivery service or feel satisfactory to its sale strategy or promotion methods or when its online sale delivery service can not let its customers feel its online sale delivery to be satisfactory. Hence, online sale delivery service performance is very important to influence Amazon's success.

Moreover, in its business model, Amazon.com also needs have these key succes factors. They may include: Building strong brand name location, because when online shoppers can remember its brand or loyalty easily when it is famous. Then they won't choose any online retail delivery providers to replace its delivery service easily. So, building one famous and confident online retail delivery service provider loyalty or brand , it can help Amazon to influence many online shoppers have confidence to choose its online retail delivery service in the first time. When they can often remember Amazon and feel it is only one online retail delivery serivce provider, the repeat online purchase chance will also increase, due to they only choose to click on its website to choose any kinds of products to buy more easily.

So, Amazon.com's marketing strategy is needed to design to strengthen the Amazon brand name, increases customer traffic to the Amazon.com web sites, builds customer loyalty, encourages repeat purchases or attracts them to clicks on its websites again to develop incremental products and retail delivery service revenue opportunities. Also, how to design its efficient products delivery value to let product buyers to feel. This factor is important to influence Amazon's products delviery service in success in online retail delivery service market. Moreover, Amazon publish service also needs to build attractive reading feeling to let readers to satisfy its reading provision needs to replace book stores or libraries.

On conclusion, Amazon ought need to continue to change its marketing strategies in order to adapt to its online retail product delivery service changes as well as lets they believe that it is one online customer care product delviery service provider to comapre other online retail delivery service providers, if it hopes to keep its online retail relviery provider top leader position in this e-commece market.

Skills technological improvement strategy
soft and hard skill to Amazon organization

Skills shortages on developing country market

Nowadays , future global job market competition will be trended serious. Any employers will expert their employees own different skills to know how to do their jobs efficiently and effectively and easily. So, future any organization employees ought considerate how to learn different kinds of skills or knowledges in order to prepare to satisfy their future employers' different new tasks needs. However, if future any new skillful needs or demands will be raised to future employers' demands. It brings these questions: what skills do global any organization employees need own in general? How to improve or raise employees themselves skills more easily and efficiently? What will happen if future employees do not learn new knowledge to improve or raise themselves skills? Why is learning any new skillful knowledge important ? What will be the possible negative and /or positive consequence if future the organizations do not need their employees to learn any new kinds of skillful knowledge?

Future developing countries need to develop their economy, so they need to employ many employees who own technical skills and /or soft skills. What kind of technical skills and/or soft skills , the developing countries' employees who will need to order to raise competiton in local job market ? I shall indicate the developing country China example. China is one developing country, employers will need different kinds of skillful labors to assist them to develop their businesses. However, China employers will face skillful labour shortage challenge. Although Chinese young age population is high, but many of them do not to be encouraged to learn enough skillful knowledge to fill future new skillful positions. So, the fast speed of training will be important to influence China supply and demand labour market to be more accurately as well as future China's the quality of labour demand number will be influenced to be raised after they have enough training to learn new skills.

How to solve future China skillful shortage of labour? Firstly, nowadays, China employers need to teach their employees to learn how to use and how to operate robotic skills in China's factories. AI robotic has been early developing, so they need to prepare to learn robotic management and operating technical and soft skills in order to satisfy future China factory automation industry development.

China is one world's factory for low-end products to high quality information products, high end technology and services. So, China will need many high skilled workers to assist manufacturers to manufacture many different kinds of products to export or local sale. Moreover, robotic manufacturing skillful workers will also need because robotic will be accepted to assist manual workers to work in China's any factories. This has led to greater demand for labour wirh upgraded skills and competence. So, it seems that China's orkers need to lern any high technological manufacturing knowledge, e.g. learning how to co-operate with robotics to raise productive efficiencies, which will be future many China's manufacturers' skills need intention.

So, when any one of China manufacturer invests robotics to work in its factory . Then, the China manufacturer's labours ought need to know how to co-operate with th robotics to raise productivities and efficiencies. Moreover, these China service industries, e.g. IT, software, accounting, finance, marketing and customer service management, e.g. waiter, property security, shopping center customer service etc. service occupations. In the future, robotics can also used to participate any one of these service industries' part of tasks in order to raise service performance. So, any one of these service industries' employees need to learn how to operate with robotics in order to achieve the most excellent servvice performances to satisfy consumers' needs. So, China service industries labours ought need to learn how to co-operate or manage service natural robotics to work together more efficiently because future China manufacturers will prefer to employ the labours who know how to co-operate and manage and control any service natural robotics more easily and efficiently in order to achieve the most excellent service performance to satisfy customers needs. Hence, it seems that China manufacturing and service workers need to spend time and effort to learn how to co-operate with manufacturing natural robotics to manufacture any products in factories efficiently or deliver any cargos in warehouses more efficiently or serve customers to let them to feel excellent service performance in restaurants or shopping centers or properties or offices receiption counters. Then, when their China employers apply robotics to participate to work in factories, restaurants, shopping centers, cinemas, offices or properties reception etc. different working places . These low skillful labours will be dismissed easily, due to robotics can replace them to manufacture any products or provide services to satisfy clients' needs in order to let them to fell robotics' performances are more excellent to compare human service labours or their productive efficiencies are more effort to compare workers. So, future China workers need to learn how to cooperate or manage or contol with robotics to work more efficiently, if they do not expect to be dismissed easily.

Future global skillful labor
soft knowledge skill need

In the future several occupations have been identified as the most frequent movers between all labour market states. The elementary occupations include: waiters, bar staffs, clearners, catering assistants, construction and security service workers, care workers, sales assistants and general clerks etc. So, the low educational level workers can learn these soft wkills to raise whose professional workering level to prepare to do these above positions in global elementary occupation job market.

The changes of employer were most frequent for IT programmers, doctors, electricians, carpenters, skilled workers in global labour market. These skilled occupations will have manpower shortage supply challenge, due to either people feel the educatonal level is under low. So, there has no many people have interest to know these knowledg to prepare their elementary careers. So, these kinds of low skilled occupations will have not enough human power supply to global labour job market also, the high skilled or educational job support.

Moreover, the high skilled occupations also encounter labour shortage issue. The skills in short supply related to experienced canadidates e.g. five years or more. For example, pharmaceutical , biogharma and food innovation industries. The occupational shortage roles include: Chemists, analytical scientists, product formulation, analytical development for roles in biopharma, quality control analyst includes pharmaco-vigilance, i.e. drug safety roles. The demand for engineering industry aspect which will aos increase the labour shortage includes process and design (research and development, quality control, automation, lean processes) are skillful labours need to help employers to achieve these intentions. They may include raising competitiveness, boosting productivity and skills availability. So, if future these above any one of occupation labours can not achieve these benefits to satisfy their employers' needs. Then, his/her average weekly or hourly wages will be reduced. It means that the unskilled labour under skilled labour wage can not increased more easily, even they own many year working experiences in any one of above these occupations. If the employer feels the labour is unskilled or below skilled level for any one of these occupations in these any one industry aspect, e.g. wholesale and retal , human health, education, accomodaton and food , construction, professional activities, financial service , public administration, and defence, transportation etc. occupations. Then, these industries' unskilled or below skilled level workers' salaries will be lower level to compare the higher skilled workers who work in any one of these industries.

The reason why future employers need to employ skilled labours. One explanation for slow recovery in demand in negative impact on investment is a prolonged period of high unemployment. This is led to job weekers left labour market or became unemployable due. So, future low skillful level will be one important factor to cause unemployment in society as well as nowadays labours ought need consider whether their skills are needed to improve in order to avoid future competition in job market.

2.1 Why do future labours need to learn worldwide readiness skills

Future employers need employees own worldwide readiness skills, such as reading , writing and arithmatic. Why do employees need worldwide readiness skills? In the future, high economic growth countries need high wage positions, high opportunity jobs which need a large number of skills required of job candidates of these positions " job readinss" and not " job training" , which support developments of these importance and widely desired skills won't only support the success to high-opportunity positions, but also be developed for future success in the competitive global economy. Because real-time business intelligence is needed for the talent marketplace to employ talent employees. So, it explains that it will have many future employers hope to employ owning readiness skillful employees to help them to develop their businesse intelligently. Hence, present employees ought need to hard to train readiness skills to prepare whose future employers' job requirements in the future competitive global job market.

2.2 Why these occupations need readiness skills

In the future these occupations will need to raise readiness skills. For example, mathematical science, teachers (post-secondary), management analysts, computer and information systems, managers, first-line supervisors of construction traders, solar photovoltaic installers. All of these occupations , employers need staffs to own good readiness analytic ability to help them to do more accurate real-time business intelligent decisions. The representative occupations include oral and written communication skills, project management, teamwork, marketing and creativity . Moreover, they need to own specific technology skill, deep science and math or even most business skills as well as these skills are "soft" skills more than hard skills. These kinds of occupation employees need own cooperative effort, creativity, problem solving, detail orientation and integrity personal characteristics, which are relevant across all knowledge and domains.

Therefore, in the future, science, technology,engineering and mathematics relevant occupations need to own more readniness and analytic skills more than othe kinds of occupations. Because these organizations need those professionals on knowledge acquisition, literacy analysis, synthesis and critical thinking skills that will impact their organizations to bring more critical thinking beneficial team culture. These occupational top skills will include oral and written communication skills, project management skill, team oriented skill, marketing and creativity skills, problem solving skill, detail oriented skill, self-motivated skills, management and analytical skills, coaching skill, business process modeling skills, work independent skill, strong leadership skills, management experience and business requirements gathering. All of these skills which will be future employers who need to employ these kinds employees who own these skills in preference. Also, all of these skills concentrate on soft skills more than hard skills. It seems that when above occupational applicants who own any one of thes skills, evn more than one skills. Then, he/she will have more chance to be selected to employ. Also occupation specific skills requirements are more needed to compare cross-functional skills for above of any one occupation. Because the high concentraton of cross-functional skills require " job readiness" and not " job training" for success, e.g. communicaton, integraton and presentation skills, entrepreneurialism and related skills, microsoft office software skills.

Of particular interest is communication, integration and presentation skills. These skills include ability to seek, evaluate and examine information and data create a reasoned position, present findings and make a case for or advocate for position. So, these skills are very important and they can help future applicants who expect to win any kinds of these positions easily. However, the hard skills can help these applicants to be more successful to win any kinds of these positions when they own these hard skills, e.g. microsoft offic, powerpoint, excel , word, microsoft project etc. softwares.

In conclusion, the global economy is dynamic and many of the skills required for positons in the future will need good technologies and work practices to be developed. The number of skills required t be successful in the jobs forecast to be most in demand in the future is growing. So, it explains that why future any one of these occupations which will need soft skills more than hard skills, due to organizations like to employ the employees who own managerial and analytical effort more than hard skills productive effort to assist their organizations to develop more easily.

2.3 Data -analysis skill needs

In the future, most organizations will have a number of jobs that include data analysis. Economists and labor market forecasters predict occupations need data analytical skill will need much. In addition, fast technological development means th types of technologies and applications workers in this field will need to be familiar with data analytical skill rapidly. It seems that data analytical jobs will have new job opportunity to employees with in-demand skills in future global labor market.

Why and how do employers demand for data analysis skills? Data analysis skills mean the ability to gather, analyze and draw practical conclusions from data as well as communicate data findings to others. The occupations include: data analyst, data scientist, statistician, market research analyst, financial analyst,research manager. In business career, many employers expect to employ statisticans, operations researh analysts, market research analysts and marketing specialists to assist their organizations to gather useful data from market in order to analyze and draw practical conclusions and finding the best solutions or methods to win their competitors.

Therefore, these data analysis jobs will have much need. Large size organizations with 500 or more employees were more likely than small or medium size organizations with 25 to 499 employees to plan hired data analysis positons in the future. For example, human source department will use big data to help make strategic decisions. How HR uses big data . HR will use big data for sourcing, recruitment, or selection, identifying causes of turnover and/or employee retention strategies or trends, managing talent and performance. Why organizations do not use big data. It is possible that they lack of knowledg expertise, the majority of organizatons will have data analysis positions within accounting and finance department, human resources department, business and administration department, information technology department, marketing, advertising and sales department, supply chain and operations department, research and development department, customer service department and other departments. So, future data analysis skill will need to used in different organizational departments.

However, publicly and privately owned for-profit organizations were more likely than government organizations to have data analysis positions in the marketing, advertising and sales function. Also, data analysis skills are required to different levels in any organizations , such as entry level, non-management / individual contributor level, mid-level management level, seniot management or executive level. The analyst, research analyst, market research analyst, scientist-based titles include: data scientists , research scientist, scientist, other descriptive titles include researcher, statistician, mathematician and other . So, data analysis positions will have many different skills to be selected to any one data analysis professional. For example, the data analysis professional can select either to learn the ability to interpret and communicate data analysis results skill or to learn how gathering or analyzing data skill. So, data analysis skill is not onlyone skill, it is more than one skill to let any one employee to select to learn.

Why do organizations need data analysis professionals? On workforce planning aspect, organizatons expect to let strategic direction and content of workforce needed for future business objectives easier, analyzing workforce: supply analysis, demand analsis and gap analysis more earier, developing action plan :

recruiting and training plans to deal with gaps more easier, implementing action plan, monitoring, evaluating and revising plan more easier. So, organizations expect the data analysis professionsla can help them to solve these challenges, such as using of advanced technology solutons to integrate disparate planning sources; data availability and format; accessing to and understanding of the organization's data and analytics, developing business case to gain support from senior management and collaboration among HR staff, managers and executive easier. Future industries need data analysis professionals may include manufacturing health care and social assistance, scientific and technical service, finance and insurance, educational services , government agencies, retail trade, transportation and warehousing, construction, utilities, accomodation, and food services, waste management and remediation services, entetainment, and creation, real estate and rental and leasing , repair and maintenance, agriculture, forestry, fishing and hunting, personal and laundry services etc.

In conclusion, data analysis job need explains why future readiness and data analytical skills will be popular needed in globl labour market , due to these both skills are labour shortage and employers will need employees own big data readiness and data analytical both skills in order to win whose competitors more easier.

2.4 What are regional dynamic skills of global labour market demand

Businessmen expect to improve better economic environment, they will prefer to recruit the most sought after skills of intelligent employees to bring positive beneficial impact to organizations. However, technology and digisation has had a significant influence on workers. Future globalization will trend digital economic development. Hence, it will influence workers' skills to be changed also. In fact, not all changes are positive because some workers will possible lose jobs, either due to new technology replaces their jobs or they lack enough effort to improve their skills in global digital economic labour market environment.

It brings this question: What are regional dynamic skills need whn digital busines environment is growing. In fact, organizations will continue to deal with skills shortages, labour markets across the global are continually changing. so, more employers and workers will need to adopt innovate working pattern, e.g. on call jobs, freelance jobs will grow popularly. The greater flexibility afforded to employ regardly.

Finally, digitalisation includes artificial intelligence, big data , online platforms. All these new technology will influence future employees how to worker. For example, they can apply online platform to work at home conveniently. So, they do not need to go to offices. They can finish their jobs and send to their employers by email easily. This kinds of job pattern can raise efficiencies and employers do not need go to offices often.

An important implication of innovating working which needs the employees who own digital skills in order to serve organizations more efficiently. So, employers are increasingly able to access demographics that were hitherto less active in labour markets. For example, future more women are joining the labour market because part time and self employment opportunities make it easier. This kinds of job pattern can raise efficiencies and employees do not need go to offices often.

An important implication of innovating working which needs the employees who own digital skills in order to serve organizations more efficiently. So, employers are increasingly able to access demographic that were hitherto less active in labour markets. For example, future more women are joining the labour market because part time and self employment opportunities make it easier to manage family with work life. So, digital skilling needs will cause many women lose jobs in possible. If the women lack digital job skills. Because high digital skill occupations need, like those requiring research, medical treatment and architectural design occupational digital skills are more common in the services sector, more women who own digital skill who can compete to win.

High digital skill occupations more easier than men because employers usually select female to do high skill occupations easier than make. However, if those professional service female employees can not learn how to apply digital skills to do these researchs medical treatmentm architectural design professional service jobs. Then, it is also different for these professional service femal employees to raise competition in global labour professional service market. So, these professional service female employees need to learn how to apply digital to do themselves jobs in future global professional service labour market. Otherwise, if the male professional service employees can attempt to learn how to apply digital skill to do themselves jobs in order to improve efficiencies and service performance to satisfy patients, such as medical service needs, school search service needs, construction firms' building needs. Then, the owning high digital technology skillful female employees will be more easier to find the professional service jobs which need digital skill more easier than the lacking digital skill female service professionals in future global digital service professional labour market.

On the other robotic communication skill need aspect, future employers expect workers to know how to communicate with robots to work efficiently in any working environment if the employers need robotc to serve their organizations. For example, communication between the robots on factory floors, and between people and robots could allow robots to start and stopr processes based on real-time conditions around them and alert people when there is a problem, so robots could increase their own efficiency if the workers could monitor themselves and determine when they needed maintenance; efficiency would also be improved if machines and robots could make production decisions on their own by. For example, ordering new suppliers when existing inputs into a production process run low. The increase in productivity of industrial robots will likely reduce the number of manual jobs on the shop floor.

At the same time, the increased output made possible by such robots will mean that manufacturers need more people in accounting, finance, sales, advertising and other roles. The increase in putput may also drive increased employment on manufacturers' supply chains. Hence, future employers expect to employ the workers who can know how to communicate with robots to work efficiently in order to raise productivity in any working environment. It means that it the worker can know how to control and communicate with the robots to work together in the team. Then, his/her communication and controlling robotic skill will help the organization's team to work efficiently and raise productivity in order to reduce time waste and human waste and resource waste considerately. So, future shortage of communication and controlling robotic skillful workers number will increase. It has much beneficial to workers who choose to attempt to learn how to communicate and control robots to work together in any working environment team efficiently. Because future employers will like to use robots to assist manual workers to attempt to raise productive efficiency in any working environment. So, the need of employees who know how to cooperate or communicate with robots whose talent skills will be useful to any future employers.

Future global business leaders will need human machine cooperation skill. This technological skill includes artificial intelligence (AI and internet of things (IOT), will reshape our working change. These machines will participate to our daily working environment. For instance, many business leaders agree that automated systems will free-up their time as well as they also believe they'll have more job satisfaction by offloading the tasks that they don't want to do to intelligent machines.

Therefore, future leaders will expect humans and machines can work as integrated teams within their organizaton in order to their workforce and machines are already successfully working this way. So, they need to expect future employees can know or learn how to work with automated systems more easily, because many jobs will be participated by automated systems, e..g simple accounting tasks, legal administration tasks etc. clerical tasks. They will be participated with (AI) technology, it learns how to cooperate with (AI) technology to finish simplt clerical tasks efficiently.

Future workers will need have autrmated system operational skills: They include that how to operate automated systems to free -up workers' time. Workers will need to learn how to operate automated system to better with healthcare tracking devices workers will need to learn how to operate automated systems to absord and manage information in completely different ways. Workers will need to learn how to operate automated systems of smart machines to work as admin. in any orking environments. Workers need be needed to learn how to operate (AI) automated machines to mak more accurate clerical tasks or efficiencies. So, the automated system (robotic) operational skillful workers' demand and number will increase.

In the future, employers need automated machine manufacturing and service with workers cooperation reasons include that clear protocols, will need to be established if autonomous machines fail. So, they need their workers to learn how to control and manage and communicate with autonomous machines skillfully. They believe move they depend upon technology, the more they'll have to lose in the event of a cyber attack. So, skillful workers are real required to let them to know how to cooperate with autonomous machines more efficiently and easily. Computers will need to be able to decipher between good and bad commands, so future employers have much chance to need the owning automated machines operating workers to assist any robots to make more accurate good or bad decision when robots and workers have need to make immediate judgement in their any related job responsibilites aspect. Therefore, future owning automated machines operating workers' skillful level will be high. It bases on automated machine manufacturing environment trend factor. Finally, future technology will connect the right employee to the high task at the right time. It implies that when future global employers began to accept to apply robots to help them to raise any productivities efficiently. It will influence many manufacturing positions which need to employ any proficient skillful workers who own automated machines operational skills to know how to communicate or manage or control , even supervise any robots to work in teams in any organizational manufacturing environment efficiently.

In the future, employers also expect employees to own sufficient digital vision and strategic skills, manifest among other things. They can know how to apply data to demonstrate any senior support and sponsorship digital technological skill. They expect to reduce a skill gap and avoid a lack of employee buying and a workforce culture to change in their digital technologicl manufacturing organizations. Future employers also believe outdated technology that can't work fast enough, data overload, privary and security concerns. So, it explains why it is possible that future employers also need digital working environment and automated robots machines to attempt to achieve raising productive efficient aim.

Moreover, it also explains why digital transformation need will be raised. The reasons include: They feel digital technology can gain employees' buying in , making customer experience a boardroom concern, achieving fair compensation , training and goals and strategy achievement more easily, tasking senior leaders with digital working environment change putting policies and technology to support a fully remote, flexible workforce , empowering lines of team work more efficient, teaching all employees how to code/understanding how to adopt to work with automatic machines or rots in any team efficiently. So, automate machine can raise efficiency in manufacturing society.

In conclusion, in the future business society, employees need to be stronger human machine partnerships. So , future manufacturing or service industries will have digital technology and automated machine robotic technology to assist workers to work in any working environment efficiently. They expect digital technology and automated machine robotic technology anticipation to workers' daily jobs in order to bring positive impacting to the customer experience from business owners to decision makers in marketing, customer service, research and developmnt and finance etc. They also expect technological productivity can bring positive relationship between technology and workers emerging technologies' impact on business and the way workers and automated machine work together.

Future organizational skillful
needs how to influence workforce
change to what kinds of employees

In the future whether in general organizations need what kinds of employees' skills, they expect employee individual own. It is one interesting question. The common skills that employees need to own in order to any duties to any organizational departments efficiently, e.g. human resource, marketing, administrative, logistic etc. different departments. For hospital, school, business, professional occupations etc. different organizations. Whether future school ought implement one system educational method to teach different common skills to students in order to let them to leave schools to jobs more easier.

Future employers need to create new technologies including automation and algorithms, in order to create new high quality jobs and improve the job quality and productivity of the existing work of human employees in any organizations, e.g. accounting department will need intelligence (AI) to assist account clerks to do simple repeating accounting job tasks in order to share their work load and raise performance efficiency or legal organizations will need (AI) to assist law clerks to do simple repeating legal draft or legal document revising job tasks . All future general clerical jobs will apply (AI) technological tools to assist human to job, it will produce a comprehensive platform for managing workforce change.

Hence, human manual(employees) need to learn how to adopt (AI) job participation to assist them to do different kinds of simple clerical jobs in any organizational administrative departments . They , clerical employees or white color workers need to learn how manage or dominate (AI) tool to improve job performance to be better. However, (AI) administrative workforce change, it is not only one kind of job automation change role in any physical offices. It influences future administrative clerks need change a more flexible manner, utilizing remote staffing beyond physical offices and decentralization of operations organizational workforce change.

Instead of (AI) participation to administrative job aspect, (AI) will also participate to manufacturing industry environment aspect, a new human-machine manufacturing workforce change will exist to any factories, warehouses working environment. Scientists predict that in present an average of 71% of total task hours across the industries are performed by humans, compared a 29% by machines. In this average is expected to have shifted to 58% task hours performed by humans and 42% by machines. In fact, nowadays, in terms of total working hours, no work task was yet estimated to be predominantly performed by a machine or an algorithm (AI). But, this picture is predicted to have somewhat changed with machines and algorithms (AI) on average increasing their contribution to specific tasks by 57% . For example, in the future, 62% of organization's information and data processing and information search and transmission tasks will be performed by machines compared to 46% today.

Therefore, these high technological skillful job change will bring negative influence to some demotive-skillful or low skillful labors to be dismissed, if they can not upgrade or raise or reskillgul their skill level to improve their analytical thinking , technology design and programming skills to cooperate with (AI) tools to work efficiently together in any organizational manufacturing or offie work environment. Because it will have many employers apply (AI) automation tools to participate with blue -color or whiate -color workers' tasks in order to raise efficiencies or improve performance in any working environment. So, it is right time to young or mid age employees need to upskill and/or reskill their rihgt type of skills to prepare future technology risch work environment changeing needs.

Future technological advances will permit an increasing number of tasks traditionally performed by humans to become automated. It seems that , such automation focused primarily on routine tasks, e.g. clerical work, bookkeeping, basic paralegal work and reporting etc. However, with the advent of big data, artificial intelligence (AI), the internet of things and ever-increasing computing power , i.e. the digital revolutions, non-routine tasks are also increasingly likely to become automated. For example, the recent development in robotics and 3D printing allow firms in advanced economies to locate production closer to domestic markets in fully aumomated factories. As a result, the future strongest incentive to automate because of their relatively higher labour costs will be reduced, when production automated will bring the negative influence to dismiss some foolish or low produtive or low skill workers , the owning high automated productive skillful workers will replace the low productive skillful workers in any factories' manufacturing environments. So, technological progress participates to raise quantity of jobs will cause result in significant job losses to low skillful workers. Because future employers will need many high automated productive employees to help them to cooperate with (AI) automated machine to work together efficiently. For example, many proportion of occupations at high risk is greatest in Germany and lowest in Korea, these countries organizations will accept to spend technology investments and education of workers to prepare future automatability manufacturing development successfully.

However, future automatability manufacturing development will bring technological unemployment in possible, due to workers need to adjust to the challenge of automation by switching tasks. Thus, preventing technological unemployment, also technological change does not just destroy jobs, but also generates new roles through its effect on productivity and the demand for new technologies. For example, it has been estimated that, for each high tech-job created in the industries , such as computing equipment or electrical machinery, some 4.9 % additional jobs are created for lawyers, taxi, drivers and waites in the local economy (Moretti, 2011).

Therefore, automated will also influence service industries' job nature change, e.g. taxi drivers need to apply (AI) automated machines to assist them to drive their taxis. When the passenger tells the taxi driver where he/she wants to go. Then, the (AI automated machine will follow the GPS road direction map to be indicated how to drive the taxi to go to the destination automatically . So, future taxi driver is one assistance role to assist the (AI) automated driving tool to dominate the (AI) tool to drive the taxi to catch the passenger to arrive the destination safety in the short time in possible. For another example, future restaurant waiters will need (AI) automated machines's assistance to help them to deliver or dispatch any foods and soft drinks to send to the identified eater's table carefully in accurate and efficient service performance way from the kitchen, in especially in the busy time and many people are sitting in the large size restaurant environment. So, future, waiter roles will be the leader , they need to manage or control or supervise the (AI) robotics how to make decisions to arrange to dispatch which foods or soft drinks to the different tables in preference immediately. Also, future law clerks need to supervise or manage the law robotics how to help them to make decisions to do revision or draft or filing legal tasks in preference in order to avoid any typing words are mistaken to type on computers or revised draft in wrong way to assist manual legal clerks' mistaken words are appearanced on any legal documents. So, the law clerk future role will be the trainer role , he/she eeds to teacher the robots how to check any words, e.g. grammers to correct them to be right grammers, or giving the accurate revision legal documents' instruction to let the legal robots to know how to revise each legal draft to prove whether which part of the legal draft will have wrong to be needed to revise.

In conclusion, future many manual workers' service or manfacturing job natures will become automated assistance to robotics. So, employees need to upgrade their skills in order to adopt new technological work nature change. So future CEO needs to prepare to learn how to apply robotic technological skills to train workers to raise efficiencies and improve performance because there are many future organizations start to apply robotic manufacturing tools to assist workers to work in any departments. Hence, future excellent CEOs must need to own AI knowledge to satisfy their organizational performance improvement need.

Skill training talent human method

Skill is an ability or effort that you need to put time to develop. Talent refers to an inborn and special ability you own it. So, when one person can attempt to learn ths kind of skill. It is possible that he can be trained to be talent person. How to Create Effective Skills Training with Career Pathing ? Your company's ability to address the skills gap is going to be the most significant issue facing HR in the next decade. Relying on the recruitment of new hires will no longer be a viable solution. Digital transformation of the workplace means that AI and automation are continually rendering skills obsolete while creating new jobs in the process. As those new roles emerge, the existing talent pool will be insufficient to meet demand. Employers will no longer be able to fall back on their default strategy of hiring new workers.

● How to improve staff skill to be talent labour ?

As the 'future of work' begins to assume a more defined shape, the majority of employers are placing more emphasis on training of their existing talent, but skills development is not moving fast enough to keep up with demand. Ongoing upskilling and reskilling can help to offset the impact on your workforce from these fundamental changes.

Creating personalized development opportunities

When it comes to developing your talent, there is no 'one size fits all' approach. To succeed in today's workplace the following steps are recommended. Your approach must become more personal, placing development at the center of your overall business strategy. Personalized development opportunities should be offered to enhance skills acquisition. This approach enables you to provide your employees with the tools they need to acquire new skills.

As well as being targeted to the individual, employees should be able to learn in their own time. Technology can help to support this. A further, critical point to note is that learning and development is not exclusively for the C Suite but should be offered to all of your employees.

- Career pathing strategy improve employee individual skill ?

Career pathing provides a clear route into all of these options, enables you to create individual learning programs for all of your employees and offers the following benefits.

Employees create their own career paths, which are aligned with your organization's business goals. All employees are guided to understand their own strengths and weaknesses and are empowered to identify key areas for development. They are inspired to work towards vertical or lateral moves within your organization, for example, through job rotation (ie, where employees assume new tasks in a different role for a specified period before they 'rotate' back to their original post). Career pathing enables HR and management to understand and analyze employee aspirations through internal mobility programs and aligns well with your succession planning program. So, career pathing strategy is one kind of good skill to raise staff efficiency or improve performance.

Skills shortages on developing country market

Future developing countries need to develop their economy, so they need to employ many employees who own technical skills and /or soft skills. What kind of technical skills and/or soft skills , the developing countries' employees who will need to order to raise competiton in local job market ? I shall indicate the developing country China example. China is one developing country, employers will need different kinds of skillful labors to assist them to develop their businesses. However, China employers will face skillful labour shortage challenge. Although Chinese young age population is high, but many of them do not to be encouraged to learn enough skillful knowledge to fill future new skillful positions. So, the fast speed of training will be important to influence China supply and demand labour market to be more accurately as well as future China's the quality of labour demand number will be influenced to be raised after they have enough training to learn new skills.

How to solve future China skillful shortage of labour? Firstly, nowadays, China employers need to teach their employees to learn how to use and how to operate robotic skills in China's factories. AI robotic has been early developing, so they need to prepare to learn robotic management and operating technical and soft skills in order to satisfy future China factory automation industry development.

China is one world's factory for low-end products to high quality information products, high end technology and services. So, China will need many high skilled workers to assist manufacturers to manufacture many different kinds of products to export or local sale. Moreover, robotic manufacturing skillful workers will also need because robotic will be accepted to assist manual workers to work in China's any factories. This has led to greater demand for labour wirh upgraded skills and competence. So, it seems that China's orkers need to lern any high technological manufacturing knowledge, e.g. learning how to co-operate with robotics to raise productive efficiencies, which will be future many China's manufacturers' skills need intention.

So, when any one of China manufacturer invests robotics to work in its factory . Then, the China manufacturer's labours ought need to know how to co-operate with th robotics to raise productivities and efficiencies. Moreover, these China service industries, e.g. IT, software, accounting, finance, marketing and customer service management, e.g. waiter, property security, shopping center customer service etc. service occupations. In the future, robotics can also used to participate any one of these service industries' part of tasks in order to raise service performance. So, any one of these service industries' employees need to learn how to operate with robotics in order to achieve the most excellent servvice performances to satisfy consumers' needs. So, China service industries labours ought need to learn how to co-operate or manage service natural robotics to work together more efficiently because future China manufacturers will prefer to employ the labours who know how to co-operate and manage and control any service natural robotics more easily and efficiently in order to achieve the most excellent service performance to satisfy customers needs. Hence, it seems that China manufacturing and service workers need to spend time and effort to learn how to co-operate with manufacturing natural robotics to manufacture any products in factories efficiently or deliver any cargos in warehouses more efficiently or serve customers to let them to feel excellent service performance in restaurants or shopping centers or properties or offices receiption counters. Then, when their China employers apply robotics to participate to work in factories, restaurants, shopping centers, cinemas, offices or properties reception etc. different working places . These low skillful labours will be dismissed easily, due to robotics can replace them to manufacture any products or provide services to satisfy clients' needs in order to let them to fell robotics' performances are more excellent to compare human service labours or their productive efficiencies are more effort to compare workers. So, future China workers need to learn how to cooperate or manage or contol with robotics to work more efficiently, if they do not expect to be dismissed easily.

In the future several occupations have been identified as the most frequent movers between all labour market states. The elementary occupations include: waiters, bar staffs, clearners, catering assistants, construction and security service workers, care workers, sales assistants and general clerks etc. So, the low educational level workers can learn these soft wkills to raise whose professional workering level to prepare to do these above positions in global elementary occupation job market.

The changes of employer were most frequent for IT programmers, doctors, electricians, carpenters, skilled workers in global labour market. These skilled occupations will have manpower shortage supply challenge, due to either people feel the educatonal level is under low. So, there has no many people have interest to know these knowledg to prepare their elementary careers. So, these kinds of low skilled occupations will have not enough human power supply to global labour job market also, the high skilled or educational job support.

Moreover, the high skilled occupations also encounter labour shortage issue. The skills in short supply related to experienced canadidates e.g. five years or more. For example, pharmaceutical , biogharma and food innovation industries. The occupational shortage roles include: Chemists, analytical scientists, product formulation, analytical development for roles in biopharma, quality control analyst includes pharmaco-vigilance, i.e. drug safety roles. The demand for engineering industry aspect which will aos increase the labour shortage includes process and design (research and development, quality control, automation, lean processes) are skillful labours need to help employers to achieve these intentions. They may include raising competitiveness, boosting productivity and skills availability. So, if future these above any one of occupation labours can not achieve these benefits to satisfy their employers' needs. Then, his/her average weekly or hourly wages will be reduced. It means that the unskilled labour under skilled labour wage can not increased more easily, even they own many year working experiences in any one of above these occupations. If the employer feels the labour is unskilled or below skilled level for any one of these occupations in these any one industry aspect, e.g. wholesale and retal , human health, education, accomodaton and food , construction, professional activities, financial service , public administration, and defence, transportation etc. occupations. Then, these industries' unskilled or below skilled level workers' salaries will be lower level to compare the higher skilled workers who work in any one of these industries.

The reason why future employers need to employ skilled labours. One explanation for slow recovery in demand in negative impact on investment is a prolonged period of high unemployment. This is led to job weekers left labour market or became unemployable due. So, future low skillful level will be one important factor to cause unemployment in society as well as nowadays labours ought need consider whether their skills are needed to improve in order to avoid future competition in job market.

2.1 Why do future labours need to learn worldwide readiness skills

Future employers need employees own worldwide readiness skills, such as reading , writing and arithmatic. Why do employees need worldwide readiness skills? In the future, high economic growth countries need high wage positions, high opportunity jobs which need a large number of skills required of job candidates of these positions " job readinss" and not " job training" , which support developments of these importance and widely desired skills won't only support the success to high-opportunity positions, but also be developed for future success in the competitive global economy. Because real-time business intelligence is needed for the talent marketplace to employ talent employees. So, it explains that it will have many future employers hope to employ owning readiness skillful employees to help them to develop their businesse intelligently. Hence, present employees ought need to hard to train readiness skills to prepare whose future employers' job requirements in the future competitive global job market.

2.2 Why these occupations need readiness skills

In the future these occupations will need to raise readiness skills. For example, mathematical science, teachers (post-secondary), management analysts, computer and information systems, managers, first-line supervisors of construction traders, solar photovoltaic installers. All of these occupations , employers need staffs to own good readiness analytic ability to help them to do more accurate real-time business intelligent decisions. The representative occupations include oral and written communication skills, project management, teamwork, marketing and creativity . Moreover, they need to own specific technology skill, deep science and math or even most business skills as well as these skills are "soft" skills more than hard skills. These kinds of occupation employees need own cooperative effort, creativity, problem solving, detail orientation and integrity personal characteristics, which are relevant across all knowledge and domains.

Therefore, in the future, science, technology,engineering and mathematics relevant occupations need to own more readniness and analytic skills more than othe kinds of occupations. Because these organizations need those professionals on knowledge acquisition, literacy analysis, synthesis and critical thinking skills that will impact their organizations to bring more critical thinking beneficial team culture. These occupational top skills will include oral and written communication skills, project management skill, team oriented skill, marketing and creativity skills, problem solving skill, detail oriented skill, self-motivated skills, management and analytical skills, coaching skill, business process modeling skills, work independent skill, strong leadership skills, management experience and business requirements gathering. All of these skills which will be future employers who need to employ these kinds employees who own these skills in preference. Also, all of these skills concentrate on soft skills more than hard skills. It seems that when above occupational applicants who own any one of thes skills, evn more than one skills. Then, he/she will have more chance to be selected to employ. Also occupation specific skills requirements are more needed to compare cross-functional skills for above of any one occupation. Because the high concentraton of cross-functional skills require " job readiness" and not " job training" for success, e.g. communicaton, integraton and presentation skills, entrepreneurialism and related skills, microsoft office software skills.

Of particular interest is communication, integration and presentation skills. These skills include ability to seek, evaluate and examine information and data create a reasoned position, present findings and make a case for or advocate for position. So, these skills are very important and they can help future applicants who expect to win any kinds of these positions easily. However, the hard skills can help these applicants to be more successful to win any kinds of these positions when they own these hard skills, e.g. microsoft offic,

powerpoint, excel , word, microsoft project etc. softwares.
In conclusion, the global economy is dynamic and many of the skills required for positons in the future will need good technologies and work practices to be developed. The number of skills required t be successful in the jobs forecast to be most in demand in the future is growing. So, it explains that why future any one of these occupations which will need soft skills more than hard skills, due to organizations like to employ the employees who own managerial and analytical effort more than hard skills productive effort to assist their organizations to develop more easily.

2.3 Data -analysis skill needs

In the future, most organizations will have a number of jobs that include data analysis. Economists and labor market forecasters predict occupations need data analytical skill will need much. In addition, fast technological development means th types of technologies and applications workers in this field will need to be familiar with data analytical skill rapidly. It seems that data analytical jobs will have new job opportunity to employees with in-demand skills in future global labor market.
Why and how do employers demand for data analysis skills? Data analysis skills mean the ability to gather, analyze and draw practical conclusions from data as well as communicate data findings to others. The occupations include: data analyst, data scientist, statistician, market research analyst, financial analyst,research manager. In business career, many employers expect to employ statisticans, operations researh analysts, market research analysts and marketing specialists to assist their organizations to gather useful data from market in order to analyze and draw practical conclusions and finding the best solutions or methods to win their competitors.
Therefore, these data analysis jobs will have much need. Large size organizations with 500 or more employees were more likely than small or medium size organizations with 25 to 499 employees to plan hired data analysis positons in the future. For example, human

source department will use big data to help make strategic decisions. How HR uses big data . HR will use big data for sourcing, recruitment, or selection, identifying causes of turnover and/or employee retention strategies or trends, managing talent and performance. Why organizations do not use big data. It is possible that they lack of knowledg expertise, the majority of organizatons will have data analysis positions within accounting and finance department, human resources department, business and administration department, information technology department, marketing, advertising and sales department, supply chain and operations department, research and development department, customer service department and other departments. So, future data analysis skill will need to used in different organizational departments.

However, publicly and privately owned for-profit organizations were more likely than government organizations to have data analysis positions in the marketing, advertising and sales function. Also, data analysis skills are required to different levels in any organizations , such as entry level, non-management / individual contributor level, mid-level management level, seniot management or executive level. The analyst, research analyst, market research analyst, scientist-based titles include: data scientists , research scientist, scientist, other descriptive titles include researcher, statistician, mathematician and other . So, data analysis positions will have many different skills to be selected to any one data analysis professional. For example, the data analysis professional can select either to learn the ability to interpret and communicate data analysis results skill or to learn how gathering or analyzing data skill. So, data analysis skill is not onlyone skill, it is more than one skill to let any one employee to select to learn.

Why do organizations need data analysis professionals? On workforce planning aspect, organizatons expect to let strategic direction and content of workforce needed for future business objectives easier, analyzing workforce: supply analysis, demand analsis and gap analysis more earier, developing action plan :

recruiting and training plans to deal with gaps more easier, implementing action plan, monitoring, evaluating and revising plan more easier. So, organizations expect the data analysis professionsla can help them to solve these challenges, such as using of advanced technology solutons to integrate disparate planning sources; data availability and format; accessing to and understanding of the organization's data and analytics, developing business case to gain support from senior management and collaboration among HR staff, managers and executive easier. Future industries need data analysis professionals may include manufacturing health care and social assistance, scientific and technical service, finance and insurance, educational services , government agencies, retail trade, transportation and warehousing, construction, utilities, accomodation, and food services, waste management and remediation services, entetainment, and creation, real estate and rental and leasing , repair and maintenance, agriculture, forestry, fishing and hunting, personal and laundry services etc.

In conclusion, data analysis job need explains why future readiness and data analytical skills will be popular needed in globl labour market , due to these both skills are labour shortage and employers will need employees own big data readiness and data analytical both skills in order to win whose competitors more easier.

2.4 What are regional dynamic skills of global labour market demand

Businessmen expect to improve better economic environment, they will prefer to recruit the most sought after skills of intelligent employees to bring positive beneficial impact to organizations. However, technology and digisation has had a significant influence on workers. Future globalization will trend digital economic development. Hence, it will influence workers' skills to be changed also. In fact, not all changes are positive because some workers will possible lose jobs, either due to new technology replaces their jobs or they lack enough effort to improve their skills in global digital economic labour market environment.

It brings this question: What are regional dynamic skills need whn digital busines environment is growing. In fact, organizations will continue to deal with skills shortages, labour markets across the global are continually changing. so, more employers and workers will need to adopt innovate working pattern, e.g. on call jobs, freelance jobs will grow popularly. The greater flexibility afforded to employ regardly.

Finally, digitalisation includes artificial intelligence, big data , online platforms. All these new technology will influence future employees how to worker. For example, they can apply online platform to work at home conveniently. So, they do not need to go to offices. They can finish their jobs and send to their employers by email easily. This kinds of job pattern can raise efficiencies and employers do not need go to offices often.

An important implication of innovating working which needs the employees who own digital skills in order to serve organizations more efficiently. So, employers are increasingly able to access demographics that were hitherto less active in labour markets. For example, future more women are joining the labour market because part time and self employment opportunities make it easier. This kinds of job pattern can raise efficiencies and employees do not need go to offices often.

An important implication of innovating working which needs the employees who own digital skills in order to serve organizations more efficiently. So, employers are increasingly able to access demographic that were hitherto less active in labour markets. For example, future more women are joining the labour market because part time and self employment opportunities make it easier to manage family with work life. So, digital skilling needs will cause many women lose jobs in possible. If the women lack digital job skills. Because high digital skill occupations need, like those requiring research, medical treatment and architectural design occupational digital skills are more common in the services sector, more women who own digital skill who can compete to win.

High digital skill occupations more easier than men because employers usually select female to do high skill occupations easier than make. However, if those professional service female employees can not learn how to apply digital skills to do these researchs medical treatmentm architectural design professional service jobs. Then, it is also different for these professional service femal employees to raise competition in global labour professional service market. So, these professional service female employees need to learn how to apply digital to do themselves jobs in future global professional service labour market. Otherwise, if the male professional service employees can attempt to learn how to apply digital skill to do themselves jobs in order to improve efficiencies and service performance to satisfy patients, such as medical service needs, school search service needs, construction firms' building needs. Then, the owning high digital technology skillful female employees will be more easier to find the professional service jobs which need digital skill more easier than the lacking digital skill female service professionals in future global digital service professional labour market.

On the other robotic communication skill need aspect, future employers expect workers to know how to communicate with robots to work efficiently in any working environment if the employers need robotc to serve their organizations. For example, communication between the robots on factory floors, and between people and robots could allow robots to start and stopr processes based on real-time conditions around them and alert people when there is a problem, so robots could increase their own efficiency if the workers could monitor themselves and determine when they needed maintenance; efficiency would also be improved if machines and robots could make production decisions on their own by. For example, ordering new suppliers when existing inputs into a production process run low. The increase in productivity of industrial robots will likely reduce the number of manual jobs on the shop floor.

At the same time, the increased output made possible by such robots will mean that manufacturers need more people in accounting, finance, sales, advertising and other roles. The increase in putput may also drive increased employment on manufacturers' supply chains. Hence, future employers expect to employ the workers who can know how to communicate with robots to work efficiently in order to raise productivity in any working environment. It means that it the worker can know how to control and communicate with the robots to work together in the team. Then, his/her communication and controlling robotic skill will help the organization's team to work efficiently and raise productivity in order to reduce time waste and human waste and resource waste considerately. So, future shortage of communication and controlling robotic skillful workers number will increase. It has much beneficial to workers who choose to attempt to learn how to communicate and control robots to work together in any working environment team efficiently. Because future employers will like to use robots to assist manual workers to attempt to raise productive efficiency in any working environment. So, the need of employees who know how to cooperate or communicate with robots whose talent skills will be useful to any future employers.

Future global business leaders will need human machine cooperation skill. This technological skill includes artificial intelligence (AI and internet of things (IOT), will reshape our working change. These machines will participate to our daily working environment. For instance, many business leaders agree that automated systems will free-up their time as well as they also believe they'll have more job satisfaction by offloading the tasks that they don't want to do to intelligent machines.

Therefore, future leaders will expect humans and machines can work as integrated teams within their organizaton in order to their workforce and machines are already successfully working this way. So, they need to expect future employees can know or learn how to work with automated systems more easily, because many jobs will be participated by automated systems, e..g simple accounting tasks, legal administration tasks etc. clerical tasks. They will be participated with (AI) technology, it learns how to cooperate with (AI) technology to finish simplt clerical tasks efficiently.

Future workers will need have autrmated system operational skills: They include that how to operate automated systems to free -up workers' time. Workers will need to learn how to operate automated system to better with healthcare tracking devices workers will need to learn how to operate automated systems to absord and manage information in completely different ways. Workers will need to learn how to operate automated systems of smart machines to work as admin. in any orking environments. Workers need be needed to learn how to operate (AI) automated machines to mak more accurate clerical tasks or efficiencies. So, the automated system (robotic) operational skillful workers' demand and number will increase.

In the future, employers need automated machine manufacturing and service with workers cooperation reasons include that clear protocols, will need to be established if autonomous machines fail. So, they need their workers to learn how to control and manage and communicate with autonomous machines skillfully. They believe move they depend upon technology, the more they'll have to lose in the event of a cyber attack. So, skillful workers are real required to let them to know how to cooperate with autonomous machines more efficiently and easily. Computers will need to be able to decipher between good and bad commands, so future employers have much chance to need the owning automated machines operating workers to assist any robots to make more accurate good or bad decision when robots and workers have need to make immediate judgement in their any related job responsibilites aspect. Therefore, future owning automated machines operating workers' skillful level will be high. It bases on automated machine manufacturing environment trend factor. Finally, future technology will connect the right employee to the high task at the right time. It implies that when future global employers began to accept to apply robots to help them to raise any productivities efficiently. It will influence many manufacturing positions which need to employ any proficient skillful workers who own automated machines operational skills to know how to communicate or manage or control , even supervise any robots to work in teams in any organizational manufacturing environment efficiently.

In the future, employers also expect employees to own sufficient digital vision and strategic skills, manifest among other things. They can know how to apply data to demonstrate any senior support and sponsorship digital technological skill. They expect to reduce a skill gap and avoid a lack of employee buying and a workforce culture to change in their digital technologicl manufacturing organizations. Future employers also believe outdated technology that can't work fast enough, data overload, privary and security concerns. So, it explains why it is possible that future employers also need digital working environment and automated robots machines to attempt to achieve raising productive efficient aim.

Moreover, it also explains why digital transformation need will be raised. The reasons include: They feel digital technology can gain employees‘ buying in , making customer experience a boardroom concern, achieving fair compensation , training and goals and strategy achievement more easily, tasking senior leaders with digital working environment change putting policies and technology to support a fully remote, flexible workforce , empowering lines of team work more efficient, teaching all employees how to code/understanding how to adopt to work with automatic machines or rots in any team efficiently. So, automate machine can raise efficiency in manufacturing society.

In conclusion, in the future business society, employees need to be stronger human machine partnerships. So , future manufacturing or service industries will have digital technology and automated machine robotic technology to assist workers to work in any working environment efficiently. They expect digital technology and automated machine robotic technology anticipation to workers' daily jobs in order to bring positive impacting to the customer experience from business owners to decision makers in marketing, customer service, research and developmnt and finance etc. They also expect technological productivity can bring positive relationship between technology and workers emerging technologies' impact on business and the way workers and automated machine work together.

In the future whether in general organizations need what kinds of employees' skills, they expect employee individual own. It is one interesting question. The common skills that employees need to own in order to any duties to any organizational departments efficiently, e.g. human resource, marketing, administrative, logistic etc. different departments. For hospital, school, business, professional occupations etc. different organizations. Whether future school ought implement one system educational method to teach different common skills to students in order to let them to leave schools to jobs more easier.

Future employers need to create new technologies including automation and algorithms, in order to create new high quality jobs and improve the job quality and productivity of the existing work of human employees in any organizations, e.g. accounting department will need intelligence (AI) to assist account clerks to do simple repeating accounting job tasks in order to share their work load and raise performance efficiency or legal organizations will need (AI) to assist law clerks to do simple repeating legal draft or legal document revising job tasks . All future general clerical jobs will apply (AI) technological tools to assist human to job, it will produce a comprehensive platform for managing workforce change.

Hence, human manual(employees) need to learn how to adopt (AI) job participation to assist them to do different kinds of simple clerical jobs in any organizational administrative departments . They , clerical employees or white color workers need to learn how manage or dominate (AI) tool to improve job performance to be better. However, (AI) administrative workforce change, it is not only one kind of job automation change role in any physical offices. It influences future administrative clerks need change a more flexible manner, utilizing remote staffing beyond physical offices and decentralization of operations organizational workforce change.

Instead of (AI) participation to administrative job aspect, (AI) will also participate to manufacturing industry environment aspect, a new human-machine manufacturing workforce change will exist to any factories, warehouses working environment. Scientists predict that in present an average of 71% of total task hours across the industries are performed by humans, compared a 29% by machines. In this average is expected to have shifted to 58% task hours performed by humans and 42% by machines. In fact, nowadays, in terms of total working hours, no work task was yet estimated to be predominantly performed by a machine or an algorithm (AI). But, this picture is predicted to have somewhat changed with machines and algorithms (AI) on average increasing their contribution to specific tasks by 57% . For example, in the future, 62% of organization's information and data processing and information search and transmission tasks will be performed by machines compared to 46% today.

Therefore, these high technological skillful job change will bring negative influence to some demotive-skillful or low skillful labors to be dismissed, if they can not upgrade or raise or reskillgul their skill level to improve their analytical thinking , technology design and programming skills to cooperate with (AI) tools to work efficiently together in any organizational manufacturing or offie work environment. Because it will have many employers apply (AI) automation tools to participate with blue -color or whiate -color workers' tasks in order to raise efficiencies or improve performance in any working environment. So, it is right time to young or mid age employees need to upskill and/or reskill their rihgt type of skills to prepare future technology risch work environment changeing needs.

Future technological advances will permit an increasing number of tasks traditionally performed by humans to become automated. It seems that , such automation focused primarily on routine tasks, e.g. clerical work, bookkeeping, basic paralegal work and reporting etc. However, with the advent of big data, artificial intelligence (AI), the internet of things and ever-increasing computing power , i.e. the digital revolutions, non-routine tasks are also increasingly likely to become automated. For example, the recent development in robotics and 3D printing allow firms in advanced economies to locate production closer to domestic markets in fully aumomated factories. As a result, the future strongest incentive to automate because of their relatively higher labour costs will be reduced, when production automated will bring the negative influence to dismiss some foolish or low produtive or low skill workers , the owning high automated productive skillful workers will replace the low productive skillful workers in any factories' manufacturing environments. So, technological progress participates to raise quantity of jobs will cause result in significant job losses to low skillful workers. Because future employers will need many high automated productive employees to help them to cooperate with (AI) automated machine to work together efficiently. For example, many proportion of occupations at high risk is greatest in Germany and lowest in Korea, these countries organizations will accept to spend technology investments and education of workers to prepare future automatability manufacturing development successfully.

However, future automatability manufacturing development will bring technological unemployment in possible, due to workers need to adjust to the challenge of automation by switching tasks. Thus, preventing technological unemployment, also technological change does not just destroy jobs, but also generates new roles through its effect on productivity and the demand for new technologies. For example, it has been estimated that, for each high tech-job created in the industries , such as computing equipment or electrical machinery, some 4.9 % additional jobs are created for lawyers, taxi, drivers and waites in the local economy (Moretti, 2011).

Therefore, automated will also influence service industries' job nature change, e.g. taxi drivers need to apply (AI) automated machines to assist them to drive their taxis. When the passenger tells the taxi driver where he/she wants to go. Then, the (AI automated machine will follow the GPS road direction map to be indicated how to drive the taxi to go to the destination automatically . So, future taxi driver is one assistance role to assist the (AI) automated driving tool to dominate the (AI) tool to drive the taxi to catch the passenger to arrive the destination safety in the short time in possible. For another example, future restaurant waiters will need (AI) automated machines's assistance to help them to deliver or dispatch any foods and soft drinks to send to the identified eater's table carefully in accurate and efficient service performance way from the kitchen, in especially in the busy time and many people are sitting in the large size restaurant environment. So, future, waiter roles will be the leader , they need to manage or control or supervise the (AI) robotics how to make decisions to arrange to dispatch which foods or soft drinks to the different tables in preference immediately. Also, future law clerks need to supervise or manage the law robotics how to help them to make decisions to do revision or draft or filing legal tasks in preference in order to avoid any typing words are mistaken to type on computers or revised draft in wrong way to assist manual legal clerks' mistaken words are appearanced on any legal documents. So, the law clerk future role will be the trainer role , he/she eeds to teacher the robots how to check any words, e.g. grammers to correct them to be right grammers, or giving the accurate revision legal documents' instruction to let the legal robots to know how to revise each legal draft to prove whether which part of the legal draft will have wrong to be needed to revise.

In conclusion, future many manual workers' service or manfacturing job natures will become automated assistance to robotics. So, employees need to upgrade their skills in order to adopt new technological work nature change.Such as Amazon is one super ecommerce organization, it ought need all different departments staffs prepare to ungrade their different kinds of skills, e.g. reading skills for KDP publish review book tasks in order to let authors can have more attractive topics to let readers can buy any Amazon ebooks to read. So, reading skills may be the essential element to Amazon any one book review staff in itself online publish business. Even ebook ecommerce platform design whether Amazon KDP publish online platform can attract to let global readers to feel enjoyment to read its ebooks , it is one essential element to help Amazon to increase e-readers number every day, so Amazon publish platform needs to improve itself ebook reading platform design improve to attract many e-readers like to choose Amazon e-reading platform to read Amazon any authors ebooks. So, E-reading platform design staffs need to upgrade themselves e-reading platform design skills. So, Amazon knolwedge workers number must need to increase in order to continue to improve its e-platform design to attract global e-reading customers or e-shoppers choose to buy Amazon any kinds of products.

Reference

Moretti, E. (2011) local labor market in O, Ashentelter and D. Card (eds.) handbook of labor economics, Elsevier, North Halland.

THREE

AMAZON ORGANIZATION RESOURCE MANAGEMENT STRATEGY

Organization tangible and intangible resources function

Any organizations must have tangible and intangible resources. Tangible resources may include: Staffs, lands, equipment, producing machines, factory etc. They may help organizations to produce products or provide services to earn profit, e.g. one shop may be the firm's tangible assets if it can be designed to be the best and provide soft music to let customers to listen and provide clourful light design , they may influence they to bring happy consumption emotion in order to attract many customers to stay long time in the shop and increases shopping chance, the salespeople (staffs) to attract more customers , they may be influenced to feel enjoy to stay long long time by their services. Although, any customers visit any shops , it must not represent that they quarantee to buy any things before they leave the shop. However, I beleive that any business , their products functions and prices is one influential factor to persuade consumers to do shopping activities, their shop design attraction feeling may be also another main factor to persuade them to do shopping decision because when the consumer feels the shop is comfortable , it will cause he/she feels enjoyable to stay long time in the shop. Consequently, shop design attraction may be another influential intangible resource factor to encourage consumers to buy any things easily, if they can be influenced to stay long time in the shop by the ship design attraction. It is one kind of feeling factor to excite consumers to do shopping decision. SO, shop may be one important organization fixed asset resource to influence consumer individual purchase desire in any business environment. It is one good exmaple organizational tangible fixed asset redsource to help any organizations to create income.

The another kind of intangible resources, they are not seen by any customers and they can not be toughed by any customers. BUt they are organizational resources, they also may help any organizations to earn income. Why can intangible resource help organizations to earn income? I shall explain as below:

Customer services and staff skills, they may be organiztional intangible resources and they may help any organizations to create income. For example, when one shop has one kindly and friendly salespeople, when any one customer enters this shop, he will say" Good morning", " Good afternoon", "Good night" and when the customer leaves this shop, he will say " Goodby". Even, when the customer has not bought any thing till to leave this shop, this salesperson also speaks " Goodby". So, all of shop visitors, when the salesperson sees them, he must speaks above words, so any one must feel he is polite person and he can represents this shop's polite image also. Although, some shop visitors do not buy anything when they are staying in this shop, but they must feel that this salesperson's attitude is polite to let them to feel. THis salesperson can bring happy feeling to let all shop visitors feel. So, he must not be complainted easily, because when this salesperson discovers any one person is staying to close to any one producg shelf location in the shop, he will walk to the person to enquire him" DO you need I help you?" politely. Although, it is possible that this person won't need this salesperson to help him, but this salesperson can let this shop visitor to feel that he does not need find any one salesperson to enquire when he feels that he needs purchase help, e.g. whether the shirt has small size stock, or the shoe has organge colour etc. product information enquiries. SO, this salesperson can let this shop visitor feels he can take care to his purchase choice behavior and he can do and purchase help in this shop any time. So, this salesperson , his excellent service performance can let any one shop visitor feels service satisfaction, instead of his essential sale customer service performance. IN fact, this salesperson may let many shop visitors to feel that he does not only considerate whether whom is his real customer in order to enquire any purchase help. The non purchase plan shop visitors may also feel his kindly customer service help during they are staying in shop any time. So, this salesperson's polite and kindly customer service attitude may influence many non purchase planning shop visitors feel happy to see him in this shop. Consequently, it explains why salespeople excellent customer service performance which may help any businesses to increase customers number. It may be one kind of intangible organization resource to any organizations. I mean that when the shop can train many salespeople to raise customer service sale performance improvement.

Overall, these excellent customer service salespeople mus thelp this business to increase customer number easily, because this shop's all salespeople thier positive emotion may influence any one shop visitor feels enjoyment when they can feel they are taking care to their purchase choice need when they are staying in this shop any time. So, the minute, that the shop visitor does not plan to choose to buy any kinds of products, it does not represent that he does not plan to choose to buy any kinds of products next minute. So, any salespeople their excellent customer service performance may influence any one shop visitor to do purchase planning decision any minute. It seems that " salespeople customer service performance feeling" may be one kind of long time intangible resource to help any businesses to earn income in possible. Hence, it explains that any organizations must have tangible and intangible organizational resources to assist them to develop their businesses in long time success. They are essential elelments to influence whether the business's customers number can increase or decrease.

For computer sale business example, its tangible resource may be computer shop and intangible resource may be computer salespeople skills, because if any visitors feel this computer shop's computer desktop or laptop products can be putted in the right and easy seeking locations on any shelves, e.g. the low range price of laptops or desktops are putted on the lowest shelf position as well as the high range price of laptops or desktops are putted on the highest shelf position. So, when the planning purchase of desktop or laptop shop visitors may compare the different design of laptops or desktops their low range price or their high and low shelves locations easily. So, laptops and desktops putting on shelves position, they may influence any one desktop or laptop buyer individual final purchase choice decision. If the laptop planning purchase visitor, he plans to buy one low price of laptop, when he discovers there are all low range price of laptops are putting on the shelf loe position. Then , he may feel convenience to choose any one kind of low price of laptop design products from the lowest range shelf location easily. So, computer shops' computer putting shelves positions may be one kind tangible resource factor to influence any one computer buyer to choose any one kind of design of laptop or desktop priduct convenience. Their computer product choice time whether it is long or short may influence their final computer purchase decision. Hence, the shop's computers ' putting on shelves positions may be one essential tangible resources to influence any one computer visitor to do purchase decision.

The computer shop salespeople computer knowledge may be another intangible factor to influence any one computer buyer decision. For example, when one planning laptop purchaser wants to know whether the laptop's any function, if he enquiries to the computer salesperson, he ften let him to feel that his explanation can not satisfy his any enquiries about the design of laptop product function knowledge, e.g. how to set up password for this computer privacy. If the computer salesperson lets the planning computer buyer to feel that he is difficult to teach him how to set up the passwrod for the computer to use. Then, the computer salesperson's innocence of computer password set up knowledge which may influence the planning computer buyers makes final non purchase decision to this computer, because his innocence can let him to feel this computer is difficult to set up password , if he is one foolish computer user.

Hence, this computer shop's all computer salespeople their computer knowledge, they may influence any one computer buyer final purchase decision. They must need to be trained to learn how to use any one new design of desktop or latop computer products before they are employed to be salespeople in this computer shop。SO, their computer knowledge may be this computer shop's intangible resource to influence this computer shop's customers number to increase or decrease every day. Hence, decision on any organizational tangible and intangible resources to the organization, they depend on whether what kind of the business needs to sell what kinds of products.

The organization is where resources come together . Organizations use different resources to accompolish goals, e.g. human resources, financial resources, physical resources, and information resources. SO, managers are responsible for managing the resources to accomplish goals. Organizational resources are all assets that are available to a firm for use during the production process. The four basic types of organizational resources are human, monetary, raw material and capital. Managing organizational resources is the ability to understand and effectively manage organizational resources (e.e. people, materials assets , budget). This is demonstrated through measurement, planning and control of

resources to maximize resources.
Company resources include tangible assets , such as its plant, equipment, finances, and location, human assets , in terms of the number of empllyees, their skills and motivation and intangible assets (such as technology, patents and copyrights, culture and reputation).

It brings this question: What makes organizational resource unique, in resource based view? Resources are available when they allow a firm to take advantage of opportunities or threats in its external environment. Many resources can either be immitated or substituted over time to any organizations. Hence, effectively managing resources helps companies more consistently deliver projects and services on time. This is because better resource management helps to improve insight into resources availability as well as improves timeline projections. Hence, the types of resources in management they may include: Human resource, natural resource, project resource, financial management, facility management, entertrise asset, public asset management.ON conclusion, I believe that a company's most important resources may be human captial, such as talent employees, their technical knowledge may be intangible resource asset to help the organization to develop its business in longf term success.

Internet will be intangible technology knowledge resource to e-commerce organization

New economy brings new way of resource management. The old loyalty and job security -based organization changes, organizations know that the assets are largely made up employees (HRM), but many new organizations begin to believe technology is important assets, such as Amazon is global ecommerce delivery service organization. It seems internet high technology is its important intangible resource to help it earn global e-buyers number increases . So , many organizations began to believe that technology will be important resource, such as internet can provide online business chance. With all the businesses are taking full advantage of internet, for example, the US department estimates that the value of retail e-commerce in 2000 year was about $25 billion, which represents less than 1% of US retail sales. Despite this, interest in e-business remains high.

- Why internet may be main technology resource to organizations?

E-commere needs strategy in order to win competitors, questions include: What criteria do customers use to choose between our firms and competitors? How do the best employees decision whether to join? What business environment attracts and keeps the best suppliers making with our firms? What characteristics draw the most royal invesdtors to our firms? e.g. Amazon . com's web site and Wal-mart's can apply internet technology resource to create each e-store to let e-buyers to choose any kinds of products to buy athome conveniently. Hence, internet technology, even future other kinds of new technology may be main technology resources to organizations, when they can help organizations to raise sale competitive effort.

I mean that digital economy will be one kind new digital resource to future any organizations. The essential piece is the knowledge, it is what give it life and what makes it an interesting and fulifulling purchase and sale channel for people to spend their time , such as e-commerce virtual organization may be leaded to let purchase and ale transactions carry on easily from online websites. Hence, internet may be main knowledge management (intellectual capital) resource to any e-commerce organizations. It is about the storage, transfer knowledge.

For Amazon publish example, e-books will be knowledge as an object, like a book in library. Amazon can apply internet technology to help it to sell any author's ebooks from its book estores. So, ebooks are Amazon's knowledge resources to help it to create readers incomes. E-books is intangible knowledge resource to Amazon . Any authors' paper and ebooks will be sold cheap price to help Amazon to attract global readers to choose to buy its ebooks from its different countries e-webstores at home conveniently.

Hence, any e-commerce organizations also need HRM (emanagers) to help them to deliver a superior value (world class capabilities) in both te virtual and physical world. E-management will be another main human resources to e-commerce organizations. Why does e-management will be future main HRM resource to e-commerce organization? The reasons may include:

E-management demands in sort of managerial/e-commerce sale strategy effort, skills at positioning the firm within a networm of industries, e-management also demands the ability to see how the firm fits into a value creation-e-management is different because doing it work requires the e-engineering of business eco-systems, e-management demands the ability to be connected to thousands of inputs about specific changes among many industry participants , such as suppliers , customers, employees, competitors, media and shareholders.

Effective e-management requires the ability to monitor developments that can change with unusually high frequency. However, it is also essential that e-managers distinguish between the few meaningful inputs and the many inputs that have limited significance, ability to sustain organizational change, effectie e-managers monitor changes in their markets. So, instead of e-commerce organizations need to employ talent e-managment staffs to help them to manage overall e-commerce organizations. E-leading staffs (HRM) is another main HRM need. E-leaders need to know how to design online brochures, e.g. online brochures simply involved putting a company's market materials on the web. in order to attract or persuade online buyers visit its websites and choose the most right price of product to buy easily. E-leaders need to lead front-office transactions which involved putting customer facing customers , such as placing on order on the web when leaving back-office activities, such as order fulfillment unchanged.

E-leaders also need to integrate online online purchase transactions in which a firm actually linked its front -office and back -office systems and processes in a fashion, e.g. most companies have developed online brochures , in order to let online advertisement tool to attract e-buyer individual purchase choice from its webstores. Hence, future any e-commerce organizations must need (HRM (e-leaders and e-managers) to help them to bring innovation in order to achieve maximize profit aim. So, internet webstores, e-leaders , e-managers may be future e-commerce organization main resources. So, e-commerce organizations, manages are actors at three levels: In the front line , as entrepreneurs, in the middle , as facilitators, and integrators, at the top as institution builders.

Hence, future new economical society, it creates e-commerce organizations number increases, when consumers began to accept online purchase transaction activities. Hence, it causes e-commerce began to feel internet (e-webstores, e-leaders, e-managers), they will be the most influential resources (intangible knowledge managment and tangible URM both resourcees to influence their success or failure.

- Why does e-commerce organization believe (e-webstore design, e-leaders and e-managers) will be main organizational resources?

The most important question: It asks when e-buyers visit their webstores, wo are their target customers and shich needs of theirs are their trying to satisfy? For exap,e many airlines , e.g. American airlines, China airlines began to feel online e-tickets sale channel is more easily than paper ticket shop sale channel, because many air passengers began to accept e-ticket/online ticket purchase choice more than visiting airline shops . They feel that they do not want to waste time to visit airline shops. They like to pre-book to buy e-ticket to pay from the airline e-websote conveniently. Hence, e-webstore design knowledge management , e-leaders and e-management webstore management skill will be future any one e-commerce organizations their main tangible and intangible resources (assets) to help their e-commerce businesses development.

On conclusion, I believe that the current economy is not a high-tech economy or an internet economy, not an m-commerce economy , but instead customer econoomy. Customers need to gather with information and access, they are demanding, fair, global price, they are demanding that compares deal with them using the distribution channel , they choose manufacturing direct and through dealers and retailers. Base on those factors, they encourage future many e-commerce organizations cause organization change traditional resouce concept, such as land, capital equipment, tangible resource began to change to e-commerce organization's intangibel and tangible resource, such as knowledge management to e-online web store design skills, e-leaders and e-managers e-stores sale management strategy and e-buyer product research and brochure online advertisement design skill. All of these knowledge management skill will be future organizations' main resources to help them to create new economic competition effort.

Organization resources defination

What are organizational resources ? What do organizational resources mean? What kinds of organizational resources are needed? What negative impact may be influenced if organizations lack enough resources to influence organizational development? Does working time belong to organizational time resources to influence employee individual efficiency e.g. how arranging enough employee to do the identified task in the most short time in order to achieve the most efficient performane? I shall attempt to identify examples to explain above questions as below:

In general, organizational resources are all assets, that are available to a firm for use during the production process. The four basic types of organizational resources are human, monetary , raw materials and capital. Organizational resources are combined, used and transofrmed to finished products during the production process. For organizational human resource example, human resource activities full under the following five core functions: staffing, development, compensation, safety and health core functions.

- HR resource

HR conducts a wide variety of activities. However, in any organizations, the major resources used by organizations are often described as follow (1) human resources (2) financial respirces (3) physical resources and (4) information resources. Managers are responsible for acquring and managing the resources to accomplosh goals. Hence, in organizational HR aspect, it may include these function, such as retirement and selection, performance management , learning and development, succession planning, compensation and benefits, human resource information systems. Because considering that for many organizations employees themselves represent a significant cost to the business, if the organization can use its employees in efficiency.

Then, it can avoid human resource in excess or in surplus on wasting challenge. Then , its employee cost or salary can be reduced. I t means that it does not need to employ in excess employees number, but the organization can still achieve itself the most efficient performance. Hence, any organizations must need to learn how to avoid " in excess employees number supply or wasting employee working behaviors" challenge . Because if some tasks do not need many employees to work together, it can still be achieved efficiency . Then , the organization ought not employee too many or excess employees to finish the kind of task. Thus, learning how to use efficient human resources, it can help organizations to avoid wasting working time to any departments employees. For example, when one factory has limited land to be supplied to become warehouse in order to help it to keep sticks. If it has excess logistic or factory workers number. Then, they are wasting working time to do not important tasks in warehouse, it means that if the factory has only one warehouse, but its area is small, it can allow maximum 50 workers to stay in the warehouse , but the warehouse has above 100 workers are staying to deliver goods in the small warehouse . Then, they must not actieve the most efficiency , even their delivery or transport goods performance will be influenced to worse by noise and crowd warehouse working environment. Hence, excess employees number in any working environment, which can not improve organizational performance or riase efficiency any organizations can not neglect " excess employees number" organizatinal HR resource arranging issue.

The solution concerns arranging the most right or the most exact empllyees number in order to supply to any organizational departments. Then, the organization can avoid wasting employee individual talent, reducing employing cost, improvig performance, achieving the most efficiency. Resource capacity means resource pool who are available in the organization to take up to appropriate human resource arrangement to assist any departmental development in long term efficiency. Hence, organizational human rsources may become talent tangible assets or foolish tangible assets. It depends on how the organization's resource capacity tasks arrangement to every employee in different departments. If the organization neglects how to arrange every employee task in the most exact or the most appropriate employees number in the department.

The department's efficiency must be caused worse, because excess employees number, it can not help it to achieve the most efficiency aim, even it may influence the excess employees , themselves feel waste working hours to do the not essential or not important tasks. Then, the organization may cause talent employee to become foolish employee. Otherwise, the organization's efficiency to be worse, because when the department has not enough employees to work. Then , any one employee may feel hard to work, his/her emotion may be influenced to negative, then his/her workig behavior may b inefficiency or lazy working. On consequence, the organization may bring economic loss, due to employee individual lasy working behavior, negative working emotion, even high working pressure may be caused, when one employee needs to do more , then the employee's task, but his/her salary can not increase. He/she will feel unfair to compare the another department employee, he /she does not need to spend long working hours or overtime to work per day. SO, any organization needs to avoid shortage employee supply or excess employee supply issue to any departments. Appropriare employees number is the best strategy in order to raise overall organizational efficiency.

- Time resource

Instead of human resource, land, raw material, earth natural resource, electricity, gas may be organization resources . Whether time may be organizational resources, organizational time management vires time as a scarce resource that must be invested as effectivity. Time is an infinite resource . If not properly managed on in an organization. It can have a negative impact on both employer's and employee's productivity. So, organizations should ensure that workers are well equipped to manage time in their duties.So, in management view, any organization managers must need to consider how to manage time, eg . how to arrange employees to work in different departments in order to achieve the most efficiency. They need to understand which resources are in short supply and focus on the prioritizing work across shared resources, they need agree on a common approach, they also need to realize resource management is an ongoing process. Thus, time is an often ignored but invaluable resource in any organization. All activities be it procurement.

An organization's time, in contrast, goes largely unmanaged. Although, phone calls, email, instant messages , meetings, they are general daily tasks to any organizations managers, but mangers need to know how to arrange the most urgent tasks in prior. For example, if the manager can not arrange a meeting to the discuss client tomorroe, as well as the manager needs to spend two hours to meeting with overall 200 employees to discuss how to solve improving efficiency challenge tomorroe. So, this manager needs to make choice whether he ought spend two hours meeting to the business client, or two hours meeting to 200 employees. If he chooses to meet the business client tomorrow, he will help his firm to win the important business chance, but he can not discuss how to improve efficiency in order to find the best method to let 200 employees to know tomorrow. Thus, tomorrow time management will be one importat time resource to the manager. The manager needs to arrange tomorrow two hours time how to plan business meting or efficiency imporvement meerting either to his 200 employees or the one business client. Because if the manager decided to meet the client, he must need to spend today time to aplan or organize how to arrange either business proposal content for the business client or organizational operational challenge questions and solutions for his 200 employees . So, today time management is also important time resource to influence tomorrow either the success business meeting or the organizational 200 employees meeting. So, it seems that time management may be one important resource to any managers more than general employees in any organizations. So, Amazon is one big organization, it employees global many staffs, it ought need to manage its different kinds intangible and tangible resources in order to achieve the most efficient departments operational aim.

Organization efficient using resources economic method
In behavioral economic view , any organizations can attempt to apply behavioral economy method to use resources efficiently. Organizational excellence framework performance measurement takes a systematic approach . One of the most effective ways of using resources and minimizing that use of work. Calculating task cost in the most efficient economic method to help organizations to reduce cost and avoid resources waste, e.g. using resource management software, technology, planning and taking a systematic approach , which aims to manage the most efficient steps to follow to finish or implement each task in the most shor time as well as avoiding excess employees number.
Organizational resource efficiency means using the organization's limited resources in a sustainable manner when minimising impacts on the organization performance. It allows the organization to create more with less and to deliver greater value with less money. HR, raw material, technology input to carry on any organizational resources efficiently ? Management is the process of using organizational resources to achieve organizational goals of using organizational resources to achieve organizational goals effectively and efficiently through planning , organizing , leading and controlling. An efficient organization makes the most productive use of its resource in the most short time and the most eficiency and the least cost aspects.

- What is efficient use of resources to any organizations in economics?

Economic efficiency implies an economic state in which every resource is optimially allocated to serve each individual or entity in the best way when minimizing waste and inefficiency. whan an economy is economically efficient, any changes made to assist one entity would harm another . Hence, budget how much spending on resources, e.g. employee saley, office and/or plant technological equipment facilities , before making resource expenditure spending decision. Budget is essnetial to help the organization to deduce resource using and excess purchase waste since budget and resource of organizations have interlock or interconnet relationship. If the organization can make exact udget, then it can avoid excess expenditure or waste resource to use. So, organizations need to acquire a talented resource pool , that can lead projects to success, when any kinds of resources are achieved to be supplied to use inn enough . For example, using an effective enterprise resource management system that delivers capabilities. Regardless of the approach and tools used, organizations must determine how to balance to use any kinds of resources efficiently. Thus, in organizational efficient resource using behavioral economy view, the organizational efficiency factor means that influences the efficiency of the organization's use if its resources can be both internal and external, e.g. how implementing strategic plans, they may include selecting what methods and resources to use, and leadning employees on guideline, working in coalitions with organizations around to deliver those needs in the most resource efficient way.

In organizational studies, resource managemetn is the efficient and one resource management technique of resource leveling, of finding the answers to the question, how to use available resource efficiently, effectively and economically ot organization resource expense. SO , resource management is the process of allocating resources and allocating.

- What is meant by economic using of resource to organizations?

Economic resources are the factors used in producing goods or providing services. Economic resources can be divied into human resources, such as labors and management, and non humann resource, such as land, capital , goods, finished resources and technology , for example, natural resource is a key input in the production process that stimulates economic growth. Natural resources have limited direct economic use in satisfying human need, but transforming them into goods and services enhances their economic value to the socirty. So, if the country has many organizations know how to use their natural resources input in that production processes. Then, they can create themselves economic benefits directly and attribute economic benefit to society indirectly.

Thus, the types of economic organizations can be identified, there are subsistence recipreocal exchange with subsistence, peasant with primary reliance on self-produced food, but containing some exhange elements, market-commercial , redistribution or state socialist. Thus organizations need to learn hoe to use themselves organizational resources efficiently. Organizational resources are all assets that are to a firm for use during the production process. The four basic types of organizational resources are human, monetary, raw material and capital. Organizational resources are combined , used and transformed into finished products during the production process. So, a business that understands how to use resources efficiently. resource management is the process of allocating resources in order for a company to grow easily.

Organizational economic is used to study transactions within individual firms and determine management approach to managing resources. It is broken down into thee major subjects: agency theory, transaction cost economic and property rights theory. Agency theory is a priinciple that is used to explain and resolve issues in the relationship between business principles and their agents. Most commonly, that relationship is the one between shareholders as principles, and company executives as agents. Agency theory is used to understand the relationship between agents and principals. The agent represents the principal in a particular business transaction and is expected to represent the best interests of the principal without regard for seld interest. So, when the relationship between shreholders and company executives is kept the best.

Transaction cost economic is understood as alternative modes of organizing transactions (governance structure, such as markets, firms and bureaus) that mininize transactions costs. This, cost is the primary determinant of such as firm's decision whether it is the most right (the best) or the worst decision. It will influence the firm ho to spend resource behavior. The cost other than the money price that are incurred in trading good and service. SO, if the organization can often make the best decision to carry on any activites. It will avoid to waste resources efficiently. For example, if transaction cost influces the commission, paid to a stockbroker for completing a share deal and booking fee charges when purchase concert tickets. The cost of travel and time to complete an exhange , it means that transaction cost. So if the organization can make the best or the most reasonable decision to carry on any business activities. Then, its transaction cost can be influenced to reduce the most level in order to bring resources economic benefit. e.g. sunk costs are indpeendent of any event and should not resulting from economic trade in a market.

Property right theory means contracted choice, through ownership, property rights theour clarifies the firm's boundary choice. The maon egal property rights are the right of possession, the righ tof excession. So, for the efficiency of property rights al scarce resources are owned by someone. IN the right property rights approsed to the theory of the firm, I assume that in the case of sale ownership by party-property rights define the theoretical and legal ownership of resources and how resources can be used by organizatin. So, above three major organizational theories can assist organizations to know how to spend resources efficiently.

The relationship between organization resources using and social resources

Resources needers may include societies needers ,e.g. government house material householders , electricity , water , natural resources needers, schools, public houses , land number and area needs etc. as well as business organiztions , office building material, office, plant, land area, number need, equipment facilities limited number . So, when global office and plant business users need to buy more land, equipment materials etc. and electricity , water. Social resources number reduces to bring resourcee shortage challenge causes. Have they have shortage relationship (resource demand number is more than supply number) between social resources need and business resource need? I shall attempt to explain this question as below:
I assume global business organization number increases, they will need many natural resources, e.g. water, electricity, gas, land to supply for office, plant building , material and staff office electricity, gas, plant , office daily essential power need. So, when global business organizations number increases, they may need to use much raw material and natural resources for equipment facility, office plant building material, even day office, plant electricity , gas power, staff drinking water etc. basic office operational needs, when global business organizations number increase.
The question concerns whether they will cause natural resources shortage to supply to social need , when global business organizatins number increases. First, I shall explains what social resources needers mean as below:

- Social resource are defined as any concrete or symbolic term that can be used as an object of exchange among people (Foa & Foa, 1980), money, information, goods and services both tangible items , such as are ususally defined the assessment of social need is of central allocation between organization needers and social citizen needers both stakeholders. So, when global human birth rate and life time increases, population number will increase, then their social resources need are also increasing, if global organizaions and population number are increasing in the same time, due to earth natural resources has limit number to supply in order to satisfy organizations and families daily resources need, e.g. building material resources are used to build either to build offices, plants or private houses , public house, lands resources are used either to build private or public houses or offices , plants , water is supplied to either office staffs drinking or families drinking, electricity , gas resources are limited to supply either offices plants use or families private or public houses use. Hence, due to all of earth, but in the same time, global offices , plants, government organizations and families numbers both stakeholders number is continue increasing. They have possible to encounter natural resources shortage issue when natural resources are using much, but they can nt manufacturers to increase by human easily.

- Can responding to resource scarcity help some kinds business grow?

Foe example, the food and agricultural business organizations, e.g. supermarkets, restaurants, they must send plactic material to manufacture plactic bags to supply to supermarket buyers to carry fruits, breads, mil, etc. foods when consumers need to buy the kinds of foods in any supermarkets, if plactic material supply number is decreasing, then a lot plactic bags can not supply to let buyers to carry their foods, due to plactic bags number is shortage , it will cause any supermarket buyers feel inconvenient when they need plactic bags to carry their foods, they choose to buy the kind of foods from supermarket to themselves homes.

So, if plactic bags manufacture material i shortage, it can not be manufactured to plactic bags to supply to global supermarket organizations. Then, the one supermarket can provide enough plactic bags to let them to carry their foods from supermarkets to themselves homes conveniently. The focus on plactic bag resource scareity is not impossible to occur to supermarket organization case. If families are often using plactic bag to carry rubbish daily at home. Then, plactic bags number can not increase to satisfy global supermarkets food plactic bags and families themselves homes rubbish plactic bags both stakeholders need. Plastic bags can not be manufactured to supply to manufacture lot plactic bags supply to satisfy global families rubbish plactic bags home users and supermarkets food plactic bas users needs. Consequently, plactic bags prices may be influenced to increases, when plactic bags demand increases, but supply decreases. It is one good exaple to explain why plactic bag manufacturered material supply decreases, it may influence plactic bags number decreases and price increases, because families home rubbish plactic bags and supermarket food plastic bags need both increase.

Consequence, supermarket cost may be influenced , due to plastic bags number also increase much, if one day shortage of plactic manufacturing material supply number is shortage. So, it seems that food plastis bags using number, they have close relationship to impact supermarket food plastic bags price, if supermarkets lack enough plastic bag number supplies, then they need to increase food price, even the supermarket may lose customers , if it can not supply plastic bags to let them to use the supermarket itself plastic bags to carry fruits, ,ilk, soft drinks conveniently. Hence, plastic bag material may be one kind of important natureal resource for supermarkets, because any one consumer may be influenced to choose another supermarket when he/she feels the another supermarket can supply plastic bags to let him/her to carry on fruits, milks, soft drinks conveniently.

Another kind of natureal resource , such as steel material for restaurants , steel material can help global restaurants to manufacture kniefs, glass sups for restaurants customers to eat food or drink , if much steels are used to manufactured cars product to satisfy car drivers' driving lesiure need , then it may also influence restaurants s' knieves, glass cups price increases, due to cost increase, restaurants need to increase food price to compensate its knief, glass cups price. even, many families feel need to buy many gloass cups to drink water, then it may also influence global glass cups price increase. If one day steel material is shortage , this kind of natural resource must influence restaurants glass cups , knief cost increases. So, their general food price may be influenced to increase. It is not fair to global restaurants food consumers.

Hence, it explains resource shortage may influence some kinds of business cost increases, as well as consumer foods, products services price increases. It means that " resource shortage may influence some kinds of businesses cost increases".

In fact, in our societies, natural resource shortage may influence any kinds of business cost increases, w.g. car manufacturing industry, if one day stell manufacturing material is shortage. it will cause many car manufacturers can not buy enough steels to manufacture cars. When, global car buyers number increases, but global cars number can not increase rapidly, due to steel material can not supply enough. Then, cars prices may be influenced to raise. SO, it seems that steel resource shortage may bring reasonable chance to let global car manufacturers to raise cars prices. When , global car buyes ‘ new car purchase needs are increasing, hence, natural resource shortage may influence some kinds of business produce prices increase in possible, when the kind of product , such as many people begin to chose to buy new cars, more than second hand cars. The, when steel material supplies shortage, it may influence new car price increases in global can market.It means that any organizations ought not waste natural resource. Otherwise, it may influence their cost increases.

Environmental resource scarcity would likely have been adaptivve in the human evolitionary parst, resources in the environment and organization resource shortage problem might alsoo effect how satisfied they were. Hence, organizations in virtually every industry face the challenge of new managing resources effectively. The influence would run the other way instability as rival, such as big data platforms for e-commerce organizations, e.g. e-book publishers, online sellers. Big data platforms lift limitations on the size of computing resources that can be applied for data, in other words, data storage and e-commerce organizations can significantly influence computing efficiency.

Hence, organizational resources may also influence computer industry information gathering intangible resources, if the electronic books publish, or online electronic commerce product sellers can gather the most up-date consumer individual purchase behavioral data in short time daily rapidly. Then, they collect the most accurate electronic books readers or the kind of online product buyers past purchase choice in order to judge whther which topics of books are the most popular or which kinds of product to the most popular to let them to implement sale strategy, e.g. whether which topic of e-books prices need to be increased ot decreased, whether which kinds of products prices need to be increases or decreased. So, the big data gathering speed is the technology resource to e-commerce market organizations.

Amazon Organizational Intangible Management Resource Strategy

Management science how applies to Amazon ecommerce organization

Management accounting concept can help organizations to do management budget strategies, e.g. margin analysis, capital budget, inventory valuation and product cost budget, trend analysis and forecast . Management accounting also called managerial accounting or cost accounting, is the process of analysis business costs and operations to prepare internal financial report, records and managers decision making process in achieving business goals. However, management accountants depend on standard financial statements containing the earning statement, cash flow statement and balance sheet. In addition , it also makes use of additional finds reports in analysizing the information of the organization including budget performance and cost reports. I shall attempt to explain how management account science can help organizations to analyze cost , why and how changes in order to avoid expense increases or excess cost cases or loss increases.

For Amazon e-commerce publish organization example, Amazon publish is a famous publish organization. It applies internet (online) channel to help authors to sell electronic books and paper books to different countries readers. It also cooperate to other publishers to deliver any its anthors books to their webstores, so when one reader chooses its publish partner webstores to buy Amazon any author books, then Amazon publish will share royalty income between them. Hence, Amazon publish may be book distribution partner to its other e-publish partners.

- How resource management can help Amazon publish to manage its cost effectively in order to increase its profit or e-books or paper books sale ability.

Amazon publish is a e-comerce organization. It depends high internet speed to help global authors to register Amazon publish's individual author account , then any global authors may download their book files to produce any ebooks and papers to sell from Amazon publisher webstores as wellas global any readers can apply Amazon publish webstores to buy any author individual paper or ebooks from its web-publish stores rapidly. So, Amazon publish must need have fast speed internet technology to support its books sale ability,

It brings this question: How much does Amazon publish internet expenditure need? Does it need to pay shops rent per month? Because Amazon publish has none any actual book shops to locate in any countries. So, Amazon publish must not pay rent to any countries for its shops. Although Amazon publish does not need to pay rent for any book shops, but Amazon publish needs to pay extra internet expenditure to US internet service provider to support its electronic webstores daily electronic books and paper books every purchase transaction, any countries author individual book electronic files download per day 24 hours . So, Amazon publish must need to pay more expenditure for internet service to support its authors and readers their electronic books and paper books purchase and sale transaction per day 24 hours.

As Amazon publish case, in its financial report indicates , it does not pay any book stores rent expenditure or book stores (shops) building building expediture on its profit and loss account, but Amazon publish must need to pay internet service expenditure to US internet service provider. Moreover, this internet service expenditure must be more amount, due to it needs to provide its webstores online book (electronic books and paper books) to sell and electronic library e-book lending service to global readers, 24 hours. Thus, internet service expenditure must be Amazon publish long-term influential transaction expenditure because, any electronic books and paper books, even e-library books borrow service and readers must need to pay visa card for borrowing book month service fee and purchase books from amazon publish e-publish webstores in any time every day.

Hence, Amazon publish must need have good management account strategy in order to predict whether different countries will have how many readers click to its different countries e-publish webstores to spend time to choose different authors books to buy or borrow to read from intenet channel. So, any countries readers budgeting number, readers reading habit behavior, e.g. US has about one million online readers click Amazon e-publish webstores , but it has only three thousands readers pay visa card to buy its ebooks and paper books from its Amazon electronic publish webstores, in this week , but next week, US has about seven thousands online readers click Amazon e-publish webstores, but it has three thousands readers pay visa card to buy its ebooks and paper books. Hence, it seems tha although this week has one million online readers click to Amazon publish electonic webstores to seek any books, but the book buyer number has only three thousands. Otherwise, although next week, it reduces three thousands e-readers click to visit Amazon e-publish webstores e-readers number , but it still keep same three thousand e-readers to choose to buy Amazon publish's books to read.

I assume that Amazon publish needs to pay a fixed internet service expenditure, e.g. US $500,000, but it design this e-publish webstores can help it to do its different countries e-publish webstores, their daily e-readers visiting number, daily electronic book and paper book sale number and daily e-readers visiting time statistics. It's electronic publish webstores can help it to record any countries' reading habits and reading taste , e.g. how many fiction , story books have sold in the week, how many non fiction books have sold in the week , e.g. business topic books have sold next week.

So, Amazon publish can use its e-publish webstores to gather above data in order to make author book topic sale choice, e.g. whether this week, US market ought sell how many consumer psychological topic book, US market ought sell how many management topic book next week. If this week US market can only sell one thousand consumer psychological topic book to compare its budget is less than one thousand consumer psychological topic books budget sale number reduces, e.g. in the week, there are two thousands readers choose to buy consumer psychological topic books from European market in this week. It implies that there are many European readers who like to read consumer behavior books recently. Hence, Amazon can attempt to concentrate on encouraging authors to write more consumer psychological books to let European readers to read within next several months.

Basic on above effects, Amazon needs to provide rapid internet service to European libraries, schools ,e-book partners to help them to promote Amazon consumer psychology topic books in order to let the European consumer psychological students, consumer psychology lecturers, consumer psychologists to know Amazon publish can provide more different topics concern consumer psychology research in order to increase Amazon 's consumer psychology book European market book buyers bumber.

As above case, I assume Amazon publish needs to pay a fixed internet service expenditure , e.g. US$500,000 per month. Amazon needs webstores to evaluate whether it is value, if it helps European schools, libraries organizations to pay internet fee, in order to let they can let many consumer psychology students and teachers and consumer psychologists to know that Amazon publish may have enough different consumer psychology books to be provided to European publish libraries, schools readers to read. For example, I assume next several month, Amazon publish needs to pay US two million internet service expenditure to global different European countries to help Amazon publish itself to promote its al different authors' consumer psychology topic books as well as it evaluates that it will sell different European countries; students , teachers and consumer psychologists readers, they have about three million readers at least choose to buy its one million consumer psychology topic authors; paper books and electronic books next several months as well as it also needs to evaluate whether it can earn more than US ten million at least royalty income after reducing author royalty from all European countries book markets.

Thus, if Amazon publish makes decision to help European countries schools, public libraries to pay internet expenditure to help it to advertise its one million consumer psychology topic authors electronic and paper books to sell. It must needs to pay fixed US$500,000 internet expenditure for Amazon publish its all e-bpublish webstores and it also needs to pay extra two million internet service expenditure for global all European countries libraries and schools per month. If next month, Amazon publish can earn more than US tem million at least royalty income after reducing author royalty from all European countries book market. Then, Amaozn publish ought attempt to make this internet service expenditure for all European schools, libraries organizations, if it had confidence to earn this royalty amount from European consumer psychology book readers, such as this Amazon publish.

On conclusion, , this Amazon publish organization case, it may attempt to apply management accounting science method to make book sale number budget, royalty income budget, even analysis to reader individual reading habit, book topic choices, book sale price evaluation in order to judge whether the kind or topic book ought concentrates on selling to which countries marekts, such as Amazin publish case, it also may choose different consumer psychology topic books to concentrate on selling to different European countries in next several months, if it can earn all European royalty income more than its internet service expenditure to European schools, libraries, then Amazon may attempt to make this decision. Otherwise, it won't be good decision.

Hence, it implies that management accounting is one kind of business management science, it can apply number to help any organizations to do right or reasonable reason more accurate as well as it is different to traditional financial acounting, it only helps organizations to record and income and expenditure, earn or loss record function. Hence, management accounting may help any organizations to attempt implement useful or effective strategies in order to improve themselves performance.

How resource management helps Amazon makes the most reasonable choice to invest different market ?

Can we apply management accounting concept to investment decision aspect? An organization's investment decision may make risk, so they need risk evaluation to decide whether the project can bring ehat benefit before they want any decisions. Risk management is the process of assessing, managing and mitigating losses . This applies to both business and investing risk management exists in many forms throughout the financial world, such as one individual investor decides to buy low risk government securities, instead of high yield corporate bonds in an example of risk managment companies and investors frequently use financial managment method like options, and future and strategies, like portfolio and investment diversification, in order to effectively manage risk.

For investment management strategy example, it is professional asset management of various securities, including shareholdings, bonds and other assets, such as real estate, in order to meet specified investment goals for the benefits of investors. Investors may be insurance companies, pension funds, corporations, charities, educational organizations or private invetors.

The term asset management is often used to refer to the management of investment funds. So managerial accounting is the process of identifications, measurement , analysis and interpretation of accounting information that helps business leaders make financial decisions and efficiently manage their day operation . The main objective of managerial accounting is to maximize profit and minimize losses . It is concerned with the presentation of data to predict inconsistencies in finances that help managers make important decisions, such as investment decision for Amazon publish book sale country market choice for which topic of books which are the most popular, in order to concentrate on selling the topic of books to the country market. So, Amazon publish needs to gather past different kinds for any one country, number data may include each author ebook and paper books sale prices, each author different book topic books sale number , in order t make which topic of book sale to which countries investment decision aims to increase readers number t o the country book sale market. So, Amazon publish may be apply these tools of management accounting to gather datas to concern book sale record. They may include: Financial accounting, financial statement analysis, book cost accounting, fund flow analysis , cash flow analysis, standard costing, marginal cost, budgetary control , management accounting tools.

- How intangible resource management skill helps Amazon publish to make investment decision?

The main aim of management accounting to investment includes planning, controlling and evaluating. Thus, the advatanges to investment may include; better decision making, increase business efficiency, simplify financial statement, raises profitability, motivates employees, cost control, reliability. Hence, management accounting means " mental accouting", it is a concept in the field of behavioral economies. Mental accouting refers to the different values of person places on the same amount of money, based on subjective criteria, often with detrimental results. Mental accouting is a concept in the field of behavioral economies. Developed by economist Richard H, it contends that individuals classify funds differently and therefore are prone to irrational decision making in their spending and investment behavior. It refers to the different values people value on money, based on subjective criteria, that often has detrimental results, mental (managerial)accounting decisions and behave in financially counterproductive or detrimental ways, such as funding a low interest savings account when carrying learge credit card balances, to avoid the mental (managerial) accounting bias, individuals should treat money as perfectly used tools when they allocate among different accounts, be it a budget account (everyday living expenses), a spending account or a wealth account (saving and investment). Also abother author indicates that managerial accounting means mental accounting, which appeared in the Journal of behavioral decision making, the begins with this definition, " mental accounting" is the set of lognitive operations used key individuals and households to organize, evaluate , and keep tracks of financial activities. He considers of how mental accounting leads to irrational spending and investment behavior.

I believe that Amazon publish may apply mental accounting concept to help it to predict whether which topic of books will be the most popular to sell to the country market more accurately. The reason concerns that it can apply all data gathering to analyze whether past has how many readers paid visa to buy the topic of electronic or paper books to prepare to the country , e.g. in this year, Jan. it had 40,000 readers buy fiction electronic books and paper books from Amazon publish US market website to read , it had 100,000 readers buy fiction electronic and paper books to read in European market website and the year Feb. It had 70,000 readers paper books from Amazon publish US market website, it had 200,000 and paper books from Amazon publish European market website. Now, it is Mar. So, Amazon publish may make assumption that fiction (story) topic book is accepted to read by American and European readers, due to US fiction readers had increased 30,000 number in past one month and European fiction readers had increased 100,000 number in past one month.

However, US and European readers number data is not enough to evaluate whether US and European fiction readers number may still keep to increase. It depends on other factors, e.g. fiction e-book and fiction paper book sale price, if one author's ficton's ebooks and paper books rising prices whether it will influence US and European fiction book buyers make book purchas decision to the author's any fictions. So, Amazon publish need s to make the author's past different kinds of fiction books sale prices record in order to judge whether his fiction book's variable price (changing price) will bring negative or positive impact to his readers' fiction book purchase decision. For exmaple, if the author (A)'s one fiction price increased 10% to ebook and paper book sale price between Jan and Feb. His fiction readers number won't be influenced to reduce, even his fiction readers number can still increase 10%. So, it implies that this author's fiction is attract or popular to US and Eurpopean fiction reader market. Amazon publish ought concentrate on helping this author (A) to advertise his fiction to let many US and European readers to know.Hence, it explains that Amazon publish may attempt to gather past every author individual writing book topic book sale proce whether it is increased or decreased how much %, book sale number in order to make book sale investment decision to concentrate on helping whom to advertise to sell to which book sale country market.

So, it seems that mental accounting concept can be applied to Amazon publish to help it to do any author individual book sale country market advertisement investment decision. For example, if Amazon publish can only spend US$10,000 advertieing expenditure to help author (A) to sell fictions to US and European both markets in Mar. , then it can help author (A) to increase 20% more fiction sale number to US and European both markets. This advertisement expenditure is worth to spend for this author (A) in fiction market.

Hence, it implies that mental accounting concept can be applied to publish investment market, such as choosing which country to sell which topic of books, e.g. US sells more which fiction or European sells more fiction or Japan sells more management business topic books or UK sells more consumer psychology business topic books. All of these issues will be any publisher's important book sale market decision . It may influence their royalty income because if the publisher makes wrong decision to sell not popular topic books to the country market, e.g. in the month, US ought have many business topic readers to choose any business topic books to buy from any publishers, if the publisher makes wrong decision to find many fiction authors to help it to increase fiction stock to prepare to sell to US book market. Then, excess fiction stock may cause low fiction price (fiction book supply or publisher's fiction stock number) is more than fiction book demand (readers). Otherwise, it can not increase business topic books royalty inocme to US book market, because it has not enough different topic, such as management, consumer psychology , accounting, economy , marketing topic business books stock to be putted on book shelves to let US readers to choose when they visit US any book shops in the month.

On conclusion, it explains why mental (managerial) accounting has close relationship to influence customer behavior in behavioral economy view. Mental accounting is a management science or behavioral science tool to help any businessmen to make the most effective or the most reasonable busines decision in nowadays society.

Management science accounting concept how to help Amazon to presict market changing

Accounting aims to help any organizations to record whether the year has what kinds of expenditures, how much of every kind of expenditure finds what factors to cause the kind of expenditure needs to be spent too much in order to avoid excess spending, measurement profict or loss level why what factors cause the year had loss or profit growth in order to achieve long term performance improvement or avoiding loss. Hence, accounting system is not only for bookkeeping record financial performance aim. Accoungint may be one kind management science concept to be applied to explain why and how market changes in order to predict whether the company ought implement which strategies to grow up its business groth or increase clients number.

The question concerns why the organization can apply accounting concpet to predict how the market will change in order to avoid profit falls down or loss causes. I shall attempt to explain as below:

For a watch product sale organization example, this watch sale compay own 100 expensive price watch brand products stock to prepare to sell, their sale prices are between US$3,000 to US$5,000 , so the watch brand prices are below than US$3000, they belong to low prices. It has 100 low price watch brand products stock to prepare to sell. Hence, every month, it keeps exact 100 high price of brand watch products stock and exact 100 low price of brand watch products stoc to prepare to sell. I assume this watch company can sell 100 low price watches and 100 high price watches in this month, but next month, it can sell 50 low price watches and 0 high price watches. Hence, it means that next watch , low prices watches sale number falls 50 number and high price watches sale numbe falls 100 number. It ensures that this company's profit may be influenced to fall by the high and low watch price client reducing number factor. However, this company still lacks data to know whether its competitors ; watch price is the main factor to influence its watch buyers number reduces or whether other factors influence its watch buyers number reduces, e.g. whether its high and low watchs are attractive or not attractive to high its watch design buyers number reduces or whether smart phone product invention influences watch users begin feel watchs have not be importnt to help them, because smart phones have time record function, they can replace traditional watch products or this month has higher unemployment rate, so it causes people do not like spend easily , in special, watch is not one kind essential product. Hence, it seems that this watch company can investigate its every month whether its low and high price watch stock sale record in order to attempt tp find whether what are the main factor to cause its watch sale number increases or decreases? I shall follow above every possible points to be investigated by accounting concept in order to explain why its watch low and high price customer number sudden reduces.

I assume that this watch company's last month and this month every high and low price watch brand's sale prices are stable. So, it seems that the influential factor won't be its " increasing sale price" to cause its high and low watch price customers number sudden reduces. If it gathered data concerns its watch competitots similar famous watch brands of general price range. It discovered their general sale prices do not have much difference between itself and their famous brnad of watchs. Also, it discovered that their these famous brand high and low price watch sale number is more than its sale number, e.g. the another similar famous watch brand company can sell 200 high price watchs and 200 low price watchs last month and 400 high price watchs and 400 low prcice watch this month. So, it seems that its high and low price of watch is not main factor to influence its watch sale number, because its high and low price watch's their price level had not changeed within these two months . Moreove, its watchs manufacture material costs had not increased within these two months. So, it ensures that its profit falls must not be influenced by watch manufacture cost increasing factor. Hence, it may depends on its accounting record to conclude the main factors influence its high and low price watch sale number reduces, they may include; poor watch design feeling to watch buyers factor, smart phones increasing need factor, unemploymenr rate rising factor.

The next step concerns how this watch company can apply accounting concept to find whether the main factor is poor watch design feeling factor, or smart phones are popular accepted to replace watch product feeling factor, or rising unemployment rate factor which one influences it s high and low price range watch sale number decreases can apply accounting cencept to investigate which is the main factor to influences its watch sale number decreased in this two months? I shall attempt to confirm this possibility as below:

Firstly, I assume this watch company's accounting record has marketing promotion expenditure, its expenditure includes advertisement fee, exhibition expense only, however, in its expenditure group accounting record, it has none design expenditure with these two months. Hence, it seems that its high and low price range fanous brands watches had not been improved by its improvement design skill method in order to improve their watch style, picture, shape, colour, function , design to satisfy watch buyers'changing watch fashion need in this competitive market. Hence, it seems that poor watch design feeling factor may be one main factor to influence its watch sale number decreases. It implies that accounting record may help it to find lacking new fashion watch design factor may be one main influential factor to cause watch buyers choose to buy other similar famous brands' watch products.

Next, whether accounting concept can help this firm to judge whether smart phones influences its watch sale number? I assume that smart phone products had been selling more than 10 years in this country in this case indicates US country. So, smart phones mus be its long time similar time seeing function competitors in US. I assume that its past 10 years high and low price range famous brand watches sale number must be more than these two months as well as it had not increases high and low price range of watches prices within this 10 years. Hence, it can depend on its past 10 years accounting record to judge whether smart phones product invention may influence watch buyers number decreases within these two months. basic on its past 10 years , accouniting record indicated that its high and lw price range watch sale number had been increasing, and it s watch price had not beedn increased and its markting advertisement promotion expense had been reducing much within 10 years. Thus, its past watching expense and watch price sale amount and profit accounting record may help it to conclude that smart phone product sale to US market is not the main factor to influence its recent high and low price range watchs sale number falls.

Finally, I shall explain whether this watch company may apply accounting concept to explain whether this month's high unmployment rate factor can influence geeral watch buyers' consumption desire as below:

I assume that this watch company employed 20 watch salespeople and their salaries range are between US$2,000 to US $4,000 per month in the first years . It operated till to this month total 20 years . However, its accounting record indicated that its watch salespeople number had been increasing from 20 to 50 number recently and their salaries range had been increading between US$3,000 to US$6,000 permonth. Hence, within these 10 years , this watch company employees number and their salaries range had been continue increasing. . It may depend on its past 10 years accounting record for salespeople salaries and employee number to reflect whether higher unemployment rate is the main factor to influence its watch sale number reduces.

I assume that within these 10 years, its unemployment rare was between 1% to 10%, in US society , although it may had 1% to 10% young people unemployed within 10 years. But, this watch company, I could also increased salespeople employees number and their salaries could also increase more significantly, even their salaries had not decreased in these 10 years. Hence, its accounting record of salsepeople salaries increasing trend , it may reflect this US watch market's local and overseas watch buyer individual buying watch desires ought not be influenced by slight rising unemployment rate factor, it is based on that this watch company will like to increase salespeople employee number, when it discovered there were many potential watch buyers visited its any watch shops every day within past 10 years. Hence, it implies higher unemployment rare won't influence watch potential buyer individual visiting to any one watch shops in US within these 10 years. So, this watch company's past salespeople salaries, employees number, and their salaries rising range record can reflect whether US higher unemployment ratio level can influence its recent high and low price range of watchs sale number decreases in US local watch sale market.

On conclusion, we can depend this watch company past 10 years accounting record to judge whether which one may be the most main fluential factor to influence its recent watch sale number reduces. I make the final conclusion that its poor watch design feeling factor ought be its main factor to influence its recent watch sale number reduces, due to it had not spend any design expenditure to improve its watch style in order to attract many watch buyers' choices within these 10 years. So, I believe that accounting concept can help any companies to revise whether what factos influence their businessess to be better or worse, instead of general booking record function.

Accounting trademark loyalty theory

In accounting theory view, any organizational goodwill or trademark, they are intangible asset because they can not touch, they are the company name. However, when the organization grows up a long time, ususally more than 10 years, if they are famous when consumers choose to buy the kind of product, they will must remember, then the organization's trademark or goodwill, company names will become the company's intangible asset in their balance sheet , financial report, e.g. Cock Coke soft drink, " Coca Coke" may be this soft drink company's trademaek , intangible asset to this soft drink company. Because any country's soft drinkers, they must remember Coca Coke brand soft drink before they make any brands of soft drink purchase choice. The reason may be Coca Coke soft drink . Its brand had been popular to be accept to be the first soft drink choice to any countries people. Hence, Coca Coke soft drink compnay must put is brand name to be intanginle asset in balance sheet, (B/S),

Why does Coca Coke's brand name (intangible asset) value may increase or decrease in B/S. The reason is simple, when general consumers feel Coca Coka drink has better taste to compare other brands soft drinks. Then, they wil choose other brand soft driks to replace Coca Coke soft drink. So, if the year, Coca Coke's any taste of soft drinks sale number decreases, then it will feel its intangible asset of trademark value is devaluation, but if its soft drink sale number increases in this year. Its intangible asset of trademark value will increase in its B/S.

Hence, it explains why Coca Coke 's trade mark value can reflect its soft drink sale number whether it increases or decreases in the year. Thus, any firms mist hope their trademark , goodwill valuation can often increase every year. The question concerns how they can often keep their trademark valuation to increase? Can the firm increase sale number , it can represent that it has long term goodwill valuation increases? Can other factors influence or impact the firm's goodwill valuation changes? I shall attempt to give

examples to explain these questions as below:
In fact, goodwill or trademark represents the company's famility whether how many consumers can remember its brand name , when they choose to buy the kind of product . So, if the firm's products are famous in market, Its products must have many consumers can remember it before they choose to buy the kind of product. So, product's familiar to publish,which ill be one measurement tool to judge whether what may be its goodwill valuation. If there are many consumers remember its brand before they want to buy the kind of products, the firm ought raise its goodwill valuation. It may make market research to enquire whether consumer will choose to buy which brand of product among several similar brands of product. It many people choose to prefer to buy its brand. Then, its brand familiar level to publis will be high grade. It may raise to goodwill valuation inB/S.
So, I think that goodwill fact valuation can not be measured by sale number or sale price or profit or loss amount. It ought be measured by market familiar level. If the product can have many people know its brand exitence in market. Then, its goodwill , intangible asset valuation ought be increased. Otherwise, if there are not may people know or they are familiar its brand existence in market. Then, its probable valuation ought need to decrease . Hence, any firms' goodwill valuation ought reflect their market familiar level for standard.
Do you feel firm goodwill valuation can represent its market value or product sale effort? In accounting principle, goodwill valuation must be measured by money. For example, Coca Coke brand goodwill valuation, in fact, Coca Coke had not pay another in B/S. Its goodwill valuation increases, it is not due to it pays its firm pays cash to buy goodwill. It is due to its capital increase. But, in fact, it does not need to increase cash to capital balance amount in B/S. Because coca Coke has not increase its cash amount, due to goodwill valuation increases. Its goodwill valuation increases, it supposes that is capital amount also be influenced to increase. So, Coca Coke 's goodwill valuation can not represent it has profit

growth. Goodwill valuation only represents it has profit growth. Goodwill valuation only represents Coca Coke's present market valuw whether it increases or decreases in soft drink market. It is not actual cash available value. So, why firms need have goodwill valuation. The reason is simple. If one day, the firm hopes to sell its busines to another. When the another potential business buyer feels this firm's goodwill valuation is high. It may persuade b make business purchase decision more easily. because he believes that there are many people are famkliar this product brnad , then they will choose to buy theis product in preference . So, good goodwill valuation can build good business sale image to help the firm can raise business sale price to anyone . Such as Coca Coke soft drink goodwill case, if it can keep high goodwill valuation, then it can persuade any businesses buyers accept to pay high business purchase price. so, B/S goodwill valuation may help any famous business to sell to anyone in the high business sale price more easily. Can goodwill valuation help the firm to predict market environment changes? For Coca Coke soft drink case example, I assume that it estimated its goodwill valuation is US 3 million , but this year, it estimates its goodwill valuation falls down to US one million. What factors influence Coca Coke feels its goodwill valuation reduces US two million in this year? I believe that is current year goodwill valuatin falls, it has relationship to whole global soft drink taste changes to global soft drinkers. The factors influence global drink makes taste changes , they may include: global soft drinkers begin to dislike to choose to drink any brands of soft drink in preference, if they feel soft drink is one kind of bad health drink. They may choose to buy freash fruits to eat to replace any soft drink. I assume that the other soft drink brand companies' goodwill valuations are decrased. It means that if other soft drink brands' goodwill valuation can increase. Then, Coca Coke may believe that there are many soft drinkers prefer to choose other soft drink brands' soft drinks to drink. So, global soft drink markets still have competitive effort. Coco Coke nees to learn how to change its taste and let soft drinkers believe its soft drink can bring health to them to compare other soft drink brands. So, it seems that goodwill valuation also helps any organizations to eveluate how market changes to influence itself product sale effort. It explains why goodwill valuation is one kind of good market changing predictable tool t any businesses in accpunting concept, instead of sale business valuation measurement tool.

On conclusion, accounting principle or accounintg concept is not only be applied to bookkeeping financial record aspect. If the organization hopes to find what factors to influence its customer number or they hope to predict whether market will ought how to change to be netter or worse. It may attempt to investigate its past every year some kinds of expenditure amount record in order to find how any why the firm itself needed to pay more or less to the kind of expenditure. It aims to research what factors may influence its past and present expenditur changes in order to find whether what the most influential factors are influenced itself buyers number increases or decreases . Hence, accounting is one kind of makret research scientific method to any organizations.

Accounting science how predicts e-commerce consumer behavior

Cash e-commerce organizations apply accounting record to predict consumer behaviors? If it is true, how e-commerce organizations can use past accounting record to predict consumer behaviors? In general, e-commerce sale transactions must need any individual e-buyers to register higher address to their e-store in order to deliver products to any one-buyer homes. For Amazon e-commerce organization, when one China client buys a furniture from US Amazon e-commerce organization, when one China client buys a furniture from US Amazon e-store. The furniture is putted to Amazon US itself warehouse. So, when the China e-buyer pays visa to buy the furniture . He needs to register his address to amazon e-store. When amazon confirms that it can receive cash from the China e-buyer visa card, then amazon will deliver the furniture from US amazon warehouse to the China e-buyer home by plane.

So, amazon must have any e-buyer address record and the product sale price record for any one country e-buyer after it comfirms that the e-buye visa card has enough money to buy the product. Thus, amazon can apply past every online transaction to follow these data to do market research, they may include: which country person buys the product, what the product is, how much to the product price, how many of different product number e-buyer purchase within the year. So, amazon can collect all above data to analyze any one country has the highest e-buyer number,e.g. in the year, there ar one million US e-buyers number, there are two million China e-buyer number,which kind of products are the most popular, e.g. soap , computer, furniture, cloth, shoe, shirt, towel, electronic products etc. what the age range is, e.g. young , old, students , workpeople, they choose to buy the kind of product, how many number , the family buys the kind of product to the e-transaction, how many goods return number to the year total e-transaction, how many goods return number to the year total e-transactions.

Hence, amazon can gather all past every e-transaction data to prepare how to predict whether how every country e-transaction will consumer behavior to predict whether how every country e-transaction will influence consumer behavior will change next year in order to let it to prepare how to implement new market strategy,e.g. how to advertise its product, which countries need to spend more advertise to promote its products, evaluate whether amazon needs to spend how much advertisement expenditure to earn more e-sale transactions number to the targe sale country.

Why does amazon's any one e-transaction's accounting record assists it to predict consumer behavior? For china target e-buyers market example, when one Shanghai city e-buyer pays visa to buy one computer from amazon e-store, if the e-transaction can be accepted . Amazon can gather the e-buyer is living in China Shanghai city, which brand of computer , he chooses to buy, how much sale price to the computer, how many of computers number , he buys, how many e-transaction times to the China, Shanghai city buyer within the year. Hence, when amazon needs know where China target market has how many e-buyers number to every city, how many e-transaction return goods and refind number, which kinds of product are the popular to China e-buyers' purchase needs, which is the highest price and the lowest price sale level to China, Shanghai city target e-commerce market every e-transaction . Thus, when amazon collestc all above China, Shanghai past one year any individual e-transaction data, it can compare whether how its China, Shanghai city.

Nest year, e-buyers behavior change in order to analyze whether which kinds of product price ought need to reduce in order to attract many China e-buyers to click amazn webstores to pay visa to buy its products or which kinds of product price may increase, when the kind of product is popular to sell to China target market, or make out of e-stock shelf decision to the kind of product when Amazon discovers the kind of product is not accepted to buy in popular from its e-store. Thus, it seems that Amazon's past any one e-transaction accountning record can help it to analyze whether how every target market its e-buyer behavior is changing in order to change next year sale changing strategy is more reasonable . Hence, it explains why e-commerce organization's accounting record may help it to analyze how future market changes as well as record how every old e-buyer customer whether he/she will choose to buy the kind of old product again or buy new product, even not buy anything from Amazon e-stores this year.

Hence, any e-commerce organization's e-stores can apply online technology skil and accounting concept to help it to learn how to analyze every year post efficient countries' cities different e-buyer individual product behavioral choice in order to judge/revise whether it ought need to change to buy its products from its e-stores conveniently. So, any e-commerce organization explains why it can attempr to apply its post every accounting e-buyer sale transaction record to make every country consumer behavior marketing analysis to compare transaction visiting shop business model more easily, because visiting shop sale model can let the seller to sell its products in its shop, when it locates in the country. But e-commerce sale model can let the product can be sold to different countries

more easily.
So, it seems that if the e-commerce organization can have good accounting record system to keep its past all e-transactions record can gather all data concerns any countries e-buyer individual address , how much sale price for the product, how many sold, and refund to the country e-buyers and the e-buyer age is young or old , male or female e-buyer purchase habit.
Can the e-commerce organizatin predict consumer behavior if it implemented inefficiency accounting record system? Firstly, we need to know good or right accounting record system can help the organization to track or find past any transactions more easily. So, if the organization has none good accounting record system , its accounting record system can not be improved efficiently. Then, its accounting record may bring wrong sale price record, wrong profit (over -profit) or less profit or wrong loss (over loss) number record. Then, this wrong sale transaction record may mislead financial performance to publis to know, e.g. current year, its sale performance is improved, but in fact, its current year sale number is less than last year sale number. Consequently, this organization can not predict its consumer behavior. Whether know to change exactly, due to it often has wrong sale number record, e.g. higher or lesser sale price record, and more or less sale number may influence its gross profit earns high amount, even if its any kinds of expense record is more orless, it will influence its net profit is more or less or less is more or less, for example, if the organization earns US one million dollar prodict this year, but due to it smore sale number transaction to cause over profit. So, its financial performance report indicated its earned US two million dollar. So, it believes its buyers number can increase, if its sale prices do not change. This wrong financial performance report many mislead it has good consumer behavior in this year. Then, it will continue implement its old marketing strategy. Consequently, its next year financial performance may be caused worse to compare present. So, it implies that wrong financial record may cause wrong consumer behavior judgement.

Can robots tangible technological resource helps Amazon to do consumer behavior prediction tasks ?

Our future will experience artificial intelligent development stage. Nowadays, we had had some tasks which can be done by robots, e.g. warehouse delivery, restaurnt kitechen dish cleaning tasks, transport tasks, even non drive manual auto driving tasks, shopping center service etc. cleaning or customer service simple jobs duties. If one day, robots cab be applied to do office tasks, e.g. accounting record tasks, they may replace account clersk, even accountants to deal simple accounting record tasks, even complicate management account analysis tasks in office working environment. If future robots can be developed to help accounts clerks as well as accountants to do simple bookkeeping debit and credit every income ot expense transaction record in order to analyze marketing research tasks, then it brings this question: Can future robots replace accounts clerks and accountants to do their accounting tasks in any organizations. I shall attempt to research the relationship between robots and accounting tasks questions as well as whether robots will bring what social influence if robots can replace future human to do any simple and complex accounting tasks for any organizations.

What is need for development of artificial intelligence to accounting tasks aspect? The first computer language used to create artificial intelligence is USP. This language is quite flexible and extensive . Features such rapid prototyping and macro are very useful in creating AI. LISP is a language that makes complex tasks simple. So it seems that it is possible tobots can learn human to do any kinds of accounting tasks, e.g. financial account record, audit check, management account analysis etc. different kinds of acounting tasks for financial , management account, audit check functions in any organizations.

However, scientists believe that artificial intelligence can help accountants be more productive and efficient. Robotic process automation RPA) allows machines or AI workers to complete repetitive, time-consuming tasks in business processed, such as document analysis, handling that are plentiful in accounting . AI can also significantly reduce financial fraud and maintenance accounting errors. Hence, the stages of AI development to accoutning industry, they may include: internet AI, business AI, perception AI, and autonomous AI ., Internet AI is thr simplest stage of AI, business AI has a limted memory, perception AI. This is the first stage in the future of AI. A key feature of this perceptive form of AI is the ability to compile and draw from past experiences, much like human to accounting tasks.

The design phase is essentially in literative process comprising all the steps releveant to building the AI or machine learning model, data acquisition, exploration, management and analsis tasks. So, it seems that future robots may be developed to help human to do simple and complex accounting tasks. Combining AI with other technologies, such as robotic, process automation can follow accountants to redirect the time that they used to spend on multiple tasks, toward performing high-value, high -impact taaks. Adding AI to accounting operation can also increase output quality by miniizing human errors. So, AI and automation won't be replacing finance and accounting professionals in the foreseeable futue.

On the contrary, as AI automates many aspects of business, there is a bug opportunity for accounting and finance professsionals to upskill themselves to meet the requirements of the 21 centurey. For AI audit task aspect, AI enables the analysis of a full populatin of data and can identify outliers or expectations. By making it possible for auditors to work better and smarter. AI will help them to optimize their time, enabling them to use their human judgement to analyze a boarder and deeper set of data and documents.

Can AI be used in auditing and accounting ? In the assurance practice, AI is being used to perform auditing and accounting prcedures, such as review of general ledgers, tax compiance, preparing workpapers, data analytic, expense compliance, fraud accounting skills. So, it seems that future AI can replace market research analysists, compensation and benefits managers , instead of financial accountants, management accountants an auditors in any organizations.For bookkeeping clerks position example, these simple account jobs are expected to decrease, by 8% 2024, and it's non surprise because most bookkeeping is getting automated if it has not been as of now, Quickbook, Peachtrss etc. accounting software that does not need any more, because robots do not need any kinds of accounting software to help them to do any simple or complex accounting tasks.

How has teachnology changed the accounting industry? Computers and accounting softeare has changed the industry complexity, with but when robots develop, it will change global accountancy professional more complex. Can robots replace accountants? Automation had brought significant changes the accounting profession over the last decaed. When some tools have made accountants lives easier. However, since robots invention, it developed these tools have also created a false debate about whether automation will overtake the global accounting industry compexity and make accountants irrelvant . The question should not be whether automation will take over accounting, but where its rreal value lives.

In fact, I believe that no any software can match the critical thinkning and trusted counsel that a human advisor offes, as valued accountants, have become business partners, where software is limited to evaluating concrete inputs, accountants can understand clients business goals and observations voice to make decisions. This allows them to serve as advisors to their clients, whether by adjusting business models in real time, or managing emplyer wellbeing . Sok, future AI development ought not replace human accountant's this kind of skill more easily.

- How robotic process automation impact on accouting industry changes?

Searching for methods to efficiently perform accounting tasks can be dated book to the 1950 s, when process mechanisation involved the use of punched cards to store and retrieve transaction data (Keenoy, 1958). Since then IT ad automation have transtormed the way accountants collect, store, process and share data through a variety of tools (Ellis, 1986); Kaye, Nicholson, 1992; Rom, Rohde, 2007). However, robotis process automation is a technology solution that allows end-users to comfigure a software robot to use existing applications to perform accounting transactions manipulate data and communcation with other systems (introduction to robotis, 2015).

Software robots can be easily programmed or trained to perform repetitive, rules-based , high volume operations by replicating human actions when accessing multiple systems, applications, and documents (Embracing robotic automation 2018). Hence, robotic accounting software can bring cost reduction to counting and finance tasks, e.g. one robotic accounting software can replace two to five full time accounting clerks, increased process speed, software robots perform routime tasks faster than employees would manage mamually (Cacity, Willcocks, 2016) . They do not get distracted or tried and thus avoid delays, cycle times decreases significantly improved process control and performance visibility, e.g the collected analytical information is much more detailed and can be used for audit and compliance checks, higher quality data (accuracy, consistency, compliance), e.g. robots can validate the data before reporting or using them future. Assuming that the appropriate rules have been thoroughly tested beforehand, data inaccuracy and quality risk decrease fill tracking and logging robots' action make internal and external audits easier and reduce compliance risks, continuous operation 24 hours a day, or none working day limits. So, robots are applied on accounting task aspect, it can bring positive impact on employees, repetive tasks taken over by robots release employees' times. They can shift their focus on higher value added tasks, solve employee morale proble,. Any accounting department staffs may feel tired when they need over time works, often but robotic accounting staff won't have tired or bored feeling.

However, robotic process, automatin may be applied on these accounting tasks aspect, they may include: internal control period end clising, general ledger, subledgers, closing , validatin of journal entries, low-risk accounts, reconsiliation, consolidation, reporting-monthly , quarterly close, internal performance and management reportng aggregating and analysing financial and operational data, external statutary report, accounts receivable and payable record-maintaining updating customer/supplier data, creating processing, posting payment, collections, billing, matching invoices, aganist sales and purchase orders, cash management, general accoutning, inter-company transactions, inventory accountancye, travel and expenses reimbursement request, audit and document expense report, payroll, stock keeping, fixed asset accouting record, tax accounting. So, the general simple accounting tasks robots will have effort to finish.

● Can robots perform the same management accounting analytical decision making skills to human management accountants tasks?

Although, robots can perform simple bookkeeping audit accounting tasks, but whether complex management accounting analytical and decision making tasks, robots can do the same level of management accounting analytical, decision making tasks to human management accountants?

I shall attempt to answer this question. How robots impact of mental accounting in valuation? No retailers show this price without considering the " 99" in end. This indicates to our mind that the price is cheaper. Its popularity can be verified gas stations all around the world. The difference between robots mental accounting issue and management accountants.

The Anchoring theory was used to verify its possible impacts on capital venture tech finds decisions, during equity trading for an initial investment starting. Management accountants ususally arrange 68% of the finds use-valuation as a basic, when 21% proposed other methods . But still use valuation and only 11% of the investors said they did not consider valuation at allo. the context considered that the human management accountant will consider that the investment would be made in a startup in early stages. That is with little or any real accounting information can image the amount of uncertainty that exists in the type of analysis?

Moreover, why do even experienced fund managers invest based on an impossible calculation> In simplity, it explains that human management accountant in order to do any investment decision. Although robotis will use alaytic mind more than calculating to estimate any investment risk in order to make investment decsion for any organizations. AI's analytic skill and human management accountant calculation risk skill be their difference on how dealing management accounting investment risk issue aspect. Even, the difference between human management accountant and robotic management accounting automation is their robotic management automation can apply mental accounting theory to judge consumer behavioral choice.

It is a new model of consumer behavior is developed using a hyrod of psychology and microeconomics. The deveopment of the model starts with the mental coding of combinations of risks and losses using the prospect theory value finction. Then, robotic management accounting automatin can attempt to evaluate of consumer purchase for the product is modeled using the new concept of " transaction utility", e.g. one family electronic firm, it is seeling rice cooker, television radio, household electronic products, it can learn how to mental accounting method to help this houseold electronic product firm to predict how any why its different kinds of household electronic products choice may change to its consumer behavior next week, e.g. robots can gather wlectronic product competitors prices data to compare itself company's same kinds of electronic product data e.g. rice cooker prices and its competitors' rice cookers prices, whether its high price , rice cookers price factor or other factors influence its rice cookers sale number decreases in this week. Consequently robotic management accounting software may help this household elecronic product company to analyze whether what are the actual factors to influence its rice cookers prces reduce in this week. It is human management accountants feel difficult to collect past price data in order to make accurate consumer behavior changes, prediction or find whther are the main factors to influence product sale number increases or decreases.

Hence, future robotic management accounting automation can learn the valuation of purchase modeled using the new concept of transactin utulitym such as this houseold electronic product case, robotic management accounting automation many learn the household budget process ,the characterization of mental accounting, in order to find whether household purchase behavior to the company's products whether what the main factors may influence its household producys sale number increases or decreased.

On conclusion, future robots can do simple bookkeeping, audit check , general daily accounting tasks, even robots can also do complex management accounting tasks, they can learn how to apply mental accounting knowledge to gather the company's past all every month different price variable data, sale number, in order to conclude whether what are the main factors to influence the kind of product sale number increases or decreased more accurately to compare human management accountants in any organizations.

Applying HR management accounting learns consumer behavior

Managerial accounting purposes to be used by management in "making by business decision: It includes product caost, budget , forecast and various financial analysis consumer behavior is the series of behaving of patterns that consumers follow before making a purchase through consumer behavior, you can also earn how customers interact with and the year products. So, any organizations may attempt to find any management account past year past per month transaction records to bring consumer behavioral change predictiver knowledge, it can help future decisions about product creation more easily.

Hence , the management accoutning knowledge focuses the process of creating organization goals by identifying, measuring, analyzing, interpreting and communicating informations to managers is call management or manerical accounting. Management accounting focuses on all accounting aimed at informing management about operational business metics. Also, any managers may attempt to gather past product number presentation date to find whether what the main factors can influence consumer buying behavioral change in its any kinds of products, the level of motivation also affects the buying behavior of customers, e.g. whether the products' sale prices sight rise, to influence customer number reduces, or whether the product's traditional old design is not more attractive or popular to accept to compare other linds of competitors' similar product design, or whether the kind of product is not popular to be accpeted to use, the another how invention of similar product ot the market is recession , it need to change another new sale market, if replaces its existence etc. different factors.

Hence, management accounting can help managers to attempt to gather past the product's sale and production past data to carry on analyzing whether what the main factor to influence its customer number reduces or increases in other to improve its sale strategy.

- Computer sale applies management accounting to predict consumer behavior

For computer sale product example, the computer saller may attempt to apply management accounting to analyze why computer buyer behavioral changes, e.g. a study of consumer behavior will reveal what kind of consumers buy computers, could they buy for home and personal use or for office, what features , they look for, what benefit o they seek including post purchase service, huw much they are willing to pay how many they are likely to buy . All of these computer buyer individual purchase behavioral analysis, the computer seller can follow its different models of laptops, desttops, prices, sale number, house or office ise design kind etc. data to research and analyze and predict hether future computer buyer individual need will how changes, in order to prepare and learn how to design new kinds of desktops and laptops to raise competitve effort.

In fact, in computer industry, the factors may influence computer buyer behavioral change, they may include core technical features, past purchase services, price and payment, conditions, physical appearanre, value added features and connectivity and ability are the main seven factors that are influencing consumers' laptop purchases choices.

- How can the laptop computer seller applies management accounting data to analyze whether which is the main factor to influence laptop buyer behavior changes?

for last month, I assume that laptop model (A) laptop computer sale price si per US$1000 and it can sold 1000 number and laptop model (B) laptop computer sale price is per US$1,500 and it can sold 2000 number.SO, it implies that although laptop model (B) computer sale price is more than US$500 to compare laptop model (A) computer, but the model (B) laptop computer can still sell more than 1000 number fo compare model (A) laptop computer last moth. It seems that model (B) laptop's attractive dsign, more fuction, rapid connectivity and mobility and attrative physical appearance main factors may influence laptop (B) model computer products sale number is more than laptop (A) model computer products last month. But, in this month, it has significant change between laptop model (A) and laptop (B). In this month, laptop modle (A) and laptop model (B) prices are not changes, but laptop model (A) can sell 3,000 number and laptop model (B) can sell only 500 number. Consequently, their sale numbers have significantly changes, laptop (A) can increase more 2,000 sale number, but laptop model (B) can decrease 1,500 sale number between these two months. It explains that although it seems that laptop (B) model has possible own attractive physical appearance, and rapid connectivity and mobility, more function to cause it can sell more than laptop (A) model computer produc. But, it ensures that all of anh one these possible factors can not help it to raise sale number in long time. It means that laptop model (B) may have other factors to influence itss sale number, e.g. other brand of laptop computers' physical appearance, more function, connectivity and mobility , features , even they can provide better value added sale service, repair service, product delivery service, feature to compare this brand of laptop seller, or its laptop model (B) buyers had lost confidence to use its laptop model () computer products, because they often need to repair and pay extra repair service fee frequently, e.g. one year has one time to two times at least per year. SO, their past poor frequent repair experience influences they choose to buy other brand of laptops. Otherwise, why laptop model (A) computer products number can sell more 2,000 number , the factor may include non rising price, none frequent past repair experiences to any one model (A) laptop buyer , their individual psychological positive feeling factor . So, it seems that gather these two laptop model (A) and model (B) past sale number, sale price data to conclude whther what main factors may influence its model (A) and model (B) laptop sale number to increase or decrease in long term.

However, this laptop computer seller can not only depend on the gathering these two months short time sale numbers ans sale prices data to model (A) and (B) laptops, in order to make the final conclusion concerns whether what the main factor can influence model (A) and model (B) laptop product sale number changes absolutely. It must need to continue to keep the long time management sale umber and sale prie data record for laptop (A) and (B) in order to conclude whether what the most accurate influential factor is that it can influence laptop model (A) and B() sale number both change in order to implement the improvement strategy for them both.

- Management accounting data can also help this laptop seller to predict future market development or whether which market will have high sale effort, e.g. Japan laptop sale market may have the highest market share ratio, among different Asia countries, or Germany laptop sale market may have highest market share ratio among different European countries next year. For example, in the last year, this laptop computer seller had sold 50,000 laptops to Japan computer market, it has sold 500,000 laptops to China computer market, it has sold 100,000 laptops to US computer market and 50,000 laptops to Germany computer market, in this year. its these laptop markets sale prices are not changed, it has sold 200,000 laptops to japan computer market, it has sold 400,000 laptops to China computer market, it had sold 200,000 laptops to

US computer market and 200,000 laptops to Germany computer market . Hence, it ensures that Germany laptop market has increased 4 times sale number from last year and Japan has increased 4 times sale number from last year. Otherwisem China laptop sale number has decreased 100,000 laptops from last year and US laptop sale number has increased 1 time from last year. So, it can imply that Germany and Japan future laptop sale number may grown rapidly to compare US and CHina laptop sale markets. It also indicates this sale trend also may help this laptop computer to attempt to find whether what factors may influence its US and China laptop sale number fells down,,e.g. whether this local laptop choices increasing factor, it laptop physical appearance is not more attraction, or slow connectivity and mobility speed ,even their model (A) and () laptop prices are higher to compare US and China local other similar brands of laptops prices.

In summary, I believe that management accounting technique can be attempted to apply to help any kinds of products to find whether what main factor(S) to influence their product sale number changes, it is one kind of good data gathering and analytical tool to help any businesses to attempt to predict consumer behavioral changes.

Organization management accounting strategy

What is organization management accounting strategy? As its most basic an organization management accounting strategy is a plan that specifies how your business will allocate resources, e.g. money, labour, and inventory to suppoty production, marketing, inventory and other business activities. IN general, the foure organizational straategy and the culture of the organization categorized into four types: Adhocracy, market and hierarchy.

The purpose of an organization management accounting strategy can be defined as the direction an organization takes with the aim of achieving future business success. Strategy sets out how an organization intends to employ its resources, including the skills and knowledge of its people as well as financial and material assets, in order to achieve its mission or overall targets. So, the key element of an organizational strategy may include: define vision, create mission, set objectives, develop strategy, outline approach, get down to tactics. However, an organizatinal strategy plan is an organizational management activity that is used to set priorities, focus energy and resources, strengthen operations, ensure that employees and other stakeholders are working toward common goals established agreement crowd intended outcomes/ results, and access organizational missions.

Adhocracy strategy is a form of business management accounting that emphasizes individual initiative and self organization in order to accomplish tasks. This is in contrast to bureaucracy which relies on a set of defined rules and set hierarchy in accomplishing organizational goals. The term was popularized by Alvin Toffler in the 1970s. Examples of adhocracy include most project or marix organizations. Among private-sector organizations, high technology firms, particularly young firms facing fierce competition are sometimes organized as adhocracies. However, important examples of adhocracy do exist in government. Hence, adhocracy is a flexible, adoptable and informal form of organization that is defined by a lack of formal structure that employs specialized multidisciplinary trams grouped by functions. Adhocracy is characterized by an adoptive , creative and flexible behavior based on non-performance. Adhocray culture in a business context, is a corpoate culture based on the ability to adapt quickly to changing conditions. Adhocracies ar characterized by flexibility, employee empowerment and an emphasis on individual initiative.

The five basic marketing strategies may include: product, price and promotion and people in management accounting strategy aspect. They are key marketing elements used to position a business strategically. A market strategy refers to a business's overall game plan for reaching prospective consumers and turning them into customers of their products and services. For example, the BSC business 2 customed marketing strategies may include : social networks and viral marekting, paid media advertising, internet marketing, email marketing, direct selling, point-of-purchase marketing, co-branding, cause marketing, conversational marketing. Hence, marketing strategy or management accounting strategy is a long term toeard looing approach and an overall game plan of any organization or any business with the foundemental goal of achieving a competitive advantage by understanding the needs and wants of customers.

Hierarchy strategy describes a relations of corporate strategy and sub-strategies hierarchically and logically consistent at the level of vision, mission, goals, and metrics , e.g. HR strategy (human resource strategy), to general, the three levels of strategy are: corporate level strategy, this level answers the foundamental question of what you want to achieve, business unit level strategy focuses on how you've going to grow.

The management accounting strategy planning hierarchy is the organization's mission and vision both of ,which should be long-lasting and motivating. At the base of the hierarchy are the shorter term strategies and tactics that unit members will use to achieve the vision. So, the basic levels of management accounting strategy are: corporate, business, functional and operational level strategy. The strategic hierarchy aims to be concept used to understand the different types of strategy decision made in a organization, e.g. michael porter , three generic strategies (cost leadership, differentation, and focus) that can be implemnted at any organizations. So, hierarchical levels of strategy managment accounting may be concerned with selection of which is the right generic strategy to implement, sale method, such as low product sale price, lot differentiation of product choice, and focus an main product feature market sale methods etc.

- The relationship between organizational management accounting strategy and avoiding resource waste

If an organization can implement good managment accounting strategy whether it can assist it to reduce any organizational internal resource waste, e.g. exceed human resource employment cost, facility used cost, using cost, efficient administration or management cost etc. essential organizational cost. Because any organizations must need to use resources in order to achieve efficient providivities, service activities, if the organization can implement effective strategy in order to measure its performance, whether strategy can assist it to judge how to avoid not essential resources spending. Can efficient strategy help organizations to avoid to waste resources? I shall attempt to explain as below:

Whether formal strategy implement can avoid formal technical measurement of scale and concentrates on the loca resource mobilization using aspect os small, medium and large organization?

What does resource mobilization strategy mean? Resource mobilization refers to all activities involved in sesuring new and additional resources for your organization. It also involves making better use of and maximizing , existing resources.What are the stepd in resource mobilization?

Firstly, any organizations need to plan od designing a resource moilization strategy and action plan, secondary , finding key elements of a resource mobilization strategy, thirdly,act of practical step to implementatin, fourth identify, fifth step, engagement, sixth step, negotiate, eventh step, manage and report, final step, communicating results.

What are the source of resource mobilization to any organizations? For example includes spreading flyers, holding community meetings, and recruiting volunteers. Material may include financial and physical capital, like office space, money, equipment, and supplies . Human resources, such as labour experience, skills and expertise in a certain field.

How does an entrepreneur mobilize resources? To exploit opportunities, entrepreneurs monilize and recombine a variety of resources, such as financial capital (e.g. cash, ot loan from a bank , human capital e.g. skills from a employees, and social capital e.g. information obtained from social contracts. Hence, the overall objectives of the resource mobilization strategy is to securce the necessary funds to deliver on the source mobilization strategic outcomes. To achieve this accurate resource used number and expenditure budget and emergency appeals will need sufficient preditable and contrributions. So, the aim of resource mobilization strategy outlines how secretariat will organize the process of prioritising, plannin, selecting projects, monitoring: broadening the resource channels, as well as coordinating with staffs for mobilising and effectively utilizing resources.

So, the genesis of resource mobilization strategy is a good, solid strategic plan, it should articulate activities that are more routine in nature and can be finded through the organizational internal efficient resource mobilization. Resource mobilization refers to all activities involves in securing . These new directions or new business opportunities are pursued using a distinct resource mobilization strategy .

On conclusion , an efficient resource mobilization plan is a term resource mobilization, it refers to all activities undertaken by an organizations to secure new and additional financial, human and material resources to advance its mission. Inherent in efforts to mobilize resources is the drive for organizational sustainability . So, resource mobilization is about an organization getting the resources that are needed to be able to do the work it has planned. Resource mobilization is more that just fundraising, it is about getting a range or resources from a wide range of resource providers for donors, through a number of different mechanisms. How does an entrepreneur mobile resources? To exploit opportunities, entreprensurs mobilize and combine a variety of resources, such as financial captial , e.g. cash or loans from a bank, human capital e.g. skill from an employee and social capital e.g. information obtained from social contract.

Why do organizations need resource mobilization strategy? The reasons may include: The principles of resource mobilization wih examples, it focuses on forging partnerships built on trust and mutual accountability . So, as to attract adequate and more predictable contributions, with the future goal of sustainability, it refers to all undertaken by an organizatin to secure new and additional financial , human and material resource to advance its mission, in efforts to mobilize resources is the drive for organizational sustainability, community mobilization is the process of bring together as many stakeholders as possible to raise people's awareness of and demand for a particular programme to assist in the delivery of resources and services, and to strengthen community participation for sustainability an dself -reliance, resource mobilization is often referrred t as " new business creaating chance" , the organization has a strong, yet flexible structure , such as writing proposal how to spend the least respurce expenditure in order to achieve the most satisfactory effective result to the organization.

Hence, developing a resource mobilization strategy plan , as the source of new business opportunities to the social and behavioral change considerations must be needed the organization as well as resource mobilization target at a minimum level should be needed to raise at transformational change happen on the ground and advocate for the products and may have to develop new business proposal.

- Can resource mobilization change improve organizational performance?

I believe that resource mobilization can help any organizations to change or improve performance to the better, even the best. I shall explain as below:

What are the sources of organizational change? Change originates in either the external or internal environments of the organization. External sources include political, social, technological or economic environment, externally motivated change may involve government action, technology development, competition , social values and economic variables.

How do organizational resources affect change? Results indicate that organizations possessing greater stocks of historically valuable resources were much less likely to engage in adaptive strategic change, but also that this resoure-driven towards change tended to have a even beneficial effect on performance . Wonder of organizational change management is easier spoken about than achieved by resource mobilization strategic in possible? Can create enterprise level value by effective process for resource allocation? The key to success involves managing organizational change , so it leads to real and lasting improvements, tailoring to resource allocation how mobilization strategy. So, nowadays, organizational capacty for change: Increasing change capacity and avoiding change overload, organization, today risk is overcommitting resources, resulting in an overload condition wih which it how allocates its resources to tbe used efficiently or inefficiently. For example, on new government regulations, ne products development or growth aspect, organizational change efforts often run into some form of human resistance. First, management staffed its human resource departments with spend most of that time in efficiency. So, whether how organizational change is better, it depends on how it changes its old resources, e.g. human resource, facility, equipment resources, even management time resources to change new improvement resources change to be better . It means providing the resources, budget, authority, credibility and commitment for the effort to truly organizational change on improvement.

● Why does organizational resource budget need?

For example, managing a human resource department involves budget planning and execution . The human resources budger refers to the finds that how HR allocates to all HR processes. Unit should include in an HR budget. It may include: number of employees, projected for next year, benefits cost increases or decreases, salary cost increases or decreases, projected turnover rate, calculation, actual cost incured in the current year, new employee welfare benefits. programs planned, other changes in policy, business strategy , it may impact costs on HR cost aspect. So, an organization needs to budget whether it will have how much on what kinds of resources spending aspect, including human resources, facility, equipment and water , electricity etc. natural resource , it budget is a tool used for planning and controlling financial resources. It is a guideline for future plan of action, espressed in financial terms within a set of period time, knowing organization's priorities, objectives and goals helps it prepare organization resource budget.

Effectively leveraging people and budget, resource management is critical for organizations to ensure . They are optimizing and allocating resources to the right initiations, e.g. from a human resource perspective, the data needed to create a new budget include the following number of employees, working arrangement tasks time, management time, employee salary cost, due to costs that only impact the human resource department and impacts the entire organization both aspects. So, efficient HR cost budget can help refine goals that reflect realistic resources and how memebers of the organization to use fund because employee retirement can be expensive and it can b increased or decreased expense in any time, when the month needs increase or decrease employees number to any departments. It depends on whether tasks rate is needed to increase or decrease. So, an organization's HR cost budget can help how it makes the most accurate HR resource expenditure.

Organizational facility, equipment, shop, office, warehouse space resource budget why is important. Office space is as an enabling resource, equipment and furniture to enhance the organization's ability to achieve efficient operations and activities of the best organizational performance. In view of this analysis, facility planning personal would be one important factor to influence whether the organizatin can spend the least expenditure to use its resource. During business growth, any facility equipment, office , shop, warehouse space must increase , moreover staff puts increasing number on existing resources, so be sure to budget in order to make another option is to least equipment instead of buying it, whether you need moving insurance for important equipment and machinery, set budget to help prevent overspending. All of the tasks that are include in maintaining a facility, such as equipment maintenance and building facilities whether are needed to improve, facility oversight, warehouse and special equipment whether is qpproriate space for customer service and uses resource dynamic of an organization's work patterns with work. It depends partly on the resources an organization is willing to invest or not, when it feels this facility resources are very important to influence its performance.

- What does organization office , shop , warehouse space resource management strategy?

Organization and using space must be land resource, if the organization can manage how to use its space in efficiency, then it can improve service performance or productive efficiency. Space management can be defined as a practice where an organization manages its physical space invnetory which includes tracking , control, supervision and utilization, planning of the space available. So, space management is the mangement of an organization's physical space inventory. Ths involves the tracking of how much space an organization has managing occupancy information and creating spatial plans. So, one efficient space resource using organization, it needs to undertake annual property assessment reviews, leverage individual projects to drive portfolio evoluation applya planning methodology on all project rises, utilize planning to define direction and scope focus on mathematics before graphics, define and collect only the required data on warehouse, shops, office, buildind space using aspect. For example, a space management ffice can give the organizatin an accurate picture of how many employees , it needs to have space for an average day, and show it the trends of demand for this space across weeks and months. This can help the organization to determine how many permanent desks could be converted to hot desks in office, warehouse or shop , saving space. For example, space managementin retail aspect, it is the process of managing the floor space adequately to facilitate the customers and to increase the sale. Shop space management is very crucial in retail as the sales volume and gross profitability depends on the amount of space used to generate those sales. Space management is a multi-step process that requires data gathering, analysis , forecast and strategizing. In prective, it involes creating a space management system that occupants throughout your organization, so whether the organization realizes it or not, every organization needs to know how to manage its space one way or another , if it hopes to improve its service or productive performance. Make use of these strategic space management and planning techniques, efficient and an unplanned, unmanaged office is not likely to magically transofrm into a well organized of productivity. So, space management is the management of an organization's physical space inventoty , employee working environment, shop product putting sheleves locatin, equipment, desk putting location. All of this tangible space physical factor may influence overall organizational service and/or productive performance and /or sale performance. So, space may be an organization's land usng resource because any organization's land using space must be limited size, they must have land space using shortage challenge if their products stock number increases, but warehouse space can not increase or shop products shelves number can not increase, but product sale number increases.

- The relationship netween organization behavior and resource using management accounting

Has organizational behavior and resource spending, they have close cause and effect direct relationship ? When one organization can perform better, whether it represents that it must spend much resource to use or when it perform poor, it represents that it must not spend much resource to use. Organizational behavior is a field of study that investigates the impact that organizational psychology and human resource management, the cause and effect relationship.

How organizational behavior effects an oganization? Organizational behaviors propose that inventives are motivational factors that are crucial for employees to perform well. It changes the way people make decisions, e.g. decision to increase or decrease resources to use, when the organization feels that it has resource shortage or excess. However, businesse that are able to encourage risks in decision making within the company culture can enhance innovation and creativity.

In fact, organizational behavior has four main elements, people, structure, technology and external environment. So , tangible and intangable resources may influence organization behavior when it is needed to change by management, e.g. human behavior in a work environmen and determines its impacts on job structure, performance, communication, motivation, leadership etc. for example, when the manager has less time to prepare how to organize this meeting process to his client. His short managing meeting plan time , intangible time resource, it can influence his business proposal to be either accepted or rejected to this client. So , time resource whether it is enough or not. It can influence this manager's client proposal meeting whether it is accepted or rejected in possible.

Every employee behavior can determine the importance of group departments in business productivity. So, it seems that resources whether they are enough , they can impact on employee's performance. As a result, managers are able to maintain better relation with their employees by effective utilization of human resource. So, cause and effect relationship plays an important rolw in how an individual is likely to behave in a enough tangible and intangible resource provided or not enough organization.

Modern organizational behavior is characterised by the acceptance of a human resource model, e.g. whether the plant can provide enough productive equipment facility and space shelf for product putting location in order to raise or improve logistic transport efficiency in warehouse. So, plant warehouse space management and shelf putting location productive equipment facility these tangible resource factors may influence warehouse productive performance. It seems that tangible resource provision amount and space management or intangible resource time management resource, they have close relationship to influence organizational behavior. Consequently, it can achieve the result either performance improvement or worse performance. So, resource and performance organizations , they ought have cause and effect relationship in resource management mobilization strategy view.

- How applying artificial intelligent management accounting solution accounting challenges

One of the biggest challenges for management accountants nowadays is the preparation to face globalization in local and global market. Globalization competition is changing government regulation and innovation in technology had to change in the market environment which have greater impact to an organization. The role of managemet accounting to AI, it may help managers to make any management strategy decision, e.g. evaluate sale price is the most reasonable, sale market choice, customer age target evaluation etc. within any organizations. Also known of cost accunting, management account of the process of identifying, analyzing and communicating information to managers to help to achieve business goals. However, the most important job of management accountant is t condoct a relevant cost analysis to determine the existing expenses and give suggestion for the future activities and make better management accounting, when management accountants need to learn how to apply these management accounting data: financial planning, financial statement analysis, cost accounting, find flow and cash flow analysis, standard , marginal cost and budgetary control, they can be made by AI.

In general, the job dutures of management accountant may include: generate sale among client accounts, operates as the point of contact for assigned customers, develops and maintains long term relationships with accounts, makes sure clients receives requested produsts ans services in a timely fashion . So, they need to learn these different management accounting technique: margin analys, capital budget, inventory valuation and product cost, tend analysis and forecasting. Future AI may be taught to learn all of these any one management accounting technique to assist organizations to make more reasonable management account strategy implementation.

The basic principles of management accounting include communication presents insight which is crucial , irrelevance information is valuable, the influence one value is estimated, credibility,recognizing the requirement, good accounting manager, they need to learn how conflict, be open to new ideas: In management accounting tehnology apply, there are three elements of management control system to develop to future Artificial intelligent management accounting technology delegated decison authority , performance evaluation and measurement systems and compensation, reward system.

Hence, accounting technology in AI development has always played a past in making the accountant's job just a played a part in making the accountant's job just a easier. Its own knowledge of technology increased to have the accountant's ability to analyze statistical values. Technology advancements have enhanced the accountant's ability to interpret data efficiently and effectively.

- Future AI management accountant may help human to the honest accounting record

However, any one managment accountant needs have good professional personal quality, honestly and integrity play vital roles in accounting because they allow investors to trust the information they receive about companies in which they invest. Honesty in accounting is the primary characteristics of the profession that allows financial decision-makers to make appropriate judgement . So, the main focus of management accounting is to assist the management of a company in efficiency performing its function-planning, organizaing, divesting and controlling . Management accounting helps with these functions in the following ways: provides data, it serves to a vital source of data for planning, for product costing method example, it is used to cost methods available are process costing, job and different production and decision making. for 3 types of controls may include: internal controls are typically procedures or technical safe guards that are implemented to prevent problems and protect organizations' assets. Future AI technology may help an organizations to do above all management accounting decision jobs ,even replace human in offices to avoid losses. The traditional management accounting technique includes" the use of performance measures, three ROI , budget systems for planning and control, divisional profit reports and cost-profit volume relationship, and breakeven analysis for decisions. The management accounting reports may include order information report, project report, competitor analysis. They are either internally aor outsourced. All of these management accounting methods, future AI can replace human accountants to do .

● Can AI be applied to help Amazon organization to implement management account strategies ?

The two widely used types of accounting are: Financial and management accoutning, for the strategic cost management techniques example, it is the cost management techniques that aims at reducing cost , when strengthening the position of the business. It is a process of combining the decision making structure with the cost information in order to do the strategy as a whole . Hence the role of management account in the organization is to support competitive decision making by collecting, processing and communicating information that helps management plan, control and evaluating business processes and company strategy . So, the strategy management accounting can be defined as the process of identifying, collecting , selecting and analyzing accounting data . So, future AI can be applied to assist accounting teams in strategic decision making and organization effectiveness assessment must be defined.

Future AI can be applied to these management accounting aspect: For methods and techniques of costing management , it may include: Job costing, advestment, salepeople,bonus, contract cost, long periods of time job, batch cost, process cost, one operation (unit or output) , cost service or operating costing, farm cost, multiple cooperation unit. The tools of cost analysis, breakeven analysis, budget cost control marginal cost analysis, cost control , minimum price analysis, standard cost development , target cost. All of these management strategies, AI can do .

The various tools and technique of marginal costing may include:

contribution, profit volume ratio, contribution : sale value , p/v ratio, features of profit volume , break even point . Hence, the AI tools can control cost monitoring in execution. For that AI can help organizations to make cost control budget, it is defined as a AI tool that is used by the management of an organization in regulating and controlling of a manufacturing organization. AI can also perform cost budget for material to any manufacturing organizations to help them to reduce the manufacturing cost , e.g. making material choice for the cheapest price.

AI can gather the product material price, e.g. standard cost and normal cost. Then , AI can help the manufacturing organization to choose the best quality of the cheapest material in order to compare whether which kinds of material to produce the kind of product can bring the high economic benefit to let consumers get more satisfactory feeling. Thus, it is future management accounting development direction for AI.

Ecommerce organization resource management strategy

Why does in this e-commerce organization situation, online webstore speed must be the most important factor to influence its sale success. Information technology internet speed, online webstore design, online transation convenience transaction feeling (tangibale and intangible both resource factors) may influence its future clients number ?

In behavioral economic view, any organizations must need to use resources to carry on any business or working activities. Resources may include: management time to managements, working time to employees, information technology etc. office computer to administration, factory equipment to plant workers, plant or warehouse land space to logistic delivery or goods shelves, electricity, gas , water to workplace , even, employees number. HR to any department tasks. So, it seems that before any organization can finish any activities, they must need enough resources supply in order to satisfy any activities need. If the organization overall itself , even overall society. I shall explain as below:

For ecommerce organizatin example, any online trading firms must need to own high speed internet information technology resource to supply to any one technologic staff store to pay visa to buy any product in the most short time rapidly. So, its online store website speeds must need to be very fast in order to avoid to delay any country clients to carry on online transaction. If the ecommerce business organization can not support efficient, high speed internet service to let any countries online buyers to satisfy its online webstore purchase service. Then, any countries‘ online buyers may choose another online store to replace to buy its similar product easily.

Hence, convenient webstore online purchase service much be very important to influence this online webstore organization. It seems that technologic online internet resource must be the most influential factor to influence this online websore organization clients number. If its online website store can not supply rapid online purchase speed to let any one country to buy its products from its webstores rapidly. Then, its clients number may be influenced to reduce. So, in this e-commerce organization situation, online webstore speed must be the most important factor to influence its sale success. Information technology internet speed, online webstore design, online transation convenience transaction feeling (tangibale and intangible both resource factors) may influence its future clients number . So, judging whether the kind of resource is the most important to influence the organization's success, it depends on whether it needs to use what kind of resource to carry on its daily activities.

In fact, one organizational change has relationship to whether its reponses can have enough supply as well as its behavior can be influenced by the resources variable , the scarcity of any kinds of resources are supplied to be used. So, I believe that whether any kinds of resources are scarcity in the organizational environment, how much they are used, these any kind of resources can bring relationship to influence how organizational perceptions, interpretations and responses.

How an ecommerce organization resource affects society?

Why has online webstore's information technology resource close relationship t influence online buyers number and social job chance?

Organizational impact to the effect on an organization has any reponses to influence how on society chance. However, organizations can also have a positive impact on the economic satisfaction of a town. More oe less jobs supply to the wociety, which can be influenced by whether the organization can have effort to buy how much resources to be used in order to carry on itself any business activities. Hence, it seems that if the organization, such as the above online website sale product organization, if it can have enough money to employ web design professional to help it to design attractive website stores to let attract online buyer purchase choice, as well as paid higher internet service fee to improve its fee to improve its online internet speed in order to let any countries online customers can still click its website rapidly, even in busy online click time. Many people click computer mouse to enter ecommerce website stores in the same time. Then, any one won't choose another websites stores to replace its online sale service easily. Even, if it can buy many advanced computers to let its staffs can use the best quality computers to follow any client's ourchase transaction in short time. When , they confirm that whether the client's visa card payment can accept and what product he has paid to buy from its webstore. Then, the staff can know where the accurate address of the country , the client's product can be delivered rapidly. It will avoid to delay any product delivery. So, if this online store seller can have enough internet information technology source to support its whole computer information department staffs to wrk efficiently. Then, it can increase more online transaction chance in success. Consequently, it can grow up its online sale business, it will create many new potisition, due to its computer information technology department must need to increase employees to help it to deal any countries online buyers online purchase service transactions and online product sale delivery service immediately in order to avoid online product delivery service to global online buyers. So, it can bring more job chance if this online webstore organization can have enough effort to buy high technological computer information products to let its online customer service staffs to use in order to improve online product delivery service store to let global many online buyers' attention . Consequently, it can apply online webstore purchase channel to apply website purchase channel to persuade many global online buyers online purchase choice to its webstore easily. So, it seems that this online webstore's information technology resource has close relationship t influence online buyers number and social job chance.

How do organizational resources affect organizational change?

IN general, resoults indicate that organizations possessing greater stocks of historically valuable resources were much less likely to engage in adaptive strategic change, but also that this resource-driven disinclination towards change tended to have a begin or even beneficial effect on performance . So, in general, if one organization lacks any one of these three important resources. It can influence this organization's performance to worse, they many include: human resource , financial resource, phycial resources and information resource. However, managers are responsible to acquiring and managing the resources to accomplish goals. If the organization can have enough resources to be used. It can bring positive impact to influence its overall organizational performance, even, when it has not any resource scarcity, it can avoid negative impacts on the society, such as increasing jobs chance. Hence, scarcity of capital, human and social resources to be provided to the organization, it will influence the organizational structure changes, even employee individual work attitude is influenced to change worse, when he/she can not have the best resources to be used in order to raise efficiency or improve performance more easily.

How to build organizatonal resource using right psychology

The psychology of management is the branch of psychology studying mental features of the person and its behavior in the course of planning, organization management and the control of joint activity. The human factor is considered as the central point in the psychology of management as its essence and a core. Hence , organizational psychology plays a very important rolw at the time or recruitment very important role at the time of recruitment taking disciplinary action or resolving disputes between employees. HR focus and expertise mainly lies in dealing with people . So , it makes sense that the study of the human mind, how to use organizational resources efficiently.

The organizational side of pschology is more focused on understanding how organizations affect individual behavior, organizational structures , social norms, management styles and role expectations are factors that can influence how people behave within organizations. In general, industrial organizational psychologists use psychological principles and research methods to solve problems in the workplace and improve the quality of life (e.g. avoiding often waste industrial resources in manufacturing process aims). They study workplace workplace productivity and management and employee working styles. They get a feel for the morale and personality of a company or organization, e.g. suggesting to use skills and knowledge relating to psychology how to reduce same productivity level, but the organizational resources can be reduced to use. It is one kind the most efficiency resources using method to any kind of organizations.

On conclusion, industrial and organizational psychologists will often use science to study human behavior organizations and the workplaces. Their aims to help organizations to reduce excess resource using in any manufacturing process in order to reduce cost. Employers who need to attempt to learn how employees use resources to do work activities, it can bring these advanaages : learning how to use neuroscience to attract the right talent, retain high performing employees, because any organizations' resources will be used in order to manufacture any products or work activites by any employees in any time.

Employees are the ones who get the job done. They know how the organization and especially ho w their specigif team works best.

So any one employee may be the important factor to influence the amount of resource use, any organizational resource use amount, it has close relationship to any employee work behavior. Moreover, resources, that is , group-level resources associated with shared relationship that foster a quality exchange of information and interaction between individuals within the workplace , helping any one employee to learn more about on the job training, use employee training optios to ensure department leader optimizes the employees' motiviation and potential retention. Aim to give opinions to employees to know how to avoid resource using waste method to achieve cost saving aim to the organization.

Can Amazon resource shortage influence consumer behavior changes?

Can bring either positive or negative or both impact to change consumer behavior when the consumer begins to feel resource shrtage occurrence to choose to buy the kind of product or consume the kind of service?

Consumer researchers have suggedsted that chronic resource scaraity, specially, an inproveished early home environment with fewer resources and high levels of instability and uncertainty can lead to chronic differences in choice behavior (Griskevicius et al. 2011). How are consumers affected by scarcity? Scarcity affects producers because they have to make a choice on how to best ise their limited resources. It also affects consumers because they have to make a choice on what services or goods to chooce. Hence, resource shortage may be situational factor influence, situational influences are external circumstances or conditions existing when a consumer makes a purchase decision. Because the kind of product is facing resource shortage issue to influence the product manufacturer can not have enough resource to manufacture the kind og product. SO, number supply is decreasing, such as cars product, if steel number supply is decreasing, it can influence global car manufacture number decreases. When global new car buyers feel that they can not buy any kinds fo new cars easily. Then, even global new car price rises, they won't influence new car buyers purchase desires. So, in new car sale market, if steel supply number reduces, global new car buyer number will not decrease easily.

How does a consumer make choice with scarce resources?

Like producers, consumers also have to make choices, since consumer resources , such as time, attention, and money are limited. They must choose how to best allocate them by making tradeoff. The concept of trade-offs due to scarcity is formalized by concept of opportunity cost. In fact, research in marketing often begins with two assumptions, by scarcity of products and/or a scarcity of resources, dfferent types of scarcity individually and jointly influence.

Consumer behavior , an integrative analysis of research finding remains that scarcity principle in consumer behavior, it refers that scarcity to the condition of resources shortages, it can affect consumer behavior. So, consumer behavior and resource shortage, they seem have close cause and effect relationship between them. For buying behavior example, when one male consumer with high shopping motivations, when he knows a scarcity arrtibute and thus are a vary limited resources, e.g. he allows to buy the product within 5 minutes , when the shop will close soon and thus a very shop time clising time limited. It can persuade the male customer to make purchase decisin immediately. So, it seems that intangible resource , such as shop closing limited time, scarcity may also be a fundamental phenomenon that influences consumer behavior, when the consumer feels that shop will close, it does not allow himw to continue to stay long time in the shop. The shop closing time nay persuade the customer to buy the product immediately.

It explains that why the influence of quantity scarcity and time restriction on consumer, this implies that when consumers' cognitive resources are not restricted by external environmental factor influence, such as shop soon closing time or web traffic to media, when the online buyer , he dislikes to spend long time to click on any website stores to choose themselves brands of the kind of product choice to make purchase decision. The online buyer may only click one website store to make purchase decision immediately.

So, it explains why online sellers can sell their products firm online stores easily, because their website stores web traffic is not busy at the moment. There are not many online buyers click themselves webiste stores at the moment. So, when there are many online buyers can click themselves webstores to choose any kinds of products in shor ttime rapidly. Then, their online sale chance may be influenced by " not busy website stores web traffic jam to media time factor".

Hence, it seems that when one consumer feels resource shortage, it may persuade the consumer to choose to buy the kind of product immediately. I suggest that people may not only differ in terms of how they choose to consume, this could include encouraging consumers , such as impact pf resource scarcity on price-quality judgement. It means that the predictable " panic shopping" in response, experiencing resource scarcity can also increase a sense of community by encouraging consumer to share shopping experience. So, product uncertainity , which is able to motivate behaviors, such as urgency to buy.

This, scarcity , also is known as paucity, is an eonomics term used to refer to a gap between the buyer purchase desire and external environmental factor, for exmaple time and money are characteristically scarce resources, to urge consumers to make purchases or else they won't guarantee next day purchase the product.

Howveer, the cost of using a resource is called the opportunity cost, the value of the next scarcity in economics connotes not that something is nearly impossible to finf. In common, consumers must choose between correct consumption and future consumption, for example, the COVID 19 crisisi may bring positive urgent time to save product, e.g. medical mouth cover protection product, when many medical mouth cover protection product buyers believe the brand of covid 19 medical moth cover protection products supply is shortage, they believe they ought buy the brand of medical mouth cover protection product supply is shortage, they believe thay ought buy the brand of medical mouth cover protection products immediately.

Otherwise, they can not find this kind of covid 19 medical mouth cover protection products to buy later. So, the anticipation to the covid 19 crisis will help some brands of medical mouth cover protection proucts, they can be sold rapidly . So, panic buying may be encouraged when the covid19 mouth cover protection product buyers feel a common brand share covid 19 mouth cover protection products shortage resource through a collection action. Hence, even the brand of covid 19 medical mouth cover protection products prices are raised, the covid 19 mouth cover buyers still choose to buy the brand of covid 19 mouth cover protection products, because they believe that they can not buy the brand of covid 19 medical mouth protection cover products later, when this brand of covid 19 medical mouth cover manufacturers won't continue to manufacture this kind of covid 19 medical mouth cover products again.

So, it explains that crisis and product sale time limited intangible resources can influence consumers to make a lot purchase decision suddenly. On conclusion, resource scarcity is essentially about current brand for a resource exceeding available supply. Resource scarcity occurs when demand for a natural resource is greater than the available supply leading to a decline in the stock of available resources.

However, limited time may be one kind of intangible resource shortage to influence consumers to choose to make the purchase decision to avoid that they lose the final purchase chance. So, the intangible limited time psychological factor may help businessmen to sell their products in short time, when the consumers feel that they have no enough time to choose any kinds of product to buy or they believe that they can not buy the kind of product later. So, resource shortage may bring position impact to influence consumer behavior in behavioral economy view.

Do they have relationship between organizational resource economic behavior and social needs?

In organizational behavioral economy view, economic systems that shape behaviors and constrain access to resource necessary to organizations and society both. People are influenced to organizations as employees, consumers. IN behavioral economy view, economics is the social science that examines how individuals, businesses and overall societies manage scarce resources. Because none resource exist in unlimited quantities, even internet technology resource , societies must establish priorities and decide how best to allocate resources in such a way that meets as many needs and wants as possible . So, organizational behavioral and economics to explain why employees sometimes make irrational business decisions , and why and how the organization employee individual behavior does not follow the predictions of economic models . Because any organizational employees are emotional and easily distracted brings , they make decisions that are not in their self interest when they are working in organization. Hence, how whether it is more or less any organizations use themselves resource. It may influence the social whether it has much or less resources to society. It can use which interact within the organization,

Why have they interaction to influence resource supply between orgaizations and societies?

In sociology, a social organization is a pattern of relationship between and among individuals and social groups. Characteristics of social organization can include qualities, such as division of labour, communication system, leadership , structure of a organization. For hospital example, it is one social organization, whether how it uses its resource , it can inluence whether society has how much resources can use. Hospital is one social resource organization (division of labour), e.g. doctors, nurses teams, cleaner teams, patient customer enquire teams, counter service teams. They are a major influence on social behavior and is the link between human nature reaching to the hospital organizational and social environment. Hoe many actual patients number , social need in the year, if the year , there are not many patients need to feel to go to hospital , then it can influence the hospital feels resource excess, or it won't need to use more hospital resource to serve its patients in the year. S, social patients needs and hospital medicine supply needs, they have close relationship every year. It means that the hospital's medicine manufacture material won't need much, it the year has not many patients or patients number is decreasing. So, shopital organzation hoe to need its resource, it has close relationship to patients number in society (nature, demographic, economic, cultural and social behavior patterns and consciousness). So, it explains why the social organization is the best of all organized human society, such as hospital organization example, its patients number will influence medicine resource need.

Another example is bus public transport service social passengers number choice to catching bus transport tool, it can influence whether how buses use oil nature resources needs. If the year , there are less passengers to choose to catch buses, they choose to catch trams, trains, ferries in preference, then due to every bus reduces passengers numer, it does not often driven , following the fixed timetable. If the bus stations often have no many passengers are waiting buses, then many buses are often staying in bus stations. Consequently, bus oil fuel nature resources need must reduce. Thus, social bus passengers number may have indirect relationship to influence buses oil fuel natural resources needs every year. It means that bus oil fuel nature resource use amount is influened by social passengers public transport tool choice needs. It is one good example bus public transport service organization seems to be one social organization.

- How Amazon e-commerce applies resource management principle to bring avoiding resource waste benefit?

For Amazon e-commerce example, it does not apply scientific management principle, due to it is not one product manaufacturing industry, it is online sale service and foreign delivery service organization. It ignores one of the key of scientific management, its creators genuinely believed that you had to pay higher wages to anyone asked to puch themselves to their physical limits. Under scientific management wages are paid to the workers as per the piece-wage system. Minimum wage is not assured, so every work needs to pay incentive wafe when he can manufacture more piece product, but Amazon believes that pay higher wages to any one can bring incentive productivity , such as it only provide online sale and foreign deli ery service to any one online buyer client, e.g. it can pay higher wage to the warehouse workers, because they need to cooperate with robotics to work hard and the human warehouse workers need to learn how to dominate any one warehouse logistic robotics to know hoe to delive and put goods to the right shelves in order to avoid to put wrong goods to the not right shelves position in warehouse.

So, in Amazon scientific management skill to workers view, its warehouse workers are smart workers, they need to know how to dominate any one warehouse robotics to do the right goods delivery to put on right shelves tasks daily. Their wages ought need to pay higher in order to avoid theig goods wrong delivery to wrong sheleves in careless. SO, Amazon feels that it needs to pay higher salary to the warehouse workers because they need have more smart and robotic control skills. When they and robotic to works together in Amazon warehouses.

So, such as Amazon warehouse workers case, Amazon ecommerce organization can apply scientific management principle to reduce resource waste. I shall explain as below:

Amazon 's warehouses have save diffeent kinds of products to prepare to deliver to different countries buyers, after Amazon had confirmed that it has receive visa card payment from online channel by each online buyer successfully. So, it must have smart warehous workers, they know how to control and dominate any one warehouse robotics to cooperate to send every right shelf position message to every one warehouse robotis to know, when the warehouse robotic receives the right product delivery to the right shelf message from the warehouse warehouse, it will delvier the product to the shelf position carefully. So, avoiding none of any wrong goods putting on the wrong shelves positions occurs easily. When, every one, there has none any wrong goods are putted on wrong sheleves positions occurrence, the spending investigation time to any wrong goods putting on wrong shelves position, it does not need to any one warehouse manager to do every day, So, Amazon does not need to waste time to do any goods putting on wrong warehouse workers number, when it applies many warehouse robotics to assist them to work in order to raise goods delivery efficiency in warehouse, e.g. Amazon warehouse can apply three logistic robotics and one human warehouse worker number to do one goods shelf delivery task. Before, it needs to employ ten human warehouse, logistic workers to reponsible to do one goods shelf delivery task. I assume that the goods shelf can put total 300 pieces of different kinds of products per day. So, Amazon can reduce none warehouse logistic workers number when it increases three logistic robotics to help them to do these 300 goods delivery task per day. Hence, its wage expenditure must decrease. Moreover, logistic robotics do not feel tried , bored, overtime work, these three robotics only follow any one of warehouse worker's message to let them to know whether which kind of product is needed to put on which number of the shelf positiion. Then, these three logistic workers can remember where the product is putted on the shelf position and help any one logisitic worker to get the right product to already deliver to the foreign buyer's home from Amazon's warehouses easily, they must raise efficiency more than only workers , they work in Amazon warehouses.

Hence, Amazon believes higher wage can enourage smart logistic workers can have good performance to dominate how every logistic robot , e.g. avoiding to send wrong message to let any one logistic robotic to put wrong product to the wrong shelf number position. SO, Amazon can apply warehouse scientific management method to avoid warehouse worker individual wrong message delviery to any one logistic robotic occurrence, when they can receive higher wage, and the three logistic robotics and one warehouse worker cooperation relationship is the most suitable workers cooperation number.

Amazon 's warehouse does not need more nine workers to often move in the crowd warehouse space environment to avoid worker accident and wrong goods putting on wrong shelves number position occurrences both. Hence, Amazon can apply scientific management method on warehouse avoiding resource waste aspect, when it decides to apply logistic robotics and workers cooperation in order to avoid wasting time to investigate whether which kinds of goods are put on where the wrong shelves number positions per day tasks occurrence in possible and it can bring delay to deliver goods to the online buyer's home. it is one good example of scientific management avoiding time waste method to Amazon warehouse organization.

Can Robotic Help Warehouses To Avoid Resource Waste On Behavioral Economic View

- Behavioral economy view whether robotic can help warehouse to avoid time and human resource waste

IN fact,robts are being used in different types manufacturing to create more efficiency with fewer resource. Robots also reduce errors, to leass waste is produced. Less waste is produced and the robots are able to final and separate the small parts more efficiently than human hands can. For example, on environment recycled aspect, robots can help reduce waste that is incinerated by efficiently sorting materials that can be recycled quickly and more efficiently than humans reducing the input poser and cost control with such processes. So, robots can bring positive affect the environment, because robots use less energy and produce less waste.

As a whole, there are multiple benefits to using robots to fight climate change,e.g. robots can prevent pollution and emissions through careful monitoring optimize the manaufacturing processes to reduce energy consumption. Moreover, robots can help with recycling, the use of robots allows facility operators some new flexibility. Most technologies used in recycling allow to sort materials. The sensing robots (sensoes) allow robots to receive information about a certain measurement of the environment , or internal components. This is essential to robots to perform their tasks, and act upon any changes in the environment to calculate the appropriate response.

- How Amazon warehouse applies logistic robots to help it to waste resource waste

Hence, although robots can take our jobs, because they can help organizations to avoid resource waste, and it can bring negative effect to influence we lose jobs. ON behavorioral economic view, robots can help employers to reduce employees number, but it won't influence organizational overall performance to be worse or inefficiency, such as Amazon warehouse applies logistic robots to assist workers to deliver the right kind of goods to put on every correct shelf number position rapidly every day. Hence, one logistic robot can replace at least 10 store workers to do goods delivery tasks every day, e.g. one store worker needs to spend one minute to find the right kind of good to deliver to prepare to arrange to deliver it to fly to overseas client. Logistic robots only need 10 seconds to find the right kind of goods from the near 200 number shelves in Amazon warehouse as well as they are putting 300 different kinds of goods on these 200 shelves in Amazon warehouse every day.

Because each logistic robot has very good memory. Each logistic robot must remember any kinds of goods , their putting number position on which shelf, e.g. when the worker needs to find the model laptop product from 300 different kinds of products,in Amazon warehouse. They are putting on 200 number shelves number following positions. IN general, human worker will need to spend about one minute to find the model of laptop product from these 200 number shelves in warehouse. For example, when one worker needs to find the brand Apple of one laptop product model: PHZ0123, when the warehouse has total 300 diferent kinds of products are putting on total 200 numbers of different shelves positions. Any one Amazon store worker must need to type this Apple brand laptop" Apple" name and its model number" PHZ0123 on the store computer as well as to search its putting on shelf number position from computer. Then, the Amazon store computer will find this laptop product to find its present putting on the correct shelf number position , e.g. 50 number of the shelf positon, or none stock record of all this model PHZ20123 laptop is sold out. So, Amazon store computer must need time to help this store worker to search this laptop product's putting on shelf number position as well as the worker needs time to walk to the right shelf number position to find this laptop product.

However, logistic robotic does not need to spend time to type this laptop product brand name and model number in order to search where it is putted on the shelf number position. The Amazon store worker only needs to speak this laptop product brand name, e.g. Apple and the kind of product, e.g.laptop and model number, e.g. PHZ0123 and its piece number, e.g. one piece number. Then, the Amazon logistic robot can follow the store worker's sound to find its past this kind of product's shelf number position memory to move to this shelf correct number position and finds it to deliver to the worker immediately. So, if the worker speaks 10 kinds f different products one time, then the logistic robotic can help this worker to find these 10 of different kinds products from their correct shelves numbers rapidly.

Hence, it seems that logistic robots can help Amazon store workers to reduce each product search time as well as logistic robots can help workers to do goods delviery tasks. So, in logistic robotic behevioral economic vire, logistic robotics can replace many workers to do product position research and delivery tasks, store workers only need to speak the kind of product name, model, brand name and delivery piece number to let the logistic robotic to know. Then, the logistic robotic can follow the store worke's sending message to find the product's past memmory in order to tell the store worker, whether the product has how many stocks on shelf, or none of stock on shelf and where is putted on . Hence, any one store worker does not need to spend much time to search where any kinds of products shelves number position are. They only need logistic robotics to help them to do any kinds of products deliver to , or 20 or more different kinds between products location and the store worker's location. It means that the store worker only needs to stay on the same location to wait the logistic robotic brings his products comes back after he speaks to let the logistic rotic to know whether which kinds of products and piece number he needs . Then, he checks the logistic robotic's all products where they are correct or not. He may put all of these different kinds of gatherng products to the lorry to prepare to send to airport to fly to another country to deliver to the overseas client's home immediately when he confirms that all goods are his correct.

Hence, such as Amazon warehouse case, logistic robotics can help it to reduce many products searching time tasks and avoiding delivering wrong product to any overseas client's home rick occurence. Also, logistic robotics can reduce store workers number, because logistic robotics can replace 10 to 20 human store workers number absolutely. Otherwise, human store workers may have errors in their product search process, e.g. finding the wrong product from shelf or putting the product to the wrong shelf number position, but logistic robotics can reduce to 0 error to put wrong product on the shelf number position or spends long time to search the kind of product from the shelf number position. So, in logistic robotic behavioral economic view, robotics can help businesses to avoid products putting on wrong shelves number position error risk, reduce store workers number, reduce product shelf number position search economic time.

Can Robotic Help Warehouses To Avoid Resource Waste On Behavioral Economic View

- Behavioral economy view whether robotic can help warehouse to avoid time and human resource waste

IN fact,robts are being used in different types manufacturing to create more efficiency with fewer resource. Robots also reduce errors, to leass waste is produced. Less waste is produced and the robots are able to final and separate the small parts more efficiently than human hands can. For example, on environment recycled aspect, robots can help reduce waste that is incinerated by efficiently sorting materials that can be recycled quickly and more efficiently than humans reducing the input poser and cost control with such processes. So, robots can bring positive affect the environment, because robots use less energy and produce less waste.

As a whole, there are multiple benefits to using robots to fight climate change,e.g. robots can prevent pollution and emissions through careful monitoring optimize the manaufacturing processes to reduce energy consumption. Moreover, robots can help with recycling, the use of robots allows facility operators some new flexibility. Most technologies used in recycling allow to sort materials. The sensing robots (sensoes) allow robots to receive information about a certain measurement of the environment , or internal components. This is essential to robots to perform their tasks, and act upon any changes in the environment to calculate the appropriate response.

- How Amazon warehouse applies logistic robots to help it to waste resource waste

Hence, although robots can take our jobs, because they can help organizations to avoid resource waste, and it can bring negative effect to influence we lose jobs. ON behavorioral economic view, robots can help employers to reduce employees number, but it won't influence organizational overall performance to be worse or inefficiency, such as Amazon warehouse applies logistic robots to assist workers to deliver the right kind of goods to put on every correct shelf number position rapidly every day. Hence, one logistic robot can replace at least 10 store workers to do goods delivery tasks every day, e.g. one store worker needs to spend one minute to find the right kind of good to deliver to prepare to arrange to deliver it to fly to overseas client. Logistic robots only need 10 seconds to find the right kind of goods from the near 200 number shelves in Amazon warehouse as well as they are putting 300 different kinds of goods on these 200 shelves in Amazon warehouse every day.

Because each logistic robot has very good memory. Each logistic robot must remember any kinds of goods , their putting number position on which shelf, e.g. when the worker needs to find the model laptop product from 300 different kinds of products,in Amazon warehouse. They are putting on 200 number shelves number following positions. IN general, human worker will need to spend about one minute to find the model of laptop product from these 200 number shelves in warehouse. For example, when one worker needs to find the brand Apple of one laptop product model: PHZ0123, when the warehouse has total 300 diferent kinds of products are putting on total 200 numbers of different shelves positions. Any one Amazon store worker must need to type this Apple brand laptop" Apple" name and its model number" PHZ0123 on the store computer as well as to search its putting on shelf number position from computer. Then, the Amazon store computer will find this laptop product to find its present putting on the correct shelf number position , e.g. 50 number of the shelf positon, or none stock record of all this model PHZ20123 laptop is sold out. So, Amazon store computer must need time to help this store worker to search this laptop product's putting on shelf number position as well as the worker needs time to walk to the right shelf number position to find this laptop product.

However, logistic robotic does not need to spend time to type this laptop product brand name and model number in order to search where it is putted on the shelf number position. The Amazon store worker only needs to speak this laptop product brand name, e.g. Apple and the kind of product, e.g.laptop and model number, e.g. PHZ0123 and its piece number, e.g. one piece number. Then, the Amazon logistic robot can follow the store worker's sound to find its past this kind of product's shelf number position memory to move to this shelf correct number position and finds it to deliver to the worker immediately. So, if the worker speaks 10 kinds f different products one time, then the logistic robotic can help this worker to find these 10 of different kinds products from their correct shelves numbers rapidly.

Hence, it seems that logistic robots can help Amazon store workers to reduce each product search time as well as logistic robots can help workers to do goods delviery tasks. So, in logistic robotic behevioral economic vire, logistic robotics can replace many workers to do product position research and delivery tasks, store workers only need to speak the kind of product name, model, brand name and delivery piece number to let the logistic robotic to know. Then, the logistic robotic can follow the store worke's sending message to find the product's past memmory in order to tell the store worker, whether the product has how many stocks on shelf, or none of stock on shelf and where is putted on . Hence, any one store worker does not need to spend much time to search where any kinds of products shelves number position are. They only need logistic robotics to help them to do any kinds of products deliver to , or 20 or more different kinds between products location and the store worker's location. It means that the store worker only needs to stay on the same location to wait the logistic robotic brings his products comes back after he speaks to let the logistic rotic to know whether which kinds of products and piece number he needs . Then, he checks the logistic robotic's all products where they are correct or not. He may put all of these different kinds of gatherng products to the lorry to prepare to send to airport to fly to another country to deliver to the overseas client's home immediately when he confirms that all goods are his correct.

Hence, such as Amazon warehouse case, logistic robotics can help it to reduce many products searching time tasks and avoiding delivering wrong product to any overseas client's home rick occurence. Also, logistic robotics can reduce store workers number, because logistic robotics can replace 10 to 20 human store workers number absolutely. Otherwise, human store workers may have errors in their product search process, e.g. finding the wrong product from shelf or putting the product to the wrong shelf number position, but logistic robotics can reduce to 0 error to put wrong product on the shelf number position or spends long time to search the kind of product from the shelf number position. So, in logistic robotic behavioral economic view, robotics can help businesses to avoid products putting on wrong shelves number position error risk, reduce store workers number, reduce product shelf number position search economic time.

Amazon organizational intangible resource management strategy

- How to implement effective intangible resources management strategy to achieve performance improvement to Amazon e-commerce organization? Why does non intangible resources effective negligence management to Amazon organization, it will cause worse performance to Amazon e-commerce organization any one e-buyer?

One efficient organization must need have efficient and effective resources management strategy in order to provide enough resources for its organization overall different departments cooperation effectively and efficiently. How to implement effective resources management strategy to achieve performance improvement? Why does ersources shortage to organization, it will cause worse performance? I shall explain the reasons as below:

For Amazon e-commerce organization example, it is one global the most large goods transport delivery service moddleman role between global online customers and their product salespeople. Amazon owns its webstores, so global any one country buyer clicks to its different countries webstores , then he/she can choose any kinds of products to buy from Amazon any one country webstore. However, the product is owned the another seller. So, any products are not owned by from Amazon any one country webstores. However, the product is owned by the another seller. SO, any products are not owned by Amazon. It only provides webstores to let global any one e-buyer to buy the product after he/she has paid visa payment. So, Amazon's role is one middleman. It needs to provide goods transport service to help the product's seller to deliver the product to whose e-buyer individual hoime in the most short time, e.g. when one China e-buyer clicks to Amazon China webstore , after he chooses any brands of computers product from Amazon China webstore, he makes purchase of the brand of comouter decision. Then, he needs to pay visa to Amazon 's China webstore . When

Amazon confirms that ie can accept payment by the China e-buyer's visa. Then, Amazon will deliver the product to the China e-buyer's home within one week or longer time, the delivery days time depends on how much delivery fee, the China's e-buyer , he can pay. So, Amazon only can receive commision infomr from the computer brand product seller. Because Amazon can build famous loyalty of rapid goods delivery service provider barnad and its different countries websites can provide above one million different kinds of brand products to let global different conuntries e0buyers to choose in order to make the most fair and the most reasonable purchase price decision from its different Amazon different countries webstores per day. So, Amazon can help its different countries sellers to apply Amazon itself unique different countries' websotes design to attract global many different countries e-buyers to click to Amazon's webstores to find any kinds of products to choose to buy conveniently.

So, such as Amazon e-commerce organization case, if it hopes to attract global different countries e-buyers prefer to click to Amazon itself any one webstore more than other firms themselves webstores . Then, it must need have enough resources (tangible and intangible) both in order to provide raoid goods delviery service and many different kinds of goods choice provision service and reasonable price consumption channel to let any one countrye-buyer feels confidence and safe payment transaction and enough product advertisement, photo, price, function information in order to make final purchase decision from Amazon itself different country webstores more easily.

Hence, the tangible and intangible resources are needed to supuply to Amazon e-commerce organization. They may include: Product photos, price information, product advertisement which are shown to Amazon's different countries webstores , enough online customer service enquiry employees number, enough computers number, enough computers number, different countries offices and warehouses number, computers, internnet technology etc. tangible resource as well as customer service enquiries feedbacks, global rapid goods delivery transport service to any one country e-buyer's home, safe e-payment channel, providing to buy global any one country sellers their products in the most reasonable and the most fair purchase transaction. All ot these issues are any one e-buyer individual purchase feeling to Amazon. SO, they are intangibel (non-tangible) resources to Amazon. It means that if Amazon can let global any one e-buyer feels it's e-purchase service provision can let they feel more satisfactory , then they will choose to buy Amazon webstores any kinds of products more than other sellers their webstores products, because Amazon webstores can provide the kind of product of different brands choice, it aims to compare whether which brand's price is unreasonable too high or which brand's product's quality is worse, or design is not very atrraction. So, Amazon's intangibale resource, such as rapid goods delivery service, online or phone customer enquiry service, webstores' products information whether e-buyers can feel satisfactory, e.g. reasonable price, clear product photo many different kinds of brands product choice. All of these intangible resources to Amazon, they may also influence Amazon's future e-buyer number absolutely.

- How can Amazon raise intangible resource number to be effective?

SO, I explain that Amazon hadboth kinds of resources. They may include tangible and intangible resources. Internet speed, whether it is intangible resources. Internet speed, whether it is rapid or slow to satisfy global e-buyers online purchase speed and non online traffic jam accidents feeling. Amazon webstores any brands of products, photos, price information images whether they are clear to let any one global ebuyer to feel when they click to Amazon any one webstores. All of these internet technology resources to Amazon any one webstore will influence Amazon e-commerce organization's e-buyers number will increase or decrease . For example, if Amazon's China webstore can not let Chinese e-buyers to feel that it can not provide different kinds of brand products photos' clear image to let any one Chinese e-buyer to see the product photo clearly. When one Chinese e-buyer clicks to Amazon Chinese webstore to find any brands of laptop products to prepare to choose one to buy. But when he clicks to Amazon China webstore, he can not feel any one brand of laptop's photo is clear to let he feels. Then, theser unclear laptop photos may influence the Chinese e-buyer forgets his laptop purchase decision from Amazon 's China webstore easily. He may clcik to the another brand of laptop seller webstore to buy the brand of laptop from the laptop seller itself webstore. SO, Amazon's webstore design may be the important intangible resource to influence global any one e-buyer's visiting Amazon's any one webstore times or reducing to do to choose to visit Amazon's webstore behavior , due to they do not click to Amazon any one webstore websites again.

I recommend that Amazon ought consider how to design its any countries webstores in order to attract global e-buyers visiting Amazon itself webstores times number increase. So, global e-buyers' visiting Amazon different countries webstores times which will be Amazon's most important intangible resources to cause its future global e-buyers number. This kind of intangible resources may help Amazon e-commerce goods delivery service organization to raise its competitive effort,, because when one country's ebuyer feels Amazon can provide the most attraction and fair purchase channel from its different countries webstores. Then, the country's e-buyer will talk to his friends, families to prefer to choose Amazon if they have online purchase desire. Because Amazon's any one e-buyer , he .she will persduade his/her friends, families to choose Amazon's e-purchase channel., if he feels it can provide excellent e-purchase method to satisfy his online purchase need. Consequently, Amazon's e-buyers number may be influenced to increase.

ON conclusion, such as Amazon case, how to decide its whether which is the most important tangible and/or intangible resources in order to raise competition effort. It depends on whether how the seller sells its product, in order to concentrate on spending to increase the kind of resources number, such as Amazon e-commerce goods sale and delivery service organization case, internet webstores design intangible image dissatisfactory or satisfactory feeling which may be the most influential global e-buyers number increases or decreases. Moreover, Amazon's internet webstores design intangible satisfactory or dissatisfactory feeling resource may also influence e-buyer before or after e-purchase service requiry feedback feeling, safe visa card payment feeling, fair and reasonable brands of products price information and different brands of product photos image seeing satisfactory or dissatisfactory feeling , they are intangible resource asset to Amazon when global any one ebuyer must need to click to its any one webstore to find its any kinds of product to make purchase decision. So, any organizations must need to spend limit money to support its the most influential intangible resource , instead of tangible resources in order to increase clients number.

On conclusion, we can increase organizational resources on these several aspects: Organizational resources are all assets that are available to a firm for use during the production process or service process, such as Amazon ecommerce organization case. The four basic types of organization resources are human, monetary, raw materials may be tangible, but internet technology may be another intangible resource to today any organizations. Improving organizational resources aim to improve efficiency, it means as the ability to accomplish something with the least amout of wasted time, money and effort or performance as well as effectiveness, such as improving internet speed, and none online traffic jam accidents occurrence easily. It means as trhe degree to which something is successful in producing a desired result success. However, we can improve resources by these way, they may include : Review who manages resources within the organization, build an-up-to date knowledge raise and company wide resource pool, manage the resource pool in line with the market, focus on education and talent employees growth, keep the customers in mind, work on quality services or products, learn to use technology , such as Amazon needs to learn how to raise high speed internet service for its webstores, and avoid online traffic jam frequent occurrent to its any one country webstore.

To sum up effective resource management strategy can help any organizations to increase resource number. Resource management is acquiring , allocating and managing the reosurces, such as individuals, and their skills, finances, technology , material , machinery, and natural resources required for a project. Hence effective effective resource management strategy ensures that internal and external resources are used effectively on time and budget, resources may be obtained internally from the host organization or procured from external resources. SO, effective resource management can help organizations to save resources being wastes and finances being spend on the wrong things, a significant cost saving factor. Hence, such as Amazon e-commerce organization, it needs to know how to learn how to apply internet technology to improve its different countries webstores design, shorten goods transport delivery time, gathering more different brands of product prices, data and phoducts photos improving safe visa card transaction secret to increase e-buyer individual e-purchase confidence. When Amazon can concentrate on effective allocate limited resource to achiev ethese objectives. Then, its global e-buyer number may increase significantly.

Management accounting science how applies to Amazon ecommerce organization

Management accounting concept can help organizations to do management budget strategies, e.g. margin analysis, capital budget, inventory valuation and product cost budget, trend analysis and forecast . Management accounting also called managerial accounting or cost accounting, is the process of analysis business costs and operations to prepare internal financial report, records and managers decision making process in achieving business goals. However, management accountants depend on standard financial statements containing the earning statement, cash flow statement and balance sheet. In addition , it also makes use of additional finds reports in analysizing the information of the organization including budget performance and cost reports. I shall attempt to explain how management account science can help organizations to analyze cost , why and how changes in order to avoid expense increases or excess cost cases or loss increases.

For Amazon e-commerce publish organization example, Amazon publish is a famous publish organization. It applies internet (online) channel to help authors to sell electronic books and paper books to different countries readers. It also cooperate to other publishers to deliver any its anthors books to their webstores, so when one reader chooses its publish partner webstores to buy Amazon any author books, then Amazon publish will share royalty income between them. Hence, Amazon publish may be book distribution partner to its other e-publish partners.

- How management accounting cocept can help Amazon publish to manage its cost effectively in order to increase its profit or e-books or paper books sale ability.

Amazon publish is a e-comerce organization. It depends high internet speed to help global authors to register Amazon publish's individual author account , then any global authors may download their book files to produce any ebooks and papers to sell from Amazon publisher webstores as wellas global any readers can apply Amazon publish webstores to buy any author individual paper or ebooks from its web-publish stores rapidly. So, Amazon publish must need have fast speed internet technology to support its books sale ability,

It brings this question: How much does Amazon publish internet expenditure need? Does it need to pay shops rent per month? Because Amazon publish has none any actual book shops to locate in any countries. So, Amazon publish must not pay rent to any countries for its shops. Although Amazon publish does not need to pay rent for any book shops, but Amazon publish needs to pay extra internet expenditure to US internet service provider to support its electronic webstores daily electronic books and paper books every purchase transaction, any countries author individual book electronic files download per day 24 hours . So, Amazon publish must need to pay more expenditure for internet service to support its authors and readers their electronic books and paper books purchase and sale transaction per day 24 hours.

As Amazon publish case, in its financial report indicates , it does not pay any book stores rent expenditure or book stores (shops) building building expediture on its profit and loss account, but Amazon publish must need to pay internet service expenditure to US internet service provider. Moreover, this internet service expenditure must be more amount, due to it needs to provide its webstores online book (electronic books and paper books) to sell and electronic library e-book lending service to global readers, 24 hours. Thus, internet service expenditure must be Amazon publish long-term influential transaction expenditure because, any electronic books and paper books, even e-library books borrow service and readers must need to pay visa card for borrowing book month service fee and purchase books from amazon publish e-publish webstores in any time every day.

Hence, Amazon publish must need have good management account strategy in order to predict whether different countries will have how many readers click to its different countries e-publish webstores to spend time to choose different authors books to buy or borrow to read from intenet channel. So, any countries readers budgeting number, readers reading habit behavior, e.g. US has about one million online readers click Amazon e-publish webstores , but it has only three thousands readers pay visa card to buy its ebooks and paper books from its Amazon electronic publish webstores, in this week , but next week, US has about seven thousands online readers click Amazon e-publish webstores, but it has three thousands readers pay visa card to buy its ebooks and paper books. Hence, it seems tha although this week has one million online readers click to Amazon publish electonic webstores to seek any books, but the book buyer number has only three thousands. Otherwise, although next week, it reduces three thousands e-readers click to visit Amazon e-publish webstores e-readers number , but it still keep same three thousand e-readers to choose to buy

Amazon publish's books to read.

I assume that Amazon publish needs to pay a fixed internet service expenditure, e.g. US $500,000, but it design this e-publish webstores can help it to do its different countries e-publish webstores, their daily e-readers visiting number, daily electronic book and paper book sale number and daily e-readers visiting time statistics. It's electronic publish webstores can help it to record any countries' reading habits and reading taste , e.g. how many fiction , story books have sold in the week, how many non fiction books have sold in the week , e.g. business topic books have sold next week.

So, Amazon publish can use its e-publish webstores to gather above data in order to make author book topic sale choice, e.g. whether this week, US market ought sell how many consumer psychological topic book, US market ought sell how many management topic book next week. If this week US market can only sell one thousand consumer psychological topic book to compare its budget is less than one thousand consumer psychological topic books budget sale number reduces, e.g. in the week, there are two thousands readers choose to buy consumer psychological topic books from European market in this week. It implies that there are many European readers who like to read consumer behavior books recently. Hence, Amazon can attempt to concentrate on encouraging authors to write more consumer psychological books to let European readers to read within next several months.

Basic on above effects, Amazon needs to provide rapid internet service to European libraries, schools ,e-book partners to help them to promote Amazon consumer psychology topic books in order to let the European consumer psychological students, consumer psychology lecturers, consumer psychologists to know Amazon publish can provide more different topics concern consumer psychology research in order to increase Amazon 's consumer psychology book European market book buyers bumber.

As above case, I assume Amazon publish needs to pay a fixed internet service expenditure , e.g. US$500,000 per month. Amazon needs webstores to evaluate whether it is value, if it helps European schools, libraries organizations to pay internet fee, in order to let they can let many consumer psychology students and teachers and consumer psychologists to know that Amazon publish may have enough different consumer psychology books to be provided to European publish libraries, schools readers to read. For example, I assume next several month, Amazon publish needs to pay US two million internet service expenditure to global different European countries to help Amazon publish itself to promote its al different authors' consumer psychology topic books as well as it evaluates that it will sell different European countries; students , teachers and consumer psychologists readers, they have about three million readers at least choose to buy its one million consumer psychology topic authors; paper books and electronic books next several months as well as it also needs to evaluate whether it can earn more than US ten million at least royalty income after reducing author royalty from all European countries book markets.

Thus, if Amazon publish makes decision to help European countries schools, public libraries to pay internet expenditure to help it to advertise its one million consumer psychology topic authors electronic and paper books to sell. It must needs to pay fixed US$500,000 internet expenditure for Amazon publish its all e-bpublish webstores and it also needs to pay extra two million internet service expenditure for global all European countries libraries and schools per month. If next month, Amazon publish can earn more than US tem million at least royalty income after reducing author royalty from all European countries book market. Then, Amaozn publish ought attempt to make this internet service expenditure for all European schools, libraries organizations, if it had confidence to earn this royalty amount from European consumer psychology book readers, such as this Amazon publish.

On conclusion, , this Amazon publish organization case, it may attempt to apply management accounting science method to make book sale number budget, royalty income budget, even analysis to reader individual reading habit, book topic choices, book sale price evaluation in order to judge whether the kind or topic book ought concentrates on selling to which countries marekts, such as Amazin publish case, it also may choose different consumer psychology topic books to concentrate on selling to different European countries in next several months, if it can earn all European royalty income more than its internet service expenditure to European schools, libraries, then Amazon may attempt to make this decision. Otherwise, it won't be good decision.

Hence, it implies that management accounting is one kind of business management science, it can apply number to help any organizations to do right or reasonable reason more accurate as well as it is different to traditional financial acounting, it only helps organizations to record and income and expenditure, earn or loss record function. Hence, management accounting may help any organizations to attempt implement useful or effective strategies in order to improve themselves performance.

FOUR

AMAZON FACILITY MANAGEMENT STRATEGY

How Amazon solves its future marketing challenges

Amazon faces what future marketing competition

Nowadays, any kinds of businessmen may apply internet to do themselves e-commerce sale channel easily and conveniently. So, Amazon needs to find strategies how to persuade any kinds of brands of sellers to choose its e-stores to help themselves to advertise, promote and sell their products to replace themselves online stores from Amazon its e-stores. It will be one long term marketing strategic problem to Amazon needs to consider how to attract global many sellers choose Amazon's e-stores to replace themselves e-stores (online sale channels) easily. How to increase global sellers confidence to choose Amazon e-stores to help them to sell their different kinds of products ? I shall attempt to indicate some useful marketing and management strategies to explain as below:

Firstly, I shall indicate what kinds of challenges Amazon will face

in future ecommerce market. Although, Amazon's cloud dominance core online sale marketplace had succeed, but it still faces many challenges.
It needs to implement useful strategies to solve in order to increase its online buyers number and online sellers number both.

` On growth challenge concerning aspect, Amazon needs to learn how to grow investors confidences to let Amazon itself can help them to apply its e-stores to help them to advertise their products from Amazon e-stores to replace Google cloud online advertisement service competitor as well as Microsoft cloud online advertisement service competitor both main online advertisement service providers. It seems that global online sellers may also choose Google and Microsoft cloud advertisement to replace Amazon cloud advertisement service.

So, Amazon's marketplace needs to find itself on the defensive for reasons unrelated to the probe improvements in e-commerce technology on the whole could mean that fewer sellers see Amazon as their primary sales channel, instead of Google , Microsoft cloud advertisement sale channel. Hence, Amazon needs to implement strategy how to help any global sellers to change positive shopping experience on traditional web stores improvement, in order to help they to promote their brands more effectively.

ON online shopping confident challenge aspect, Amazon became the dominant e-commerce marketplace in the world by offering hundreds of million of products at competitive prices. However, Amazon will face third-party sellers participation to cloud market online sale agent competitive challenge. Third-party sellers , such as Google, Microsoft have made up an increasing share of products on Amazon in recent years, roughly 58% of sales on Amazon were key third-party sellers, but that comes with its own host of problems, including fakes, counterfeits and unsafe products that Amazon has not been able to successful compete easily in third party cloud e-commerce sale market. Past surveys have shown that Amazon is among the most trusted technology brands out there, but if it gains a reputation as a sketchy products, some consumers could not to do their shopping at first past sites. Hence, Amazon needs to let global many sellers believe that it is the best third party cloud advertisement service provider to compare its another third part cloud advertisement service providers , such as Google. Microsoft in order to persuade many global sellers choose to use its cloud online advertisement service.

What is Amazon marketing strategy? Amazon uses the high runner strategy to market its products. This strategy was data to uncover which products are in the highest demand in every category . Amazon's pricing strategy and bids heavily on advertisement to pull people to those sellers themselves products. In future, Amazon's marketing strategies include: SEOP, cheap price advertisement, user-generated content, video marketing, dedicated website. Hence, Amazon's future marketing strategy or communication strategy aims to increase customer traffic to Amazon websites, create awareness of products or services, promote repeat purchases, develop incremental product and service revenue opportunities.

However, Amazon can improve marketing strategy to help its sellers to boost their products sale by providing free shipping, reviewing [product sale analytics, testing different advertising methods. So, Amazon has three big market sale channels, the retail marketplace, Amazon Prime, and Amazon web services. Moreover, Amazon needs to build effective growth strategy. It's Amazon's secondary intensive growth strategy. It aims to generate more revenue from markets where the company currently operates because Amazon is depended on its customers, which is why when consumerism grows, the business by default grows. It means that whose global e-commerce online e-stores purchase market grows, the global visiting shops market customers number will be influenced to fall down. So, it implies that they have close customer number relationship between e-stores customers number and visiting shops customers number to different kinds of businesses.

Even, future Amazon business may have this competitive strategy, it can be described as cost leadership taken to the extreme strategy. Cost leadership strategy seems as cheap , bulk products sale, such as " discount stores " sale method. All of Amazon's products are sold by the cheapest sale product method. So, Amazon marketing communication mix integrates print and media advertising, sales promotions , events and experiences, public relation and direct marketing. Amazon places a particular focus on print and media advertising and sales promotions elements of the marketing communication channels. So, Amazon was direct marketing. It is so advanced that they see what their customers are searching for, offer products, that are the same of similar and send their emails for when the price changes for an item, the customers have been eyeing up.

However, Amazon's management principles of leadership in organization, it is also important to influence organizational growth. It can drive Amazon to boost sale, they include: customers obsession, leaders start with the customer and work backwards, leaders are owners, invent and simplify, learning and be curious. Hiring and developing the4 best, insisting on the highest standards. So, Amazon company makes include customers are at the top of the company's interests, Amazon wants to make everything as simple as it is possible. Hence, Amazon applies intensive growth strategy. It is a growth strategy that focuses on cultivating new products or new markets and sometimes both. Amazon aims to help its any kinds of product sellers to bring new online advertisement experience feeling to let online buyers to aware their new products existences.

Hence, Amazon needs to help its sellers to change their e-business model from " direct sales" to sales-and-service model, aggregating many sellers under one virtual roof and receiving commission from the other companies sales, because Amazon needs to make income through its online retail e-stores, subscriptions and web services, among other channels. Retail remains Amazon's primary source of revenue, with online and physical stores accounting for the biggest share. Essentially , Amazon is choosing growth over profits. And, Amazon is able to lose money to help its sellers grow their markets shares from e-business model.

In fact, most Amazon sellers market least US$1,000 per month in sales, and some super-sellers make upward US$250,000 each month in sales. However, Amazon also helps someone without cost to create selling, such as Amazon publishers. So, Amazon publishers do not need to spend any cost to sell e-books or paper books when they download their books on Amazon publish. Hence, Amazon can attract many different countries authors choose to cooperate to sell their books from Amazon publish platform. It means that Amazon's business model , which was initially based on ecommerce had changed and now incorporates entertainment, music, cloud computing, meal delivers etc. e-publishing etc. Although, Amazon sells a lot more through its subsidiaries, the core Amazon busi9ness model is based on an e-commerce market platform . Amazon sells products or the platform but, also allows third-party sellers to sell consumers.

How does Amazon future business model? Amazon future business model ought depend on geographically and terms of products and services offered to help its different kinds of product sellers to sell their products, such as continue expanding on selling music, videos, electronics, video games, software, houseware, toys, games, e-books as well as attracted customers were Amazon its personalized recommendation tools and customers reviews, this developing a community of consumers , which is essential free online service to any one Amazon customer.

So, Amazon will obsession rather than competitor focus, passion excellence, and long=term, thinking. Amazon must continue focus on those operations in order to grow income. They may include: Amazon marketplace business model, Amazon asks for a fee from its sellers to promote and advertise their products, Amazon's subscription business model has been vital to the brand growth. In exchange for a monthly fee. Subscribers have access to the platform's video and music streaming catalog, free two days shopping, unlimited photo storage etc.

Amazon was services business model, it is a low cost complete IT structure platform, whose services are contracted by companies, organizations, and institutions around the world. Amazon kindle, business model, it is Amazon's e-reading service, users can buy, browse, and download books, magazines and newspapers , available at kindle store. Amazon patent business model, it has more than 1,000 patents, several of which are licensed by other campaigns. Amazon advertising business model, it is Amazon ad. Platform offers sponsored ads and video. It is a very efficient marketing channel, since the audience there with the intention of buying. Hence, Amazon 's customer segments may include: sellers, buyers and developers. Sellers are all the companies that use Amazon's e-commerce platform to sell their products to all the community involves with Amazon web-services.

Amazon's cloud computing platform, As its own website states, they are customers and partners, e.g. any public sector or private sector organizations. And the buyers are global people, who acquire products and services through Amazon's channels. So, Amazon can track its custoOmer based on some characteristics, such as interest, engagement, and personnel information (e.g. gender, geographical space, language among other), ion order to predict any countries potential consumer behaviors more accurately.

Hence, Amazon's business model is based on three value propositions: low price, fast delivery, and a wide selection of products in order to let consumers feel these benefits, e.g. convenience to connect to Amazon's any web stores to buy any kinds of products, with an reasonable price, safe and reliable delivery service. Also Amazon can build long term good relationship to its global buyers from its web stores, such as product reviews, and comments on the platform, telephone, online chat and email contact. Aside from Amazon's online resource, other key resources to bring Amazon's benefits, they may include physical spaces of the company, such as offices, warehouses, supply chain structure and automation etc.

In fact, human resources are essential for Amazon , which needs to help it to operate daily online purchase and sale activities effectively, such as Amazon's e-stores designers, engineers, developers. Hence, Amazon key partners may include: world wide different brans of product sellers, affiliates, bloggers who earn a commission for any referrals that need to a sale. In addition to helping with sales, they also promote traffic to the Amazon platform. Amazon's platform independent software vendors, who adapt Amazon's online platform technology to work, content creators , they are independent authors, who can publish their works through kindle direct publishing, subsidiaries, include companies that provide storage spaces, stores and systems, in additions to brands and products, developed by Amazon itself, such as Amazon essentials, Amazon elements, kindle , Alexa etc.

Also, Amazon needs to know how to let its future cost structure to reduce in order to achieve saving cost benefit in long time. Its cost structure includes its complete IT structure, customer service center, software development and maintenance, information security, marketing as well as expenses involved in maintaining its physical spaces, such as fulfillment centers, sortation centers, and delivery stations. Hence, future Amazon will need to implement useful methods to help its any departments to reduce operational cost as well as have to persuade partners, sellers, product buyers to help them to raise sales growth, earn more commissions, bringing advertisement effectiveness, subscription income growth, web service growth and patents income.

Amazon's main competitors may include: online stores, Walmart, Alibaba, Otto, Jingdong, ebay, fliplcart, Newegg, ralcuten. So, if Amazon can persuade these any one online competitors to be its future partners, Then, it may reduce its online competitors number significantly. However, Amazon SWOT analysis indicates its strengths may include: Building famous e-commerce brand valuation, customer orientation, such as reasonable prices, personalized suggestions, and reviews make a loyal consumer community, innovation, it always develops new products and services, when improves its regular business, it does not maintain physical stores and has little inventory. It is able to keep a low-cost structure, large selection , it owns an extensive product mix, allowing customers to buy anything on the same platform, more global third-party sale partners, logistics . Also, Amazon's weaknesses may include: limitable business model, kindle e-book publish faces many e-publish competitors, employee workplace conditions may feel worse , focusing dependence on distributors, that exposed Amazon to a wide range to issues, especially considering renegotiation of terms. But, Amazon also has these opportunities, such as expansion. Amazon can expand its operation in developing countries, increasing physical stores number, it can make some big purchases, such as acquisitions and that can increase market share and reduce competition. But, it also has threats, e.g. some government regulations can threaten Amazon distribution inside some countries, exploitations , labor, cybercrime, it can threaten the security of the platform and its users, it faces strong competitors, A video streaming service, such as Disney Add, HBO,. Netflix.

Moreover, it can not estimate when economic recession , online stores are not adapted to alive to economic recession and uncertainty can impact Amazon's sales, fake reviews, customers rely on reviews to make purchase and Amazon needs to have more positive product review more than negative product review from its online customers.

On conclusion, Amazon is one good case to explain future any kinds of e-businesses will face what challenges in order to decide how to implement effectiv3e strategies to help them to solve any possible not predicted challenges in order to raise competitive effort.

Amazon Facility Management Strategy

Facility management functions

Why do many organizations begin to feel facility management importance? What are the real functions that when one organization can attempt to achieve facility management strategy? The main functions of facility managment may include. For example, when sale manager is is directly responsible for managing the performance of salespeople, facility managment seems that it can not help any salepsople to increase sale number, they have no direct relatonship, but in fact, any salespeople must need to stay to sell any products in the shop. SO, the shop's facility environment may have indirect relationship to influence customers purchase emotion, when they enter the shop. If the shop's facility is more attractive, it may let customers to feel comfortable to stay long time in the shop.

So, facility management influences people, processes, the building and technology to be improveed better in order to achieve good job performance or sale performance both in possible. This serves many broader goals, improving efficiency, and productivity and creating a positive workplace culture, coordinating desking arrangements, managing employees, facilitating moves and spaces utilization, handling emergency planning benefits to any organizations.

Hence, the facility management function to service aspect, they may include submitting a work order request rapidly (raising efficiency) , when the shop can be designed to have more space for service staffs to contact customers , it aims to let they feel comfortable to stay in the shop, reserving space and visitors and handling emergency action planning more easily. When the shop customer service counters have have effective enquiry place facility enviroment for customers and customer service staffs in order to let they can feel comfortable to stay to enquire and answer in the shop's service counters in long time.

ON physical building improvement aspect, effective facility management many provide repair, maintenance, and building improvement, workplace , cleaning , on-and-off site property management , e.g. improving security places to avoid theft occurrence easily. Moreover, more importance is needed for facility managers to understand and use technology, workplace management system aggregate data, which drives crucial decisions about how to run the business and shape the workplace, a modern facility management building, offices , factories , shops even living houses in order to raise amart building concept comfortable feeling to let house owners, shops staffs and customers factories workers, office staffs to feel smart facility management system lay let them to feel comfortable when they are working or living in the smart building. So, amart facility management system may bring these functions: Researching IOT devices based on data collection needs, integrating IOT devies into everyday facilities processes, determining the cost, ROI and using aggregated data to better understand the workplace.

Hence, in one smart building, facility management system can collect and analyze data from networked technologies to get insights about the workplace. This fuels better decision-making on how to optimize the work environment for the people using it. For example, all smart office technology relies on data collection , access control system supports safety, when automation technological streamlines processes. And when these's a data component to any networked device or software, the true benefit of most technology is in its function. So, future smart offices , houses, factories etc. building will be needed to apply facility management technology to let any one feels comfortable when they need to use the building smart office or house or factory automatic turn off light facility when the office facility management system can help all the building all offices to turn off the light or central air condition automatically in order to save power or reduce energy waste in any office inside working environment any time when the facility management samart system ensure that none any one is staying in the building any offices.

Hence, facility management ought bring these benefits to any business office users or house living users, they may include tha complete management and maintenance of the buildings, people and assets of the business, it enables a more cost-effective working process within the business, it improves the efficiency of the business, e.g. raising workers productivities when they need to stay long time in the factory to manufacture any products, if they feel the factory environment is more comfortable and safe to let them to work, their emotion may be influenced to feel more happy to work, even raising the product manufacturing number more efficienly, it improves the efficiency of the business, it helps to manage health and safety requirements in accordance with industry requirement, helping a workplace run at maximum efficiency, e.g. cost reduces, space optimization , creating a comfortable feeling in a better workplace, outsourcing facility management service may brings better service delivery, more variety snf flexibility, today's employees and tenants expect more then just clean restrooms and adquate lighting to create and enhance great company cultures.

So, FM provides and manages a variety , it supports services in order to organize all the organization's functions more efficiently. It focuses on the integration of primary activities on both strategic and operational levels. Moreover, facilities management can be defined as the tools and services that support the functionality, safety and sustainability. For outsourcing facilty managmeent advantage., it may involve turning over the complete management and decision making authority of an operation to somebody outside organization. It may help businesses to maximize returns on investment and establish long term competitive advantage in the markplace.

Hence, the types of facility management may include: cleaning, hardware inspection and maintenance, transportation, security service, fire safety. However, there are some differences between facilities management function and property management funciton. In general, facility management and office management are concerned with the people using the space, when property management concerned with the space itself only, e.g. the physical building shell and rented offices etc. buildings.

Facility management brings what benefits
Facility managment brings what benefits to organization
Can facility management bring social benefits? What benefits do facility management bring to our societies? What are social responsibilities to facility management? Why do our societies need facility managment services? I shall attempt to explain as below:
IN fact, ay organizations will need facilities management services, because it can bring continuous development benefits on economy, environment and society aspects, e.g. minimising waste to landfill form the organization, when the organization has effective facility managment service, increasing supply chain opportunities, when the organization can apply facility management skill to arrange how to let worehouse or store space can keep goods to put on corrective positions and more space to put their goods in warehouse. So goods can be transported to move more easily when the warehouse can have effective transportation to different countries more efficiently in short delivering time as well as when global warewhouses can have effective facility management service to be arranged how to store their goods in warehouses efficiently in order to bring rapid transportation benefits between the country and another country. It is significant " rapid goods transportation deliving benefit" to any organizations. For Amazon example, it needs to manage different goods to keep to its different countries warehouses in order to transport goods to fly to different countries customers' homes every day by air plane rapidly every day. If Amazon can have effective warehouse facility management strategy to manage how its different kinds of goods to be putted on its shelves in its different countries warehouses. Then, it's logistic workers won't need spedn much time to seek any goods on shelves in order to deliver their goods to fly to another country in short time efficienly. So, Amazon warehouses facilties managment service can help its organization to provide efficient delivering service.
How can facility managers satisfy the needs of customer when such

needs changing so frequently to their organizations? Organizational justify theory indicates that where managers do not have resources available tomeet employee demands. The procedures used to divide what resources are available may be used to achieve satisfaction. How can facility management satisfy needs of customers when both these needs and environments in which they are operating change as frequently? How to match unpredictable space demand with supply? How to manage refurishment of out dated facilities, dealing with the competing space and service demand of different deparrments.

So, it brings this question: How can facility and accommodation management groups appease their customers in the intermediate term? SO, it seems that facility management can raise our social organizational justice benefits, such as improving service performance and raising customer satisfactory feeling for the organization's efficient service performance.

IN fact, efficient facility management strategy may help our social any organizations to earn these benefits. They may include: Influencing empllyees' perceptions fair procedural fairness in our social orgnaizations, the provision of timely feedback and effecgtive communication of the basis for decisions. So, effective facility management may help global organizational managers to know hoe to allocate new space that has become available to let employees to feel enjoyment to work in order to raise efficiencies or improve productivities. It will create any country's GDP growth when the organization can implement effective facility management strategy. Hence facility management can bring benefits to improving customer satisfactions, improving productivities and raising efficiencies. Then, our social organizations will have more social benefits, when GDP growht is caused by facility management service improvement to any global organizations.

Brochner (2003) pints out the reality that innovation in jointly FM brings benefits to organizations , developing goods and associated services in manufacturing is starting to surface, when the connection between facillity design and management is still weak,

IN organizations, FM can meet organizational business need more appropriately, atract customers more are easier to manage and controp and operated more cost effectively, respond better to occupant needs.

After all, design has an effect on sales efficiency, staff, profit , capital investment, and maintenance cost(Ransley and lngram , 2001). These factors are the concern of facility management as much as they relate to the organization's core business success. Therefore, managing FM requirements during design is necessary for an organization to achieve its goals after occupancy a newly build facility.

For airport facility management case example, an effective management of the facility , aimed at successfully satisfying both the airport ownership and the passegners (air plane travellers) customers, should be based on agreement, network and strategic allience with FM functoins from other airports, they can apply outsourcing FM strategy to provide facility management service during travellers are staying in their airports, they can feel enjoyment in airport environment, then their shopping desire and again visiting the country's airport desire will be influenced to raise, when the country's airport can provide comfortable FM airport facility to let them to feel. Hence, FM can raise customer service perofrmance with firm's objective and service processes, drive performance improvement and increase client satisfaction, such as airport travelling places whehter how FM may influence travellers to stay how long time in the country's airport. It means that when the airport is more attraction, e.g. design is attration. Then , the airport can persuaded travellers to stay long time in the airport. Consequently, their shopping chance will increase in the airport.

Facility managment brings what benefits to economy

The economic benefits of FM organizational design . Evidence is growing that FM may help buildings provide financial rewards for building owners, operators and occupants. FM buildings typically have lower annual costs for energy, water, maintenance / repair, reconfiguring space because of changing needs, and other operating expenses. These reduced costs do not have to some at the expense of higher first costs, Through FM design and innovative use of high quality of materials and equipment, the first cost of FM building can be the same as or lower than that of a traditional building.

Morevoer, some sustainable design features have higher first cost, but the payback period for the incremental investment often is short and the lifecycle cost typically lower than the cost of more traditional buildings. In additional to direct cost savings, FM buildings can provide owener and socieyt benefits, for example, FM building features can promote better health, comfort, well being and productivity of buildings, occupants , which can reduce levels of absenteeism and increase productivities. Moreover, FM buildings can also often owners economic benefits form lower risks, longer building lifetimes, improveed ability to attract new employees, when they feel office environment or warehouse , shop working environment are more comfortable to let they feel, when they are staying in these FM workplaces, reduced expenses for dealing with complaints, and increasing asset value.

Overall, Amazion FM office and warehouse buildings also offer society as a whole economic benefits, such as reduced cost fomr air pollution , damage, avoiding landfills, wastewater treatment plant, power plants and distribution lies. So, low first cost and later repair / manintenance expense reducing or avoiding. Consequently, above of these will be FM building's long time economnic benefits, social benefits and organizational benefits to the building owner, its clients and our societies.

Facility management can reduce
maintenance service expenditure

Facility management provides a variety of non core operations and maintenance services to support any organizations' operation. For logistic organization example, it is possible to provide effective maintenance service to warehouse in order to reduce warehouse facilities to be damaged to bring to spend to buy any new equipment facilities expenditure. So, when the logistic compnay's warehouse facilities can be maintenanced to be the best quality. Then, they can be used these warehouses' machines facilities again. Their performance can assist workers to manufacture any products to keep the most efficiently an raising the best production performance in whole manufacturing process. Then, this logistic company's facility management department can bring to avoid purchase any new machine facilities expenditure spending. One to these warehouses' production machine facilities are kept in the best productin performance environment evem in long term production need.

The logistic industry's facility management department can create cost savings and efficiency of the warehouse's workplaces. It's machines facilities (producton machines) are dealt with the maintenance management of the physical assets maintenance service. FM (facilities management) has been being applied to industrial facilities in logistic and warehouse industry long term as well as maintenance plays a significant role to ensure the full service and the warehousing system, including both building components and equipment in warehouse.

Maintenance service is needed to bring a certain level of availability and reliability of a warehouse facilities system and its components and its ability perform to a standard level of quality. So , it seems that logistic industry's warehouse asset cost reducing. It depends on whether it has one facility management deparrment to provide maintenance service to itself warehouse workplace's production machine facilities and warehouse building itself in order to let workers t feel the manufacturing machines can bring good manufacturing performance to assist them to produce any products in one safe warehouse workplace environment. Hence, the performance measurement of warehouse maintenance issue will be valued to be consider to every warehouse manager and facility manager in logistic industry.

In logistic industry, (FM) works at two level on the one hand, it provides a safe and efficient working environment, which is essential to influence warehouse workers whether how they perform to do their manufacturing tasks or logistic goods delivery tasks in warehouse. When they feel the warehouse is safe environment to work. They will not need to consider anywhere has risk to cause they die by accident in warehouse. Hence, they can concentrate on doing their every tasks . On the other hand, it can involve strategic issues, such as property (warehouse workplace and management, strategy property decision and warehouse facility, e.g. manufacturing macine, facility maintenance and checking planning and maintenance planning development.

However, reducing the operating expense issue will be the main aim when the logistic company feels that it has need to set up one in-house facility management department to carry on any maintenance service for its warehouses' any workplace property and manufacturing machines facilities. So, when the logistic company decides to implement one facility management department, it needs to ensure its facility management department can bring the minimum level of keeping manufacturing performance and efficiency to its warehouses' any manufacturing machines and warehouses' property to avoid to be damaged in shourt term, such as loss of busness due to failure in service, provision of project to customer satisfaction, provision of safe environment, effective utilisation of workplace space, e.g. warehouse effectiveness and communication between the workers and the logistic managers in the warehouse workplace , due to the warehouse's space is not enough maintenance service reliability to the logistic company's warehouse, responsiveness of the warehouse's worker individual negative emotion problem, due to hs/she often feels need to work in one unsafe warehouse working environment. Hence, it seems that poor or unsafe warehouse working environment can influence workers feel negative emotion to work to bring low efficiency (inefficiency) or under productive performance in warehouse. It has relationship to influence they to bring psychological negative emotion feeling to work when the organization lacks one effective warehouse management repairing service to be provided to the warehouse's facilities and properties' maintenance needs in order to avoid ineffective measurement and misleading of performance.

Hence, the logistic company's facilities management department often needs to be reviewed whether irs maintenance service level is passed to achieve the lowest repair (maintenance) service standard to its warehouse itseld property and manufacturing machine or warehouse delivery tool facilities or warehouse lamps' light whether is enourh to let workers to see anything clearly to avoid accident occurrence or see anything to work clearly or the warehouse space areas are enough to let they can have enough space to walk or communicate to their team supervisors or deliver any goods more easily in the short distance between the worker's sending goods location and the delivering goods destination in order to avoid because the lacking enough space to cause the accident occurrence , due to the space is not enough to let they deliver their goods to any locations in warehouse.

Hence, it seems logistic company's (FM) department can contribute to the organization's mission, such as avoiding warehouse accident occurrence, inefficiency, inadequancy and unavailability of the facility for future needs when the warehouse lacks enough space areas to bring poor performance of facility and dangerous warehouse itself property in warehouse, e.g. safe and reliable operations of material handling equipment and maintenance of warehouse facilities, grounds, sesurity system, utilities, plumbing, heating , enough lightins system, air conditioning, warming heater, fire protecton, security system alarm etc. facilities in warehouse.

Hence, it seems that if the logistic company expected to reduce to spend lot of excessive manufacturing machine purchase expenditure, lossing of workers' life or bring workplace accidents , due to poor warehouse workplace environment, even bringing lawsuit compensation claim loss , due to the worker individual accident or death is caused from the poor warehouse facilities, or bring negative emotion to let the workers feel they are working in unsafe warehouse workplace environment. Then, it ought choose to set up on facility manageemtn department in order to provide enough maintenance service to its warehouse to avoid these non essential expenditure causing , due to these poor warehouse facilities factors.

Hence any logistic company ought choose to set up one itself in -house facility management department, it be better than outsourcing its all facilities service to one facility mangement (maintenance service provider) to help it to deal any kinds of maintenance service in warehouse. Because it is long term maintenace need to its warehouse's any machines and warehouse itself properties. If it chose to find one outsourcing facilitiy management maintenance service provider to replace its in-house facility mangement department to deal all related facilities maintenance tasks in warehouse. Then, it is possible that it needs to pay long time facilities maintenance service fee to its outsourcing facility management maintenance service provider more than itself facility management maintenance service provision department.

In conclusion, to decide whether the company ought need or not need facilities maintenance service or either set up in-house facility management department or outsource one facility management maintenance service provider. It depends on whether its organization has how many facilities are used in its workplace, how many staffs are working the workplace, how much size of its workplace, its workplace is office or warehouse or factory, how long time of its facilities' useful time etc. factors , then it can decide whether it needs or does not need one facility maintenance service deparment or outsouring facility maintenance service provider to help it to deal any facilities management problem in its organization.

Facility management role in
Amazon warehouse and office organization

When one company feels that it has need facility management service. It can choose to set up either in-house facility management department or seek one outsourcing facility management service provider to help it to arrange any facility management service need. However, this facility management role is only one for the

organization. It concerns this question: What facility management maintenance function can bring the benfits to the organization?
It can define that all services required for the management of building and real estate to maintain and increase their value, the means of providing maintenance support, project management and user management during the building life cycle, the integration of multi-disciplinary activities within the built environment and the mangement of their impact upon people and the workplace. In traditional, (FM) services may include building fabric maintenance, decoratin and refurbishment, plant, plumbing and drainage maintenance, air conditioning maintenance, lift and escalator maintenance , fire safety alarm and fire fighting system maintenance, minor project management. All these are hard services. Otherwise, cleaning , security, handyman services, waste disposal, recycling, pes control, grounds maintenance, internal plants. All tese are soft services. Additional services, might also include: pace planning, things moving management, business risk assessment, business continuity planning, benchmarking, space management, facilities contract outsourcing service arrangement, information systems, telephony, travel booking facility utility management, meeting room arrangement services, catering services, vehicle fleet management, printing service, postal services, archiving , concierge services, reception services, health and safety advice, environmental management.
All of these services will be every organiztion's in-house facility soft or hard services needs. So, it explains why some large organizations feel need one effective facility management department to help them to arrange how to implement facility serivices efficiently in order to achieve cost reducing, raising efficiency and performance improvemen aims because one effective facility management control system can influence employee individual productive effort to be raised or reduced indirectly.
However, (FM) can be selected either setting up one in-house (FM) department or outsourcing its services to one facility mangement service provider to help the organizatin to solve any kinds of

facilities maintance service problems. One on-house (FM) department is a team, it needs employees to deliver all (FM) services. Some specialist services are needed to be outsourced, when the service is on expertise in the company. The no expertise services will be outsourced to simple service contracts, e.g. lift and escalator (FM) department will have direct labour, but it can outsource some specialist to help it to do some complect facilities management service. So, the team leader can of can manage whose team staffs, such as maintenance technicians run low risk operations . Otherwise, the outsourcing facility management service provider needs to help it to operate high risk operations or maintenance vital plant facility management service. Anyway, it can set up in-house (FM) department to arrange specialist direct labour and outsourced (FM) services to more than one facility management service providers to do different kinds of (FM) services. One of these outsourcing (FM) service provider, who can arrange sub-contractors to assist it to finish any (FM) services of it's outsourcing (FM) services are more complex to compare the other sub-contractors (third parties).

- What is a facility manager's role to provide quality service to satisfy its user needs?

We need to know how quality can be defined in facility management and why it should be defined by the customer? How facility managers can find out customer (user) needs? What are the difficulties in finding out users' needs and in delivering quality services? Whether improving quality always means requiring higher cost?

In general, facility manager's major responsibilities may include these major functional areas: longer range and annual facility planning, facility financial forecasting, real estate acquisiton and/ or disposal, work specification, installation and space management, architectural and engineering planning and design, new construction and/or renovation, maintenance and operations management, maintenance and operation management, telecommunications integration, security and general administrative services. When the facility manager had implemented any one of these FM services for those user. How does he/she provide excellent (FM) service quality ot let whose users to feel satisfactory?

In fact, quality issues can not be considered without customer-oriented perspective service quality involves a comparision of expectation with performance. (FM) service quality is a measure of how well to service level delivered matches customer expectation. So, these issues are (FM) service user's general measurement level requirement. The (FM) manager needs to achieve these the minimum performance measurement level to satisfy whose (FM) user's needs.

However, (FM) service quality has three characteristics: Intangibility, heterogeneity, inseparability. But in fact, (FM) service delivered may be through tangible physical aspects, e.g. factory plant workplace building, machine equipment maintenance, intangible (FM) services, e.g. managing space moving in plant to let staffs to work, managing outsourcing cleaners to clean factory equipment. However, all (FM) service performance often varies, due to the behavior of service personnel. Hence, a well developed job specification and training can help to improve the consistence of services of (FM). Any (FM) productin and consumption of many services may are inseparable and they are ususally interactions between the (FM) client and the contact person from the service provider.

Hence, it seems that service quality is considered as hard to evaluate. In (FM) service quality, it includes physical quality and interactive non-physical service quality. Physical quality is tangibles: The appearance of the physical facilities, equipment, personnel and communication materials. Non-physical services quality means reliability: The ability to perform the promised service dependably and accurately; responsiveness means the willingness to help customers and provide promopt service to let user to feel; assurance mans the competence of the system in its credibility in providing a courteous and secure service and empathy

means the approachability, ease of access and effort taken to understand customers' needs.
Hence, a good performance of (FM) manager , he/she ought satisfy the user's tangible and non-tangible both service quality needs. I recommend that he/she can attempt to predict what are the (FM) customer expects in each (FM) service needs. Then, it can make decision what aspect(s) will be the (FM) users major (FM) service need and what aspect(S) won't be the (FM) users major (FM) service need. Then, he/she can make more accurate decision to arrange time, human resource , cost spending amount arrangement whether when it ought concentrate on finishing the (FM) major service tasks as well as whether how he/she ought finish the major (FM) service tasks to be more easily, e.g. how to arrange staffs number to finish, how many the minimum staffs number is needed to be arrange the major (FM) service tasks, time arrangement is important factor, because it can influence whether he/she ought finish the major (FM) service tasks today or tomorrow or later in order to have enough time to finish other non-major (FM) service tasks. Instead of time management, staff number arrangement is also important factor , if he/she arrangeed the excessive staffs number to do the (FM) major services tasks, then it is possible that it will have shortage of staffs number to finish the non-major (FM) service tasks on the day. So, avoiding either majoe or non-major (FM) services can not finish on the day. The (FM) manager needs to predict when the major (FM) services and the non-major (FM) services which are necessary to be finished in order to have enough time and staffs to assist him/her to finish every day major and non-major (FM) servie effectively. Then, the achievement of his/her (FM) major and non-major tangible and non-tangible services , it will have more chance to be performed efficiently by his/her managed staffs.
In conclusion, in any organizations , (FM) manager needs have good predictable effort to evaluate whether when his/her managed team need to finish the major and/or non-major (FM) tasks as well as whether how he/she ought arrange the accurate time and staff

number to finish any major and/or non-major (FM) service tasks on the day. Then, his/her leading of (FM) service team can be managed to work more efficiently in order to satisfy her/his (FM) service user's needs.

How (FM) space moving management
can bring valued add to Amazon organizations

There are interesting questions: How (FM) can bring value-add to avoid loss or earn more profit to the organization? Can it influence employees to raise performance and improve efficiency ? Some organizations' (FM) service need which is necessary in order to let employees can raise productivity.

It is based on these assumptions: I assume the organizations have completely either outsourced or in-house their (FM) facility management departments will gain more effect on added value than they have no (FM) function as well as organizations have a strong coordination with the (FM) department will gain more added value than organizations with a weak coordination. Organizations in the profit aim can gain more added value than organizations in the not for profit aim sectors.

In fact, any organization is difficult to confirm it has relationship between improving performance, raising efficiency and owning (FM) function in its organization. (FM) could have to do with the attraction of easy but incomplete indicators of efficiency rather than the necessarily and less direct measures if the effectiveness and the relevance of space moving useful management, e.g. whether building has the enough space to let employees to move to work easy in order to raise efficiency, whether the building has excessive furniture and equipment number and they are putted on wrong places to be caused employees move difficulty in the building in order to influence productive performance.

However, how to arrange space moving management to equipment, e.g. copying machines, faxes, productive machines, they are putted on the locations where have enough space to let employees to move to another locations. For example, the building floor has more than 50 employees, but its space is not enough to let these 50 employees to move to any locations to let them to feel easily often. Then, it is posible to cause they feel nervous pressure and they can feel difficult to work , when they are working in a small office space or factory space or warehouse space. Then, the consequence will be under-predictive efficiency or poor performance to any one of these 50 employees in this office or factory or warehouse.

" Facility management is responsible for coordinating all efforts related to planning, designing, and managing buildings and their systems, equipment, and furniture to enhance. The organizations abilty to compete successfully in a rapidly changing world." (F.Becker)

The author explains equipment, workplace internal space designing, furniture space putting location arrangement will have possible to influence employee individual productive performance or efficiency to be raised or reduced in the workplace. Hence, it seems that, in the value chain (FM) belongs to the activity part of the firm. To make the facilities cooperation with each office or factory or warehouse using space moving facility management. Facility space moving management must be linked strategically, tactically and operationally to other support activity to add value to the organization's office or factory or warehouse space moving management arrangement more effectively.

Thus, how to arrangement space moving management issue it will have possible to influence the organization's employee individual productive performance and efficiency in whose workplace. It seems that (FM) space moving management arrangement have indirect relationship to influence the organization's employee individual performance and efficiency , due to they need often to work in the workplace, if they feel moving difficulty , or excessive equipment , furniture number is putting into the small office, factory or warehouse locations, or they feel the office or factory or warehouse has excessive (a lot of) staffs number to work in the small space of office or factory or warehouse. Then, they can not concentrate nervous on finishing every tasks in possible. In long term, their efficiencies will be poor or inefficiencies or their performance won't be improved or causing poort performance in possible.

Instead of the not enough space moving and excessive staffs number factor, it will bring another question: Can enough information systems equipment cause a more efficient and improved performance to the organization staffs in the workplace? I assume that the office has 100 employees and it has only ten copying machines. So it means that ten employees use one copying machine. Hence, it brings this question: Is it enough to provide only ten copying machines to average ten employees to use? It depends on other factors, e.g. whether any one of these 100 employees needs to print how many documents per day , whether the five copying machines' locations are far away to separate different locations or they are stored in one printing room in the office, whether the day has how many staffs are absent, whether the day has how many printing machine(s) is/ are broken to need to be repaired. Hence, these unpredictable external environment factors will influence whether the five copying machines number is enough to let these 100 employees to use in the office every day. Hence, facility manager ought need to spend to observe average their copying behaviors every day in order to make data record. Many employees need to use copy machines to print documents, average how many document's page number, they need to print, how much average time spending to print their documents, average how many staff absent number on the day. Even, if the all five copying machines are stored in the printing room, calculating the staffs number whether how many staffs need more than five minutes to walk to the printing room to print their documents many staffs need to spend five minute to walk to the printing room, and they have other urgent tasks to wait to finish. It is possible to influence their efficiency, due to they often need to spend more than five minutes to walk to the printing room to print documents. If there are many staffs need to often to print documents, but their printing task will have many time, e.g. 20 separate printing tasks. Then, they need to spend at least (20x5) 100 minutes to spend time to walk to the printing room to print their documents. It must influence that they should not finish the other urgent tasks on the day. If there are many staffs to spend much time to walk to the printing room in the least 20 separate printing time or more on that day. All the facility manager needs to evaluate whether all the five copy machines are stored in the printing room whether it is the best location decision or they ought need be separated to put on different office locations in their workplaces, even he/she ought need to evaluate whether it is enough copying machines number, when the office has only 5 copying machines. He/she ought need to buy more copying machines number to satisfy any one of these 100 employee individual copyiing task need.

In conclusion, effective office or factory or warehouse space moving facility management will be one part task of (FM) function. If the office or factory or warehouse can have accurate equipment, machine , furniture number to avoid excessive or shortage number problem to cause employees often feel moving difficult problem in their workplace when they need to move to another location to work in office or warehouse or factory as well as whether the staff needs often spend time to wait the another employee to use the copying machine to print whose document or fax machine to deliver whose document. Then, it is not that fax or printing machines number is not enough to provide the employees to use in the office or warehouse or factory workplace.

Hence, (FM) includes space moving facility management to equipment , machines, furniture number as well as choosing anywhere is(are) the suitable location (s) arrangement to putting or storing these facilities in workplace as well as decision of the staff number and the workplace area size whether it has excessive staffs number to cause these staffs need to work in the small area size of office or warehouse or factory workplace. So, the organization ought need to decide whether it needs to reduce the office's staffs number to let them to work in another more suitable locations in another workplace. Hence, all these facilities space moving management and staffs and workplace size issues will be (FM) manager's consideration issues, because these external environment factors will influence employee individual efficiency and performance to be ppor to cause low valued to its organization in long term in possible .

Reference

Becker, F. (1990). " Facility management : a cutting edge field?" property management 8 (2): 25-28.

Predictive the choosing right
data asset and (FM) analytics
solutions to boost public
transportation service quality

Can gather the choosing right data public transportation service station facilities asset and analytics, it can give recommendation to help any organizatin to boost service quality? (FM) analytics data can be applied to public transportation service industry to be supported how and why the train, train, ferry , ship, air plane, underground train public transportation tools' time arrival and leaving information notice board and automated ticket paying machines facilities are putting on or stored any where locations in order to boost passengers to feel their facilities locations are convenient to let them to buy tickets and see the arrival and leaving time for the next public transportation tool from the information notice electronic board machine. So, it seems that these public transportation tools' station facilities locations can influence passengers to feel the public transportation service company how to consider to its passenger's buying ticket needs and next public transporation tool's arrival and leaving time information needs in order to boost its passenges use service quality and let them to feel better service reliable performance in any train, tram, ferry , ship, underground tram, airplane stations.

As these public transportation service organizations need to learn data analytics represent an opportunity for its ticket paying machine equipment facilities as well as the next transportation tool arrival and leaving time information notice board electronic equipment facilities anywhere the locations are the most suitable to put on or store these equipment to let passengers to walk to the ticket paying machines to buy the ticket to catch the train, tram, underground train, ferry, airplane, taxt, ship more easily. So, they do not need to spend more time to find these facilities locations and spend more time to queue to wait to buy ticket to catch the public transportation tool in stations conveniently. Instead of where is the seeking ticket paying machine location, where is the next public transportation tool arrival and leaving information notice time , these both issues will be any public transportion tool's passenger's main needs.

Hence, how to spend time to seek where the next public transportation tool's arrival and leaving time information electronic notice machine location and where the ticket paying machine location , these both factors will influence any passengers' positive or negative emotion causing. For example, if the passenger feels diffcult to find the ticket paying machine in the large area size train station or /and he/she feels difficult to find the train time arrival and leaving information to let him/her to know when the next train will arrive the station. Due to he/she feels difficult to find the train ticket paying machine, he/she needs to spend much time to find any one tickeet paying machine in the train station. Then, it will influence him/her to choose another public transportation tool to replace the train public transportation tool, e.g. he/she can choose to catch tram, underground train, taxi, bus, ferry, taxi, ship to replace train. So, it seems ticket paying machine and time arrival and leaving information notice electronic equipment 's location putting or stored choice will be one factor to influence the passenger to choose another kind of public transportation tool to replace train at the moment. When, he/she feels that he/she arrives the destination in the most short time. Then, the public transportation service organization (FM) manager has responsibility to evaluate whether there are enough ticket paying machines number to let passengers do not need to spend more time to queue to buy tickets to catch the public transporation tool in short time as well as there are enough time arrival and leaving for next transportation tool to let passengers to know. It will be their concerning issues when they arrive the public transportation service tool's station.

Hence, predictive passenger individual walking behavior can help the public transportation service organization to choose whether where are the most convenient and attractive locations to let the ticket paying machines and the arrival and leaving time information electronic board machines to be putted on or stored in the suitable station positions in order to let many passengers can find these essential facilities in stations very easily. So, gathering data concerns passenger walking behavior in the public transporation service any stations, which can help the facility manager to make more accurate evaluation to attempt to predict whether where the locations are common places to let passengers to choose to walk daily or where the locations are not common places to let passenger to choose not to walk daily in general. Then, he/she can apply these data of different locations in the stations to evaluate whether anywhere they will have many passengers to choose to walk or whether anywhere they won't have many passengers to choose to walk in order to make more accurate decision whether anywhere are the most suitable locations to let the ticket paying machines and the time arrival and leaving information electronic board equipment to be putter on or stored in order to let them to feel it is so easier to let them to find.

Anyway, calculating each station's passenger number per day issue is important to predict whether where , there are many passengers choose to walk or where, there are not many passengers choose to walk in these different public transportation service stations in order to evaluate whether where the stations' different ought put on paying ticket machines or time arrival and leaving information electronic boards in order to let they feel very easy to buy tickets and seeing the next arrival and leaving time information for the kind of public transportation service tool conveniently in the different stations. Moreover, if the station has no enough ticket paying machines number to be supplied to let passengers need to spend more than ten minute time to wait to buy ticket to catch the kind of public transportation service tool in every queue every day. Then it will cause them to choose another kind of public transportation tool to catch go to working place or entertainment place to replace it to on that day. Then, it will cause these passengers who often do not like to queue in the kind of public transportation service tool's any stations, who will not choose to go to anywhere of this kind of public transportation service tool's any stations again. Hence, in long term this kind of public tranportation service tool will lose many passengers. Thus, calculating each station's busy time of passengers number , which can predict when it is the busy time and it can make more accurate decision whether the station has need to increase enough ticket paying machines number in order to bring enough supply number to satisfy passengers' ticket purchase need in the busy time.

In conclusion, gathering above all stations' public transportation service equipment facilities number, storing positions datas and every station's passenger walking behavior datas, they are necessary to any public transportation tool service industry, because these equipments' number and storing locations will influence them to make decisions to choose another kind of public transportation tool to replace it's transportation service if they often feel difficult to find these facilities in its different stations. Thus, it is part of task to facility manager's responsibility if the public transportation service organization expects it won't lose many passengers , due to these external environment factor influence and it also implies cheap ticket price does not guarantee the passengers will choose to catch this kind of public tranportation service tool to go to anywhere.

The relationship between facility management and productive efficiency

It is one interesting question: Can facility management function bring benefits to raise productive efficiency to organizations? I shall indicate some cases to attempt to explain this possible occurrence chance as below:

- Facility management benefit to office workplace

In private organizations, when the firm has facility management department, whether it can bring efficient administration to influence clerks to work efficiently in office, e.g. reducing administrative time or shortern time to work in administrative processes, in order to achieve minimizing clerk number labor cost. How to design office facilities to let office staffs to feel comfortable to work and reducing their pressure to work. It seems that office working environment will influence office staff individual performance. If the office workin environment could improve efficiency and creativity of services to satisfy office workers' comfortable working environment needs. It will reduce every administration manager's working pressuse when he/she needs often to find methods to attempt to encourage whose administrative clerks to avoid to waste working time to do some non-major administration tasks.

Hence, how to design or allocate or arrange office any facilities' stored locations or whether how many equipment number is the enough to store in the locations, which will influence office employees' working attitude in order to raise or reduce their administration tasks efficiency indirectly, e.g. the office is clean or dirty, whether office receiption has enough information telephone switchboard operation facilities, whether every clerk's table has enough computers number to supply to every to use, whether internet speed is fast or slow in order to let any employees can send and receive email to communicate or download any document from internet in short time, whether data processing and computer system maintenance service supply is enough to be repaired to employees' computers immediately when their computers are broken to wait repaire, whether website editing facilties operation whether is enough to link to office every staffs in order to let any office staffs can apply internet to do their tasks conveniently in short time.

Hence, all of these general office equipment facilities whether they are enough supplied and their stored positions anywhere are the suitable to assist any clerks to work conveniently, they will influence every office employee's administrative and productive efficiency indirectly as well as all faxs, copying machines, computers, whether internet linking maintenance service time is short or long to prepare to any office employees to use conveniently any time, these different issues will also influence every employee individual efficiency in office. Hence, it concludes that office working environment, facilities supply number, facilities maintenance service and facilities location storing both factors will influence employee individual administrative productive efficieny in office.

● facility management benefits to service working environment

Can effective facility management improve service working environment to raise employee individual work performance? It is a concern about the quality of service to its customer question. The term" standards and goals" are often used to measure staff individual service performance whether he/she can serve to customers to let them to feel this staff's service performance or attitude is good or bad.

Is the service workplace working environment facilities enough, it will influence customer service staff individual performance.

For shopping center service industry case example, for this suitation, e.g. shopping center's facilities are enough or are placed to the suitable locations in order to let the shopping center's customers to feel comfortable to shopping when they enter this shopping center as well as whether the shopping center's facilities can influence the customer service staffs to serve whose shopping customers easily or difficult, due to whether the shopping center's facilities whether are adequate supplied or their locations are the best suitable positions to influence their service performance to let them to feel easier or comfortable to serve their customers in any large size shopping centers. For example, whether the lamps' lighting energy is enough to let the shoppers to feel safe to walk to visit any shops when there are many shoppers were walking to cause crowd and they feel diffuclt to walk to avoid any body contact to any one in busy time when the shopping center has no enough lights to let them to see anywhere in the shopping center's dark environment. Then it will influence customer service staffs to feel difficult to find any shopping center customers, e.g. when two shopping center customers are fighting in one location where is far away to the shopping customer service staffs and securities in the shopping center, because the shopping center is large and it has no enough light to let the customer service staffs and securities to find their frighting location to deal their fighing behavior and other shopping center's shoppers will feel very dangerous to walk their fighting location to avoid to close them. Then, it will has possible to cause death or hurt to any one of these two fighting shoppers ,even other shoppers' lifes. Because the shopping center's securities and customer service staffs who need to spend much time to find their fighting location, it will delay they can bring the policemen to their fighting location when they arrive this shopping center's destination in short time in order to solve their fighting behavior to influence all shoppers' lifes in this shopping center. Hence, the shopping center whether it has enough lamps number and the lamps' light whether is enough, these lighting facilities will influence any shopping center customer service staffs and securities who can spend less time to arrive any locations to deal any urgent matters.

For another suitation in shopping center, if the shopping center has no enough paying telephone service facilities to supply shoppers to phone to anyone when they feel need to phone to any in the shopping center. Then, it will lead to some shoppers decide to find where the shopping center's receiption's telephone to supply to them to phone call to anyone. If ther are ten shoppers are waiting to use the shopping center's receiption's telephone to phone call to their friend or family within one minute. Thus, it will influence the reception customer service staffs feel difficult to arrange how to distribute the only one telephone to these ten shoppers to use to phone call their friend or family when they are queuing within their one minute waiting time in the shopping center's reception. If these ten shoppers can not use the receiption telephone to phone call anyone. hen, they will feel disatisfactory and complain to the reception service staffs unpolitely. So, lacking enough facilities in the shopping center's any where, it will possible to influence their shopping centers' shoppers to feel all shopping center's service staff individual performance to be poor. It means that if the shopping center expects to improve customer satisfaction to its customer service staff's behavioral performance, it meets have enough facilities to be supplied in the shopping center to let its shoppers to feel it is one comfortable and safe shopping center. In conclusion, shopping center's facilities will have possible to influence shoppers' feeling to evaluate its customer service staffs to evaluate whether their service attitudes are good or poor indirectly.

- Can facility management improve productivity

The productivity means resources (input) is therefore the amount of products or services (output), which is produced by them. Hence, higher (improved) productivity means that more is produced with the same expectton of resource, i.e. at the same cost is terms of land materials, machine, time or labor. Alternatively, it means same amount is produced at less labor cost in term sof land, material, machine, time for labor that is utilized. So, it brings this question: How can facility management improve productivity? I shall explain as these several aspects, it is possible to be improved productivity from (FM) successfully.

Improved productivity of farm land: If the farming land has better facility management to bring advantages by using better seed, better facilities of cultivation and most fertilizer. It is in the agricultural sense is increased (improved). So, facility management can bring benefits to any land resource to raise productivity in possible. It implies that the productivity of land used for better facility management of industrial purposes is said to have been increased if the output of products or service within that area of industrial land is increased output aim.

Improved productivity of material: If the factory has improved better equipment by facility management method to assist skillful workers to raise the manufacture cloth number, then the productivity of the cloth number is improved by (FM) method.

Improved productivity of labour: When the factory has good manufacturing equipment facilities to be supplied to improve methods of work to product more producing number per hour, then (FM) improved productivity of worker. Hence, in any workplaces, when organization has good facilities, it will influence employees to raise productivities in possible, because they need often to improved equipment facilties manufacture products to achieve higher producton number aim.

- Can facility management raise bank employee productivity

Bank workplace environment is busy, the bank counter service staffs need to contact many bank clients to help them to serve or withdraw money from bank's counters. Whether does the quality of environment in bank workpace will influence the determination level of employee's motivation, subsequent performance productivity in bank working environment. For example, if the bnk's staffs need work under inconvenient conditions , it will bring low performance and face occupatinal health diseases causing high abenteeism and turnover.

In general, bank size is usually small, it will have many bank clients enter bank to contact counter staffs to need them to help them to save or withdraw money. So, it will bring air pollution the crowd queue in every bank counter challenge when the bank has many people are queue waiting in counters to queue. So, bank working condition problem relates to environmental and physical factors which will influence every bank counter staff individual working performance to serve bank clients satisfactory. However, bank staffs need to deal many documents concern every client personal data every day. So, they need to spend much time to use computer and painting machines. This is particularly true for these employees who spend most of the day operating a computer terminal in bank workplace. As more and more computers are being installed in workplaces, an increasing number of business has been adopting designs for bank offices installment. So, bank needs have effective facilities management design because of demand of bank staffs for more human comfort.

An good equipment facility management for bank staffs to use conveniently, it is assumed that better workplace environment can motives bank employees and produces better productivity. Hence, bank office environment can be described in terms of physical and behavioral components to influence bank staffs to work inefficiently. To achieve high level of abnk employee productivity, bank organizations must ensure that the physical environment in conductive to bank different department organizational needs, facilitating interaction and privacy, formality and informality, functionalit and disciplinarily, e.g. house loan or private loan departmets, counter service department, visa card application department.

Thus, in a high safe privary facility management working environment will let different department bank staffs feel safe to worry about privacy loss in possible. So, the improving bank facility to bring safe and high privacy to avoid bank client individual loss in working environment issue, the facility management can be results to bring these benefits, such as in a reduction in a number of complaints and absenteeism and an increase in productivity.

- Can (FM) create value to organization?

(FM) can reduce managing facilties as a strategic resource to add value to the organization and its overall performance, e.g. saving the energy in building and take care of shuttle buses and parking facilities space management for brikes, on economic efficiency and effectiveness, or good price and value for the organization.

If the organization expects to apply (FM) process to save energy, it depends on possible input factors, i.e. interventions in the accommodation facilities services. So, it seems that the organization expects to save its energy consumption in its building. It needs have goos space management facilities between parking its shuttle buses and brikes in its property's car park.

Why does space facility management is important to influence efficiency and productivity. For one school's building example, when the school decides none of the two gymnasiums student sport entertainment centers to be built in order to reduce financial cost and higher benefits. Remarkably, the use of space with the school overall strategic goals , such as creating spaces that better can support the teaching, motivate students and teachers, attract more students and increase the utilisation of existing space to accomodate an increasing number of students.

If it hopes to make high quality teaching facilities on student's choice where to study. The school will need to choose to build either one comfortable and new design facility teaching accommodation or build two gymnasium sport entertainment centers in its limited land space either for students' learning or sport aim. Due to it feels new teaching accommodcation can make more attractive to increase students numbers to choose it to study more than building two new gymnasusm sport centers to let them do sport in school.

Hence, space choise (FC) management strategy will be one important considerable issue, when the organization has limited land space resources to make choose to build any constructions in order to increase many clients number. Such as the school organization has limited stortage land resource to let it to build either two gymnasium sport entertainment centers or one new teaching accommodation in order to attract many students to choose it to learn. Hence, it needs to gather data to make more accurate evaluation to decide how to apply its space facility to choose to build these both kinds of buildings in order to achieve the attractive student learning choice aim, so whether teh two sport entertainment activity centers or one new teaching accommodation choice, it needs to gater information to decide whether the school ought to choose to build which kind of building in order to achieve the increase of student number aim, so space facility management will be this school's land shortage problem.

The relationship between facility management and Amazon online consumer behavior

How and why shop facility management can influence consumer individual shopping behavior? If it is possible, what shop facility management factors can influence their consumption decision when they enter the shop to plan to buy anything. I shall indicate some shop case studied to expline whether how and why every shop's facility management can influence consumer individual consumption desire when any one consumer enters any shops.

- Shop's low ceiling height location (FM) influcence consumer behavior

Can the shop's ceiling height influence shoppers' shopping behavior? Can the shops's variation in ceiling height can influence how consumers process information to decide to make purchase decision in the shops, e.g. for this suitation, when the consumer enters the shop, he/she feels the ceiling height is low and it has a lamp wil contact his/her head in possible. So, he/she chooses to move far away from the low ceiling beight location in the shop. It is possible that shop's ceiling low height and the lamp locates at the ceiling low height position will influence many customers' choices to leave the low ceiling height and lamp location, then the shop's low ceiling height will have possible to influenced many customers to choose to find the another shop to buy the similar kind of products , due to the lamp locates in the low ceiling height, so this lamp and low ceiling height will be possible factor to influence any shoppers who won't choose to walk to this dangerous location in the shop. If the shop's all spaces are ceiling height and it has many lamps are located at the low ceiling height spaces. Then, it will be serious to cause many shoppers do not want to spend too much time to choose any products in the shop because they feel dangerous to walk to the any low ceiling height lamps' locations in the shop.
Hence, hoe to design the different concept may be activated by the showroom ceiling if it were relatively high, as it tends to be in mall

stores, versus low, as it is in most strip mall shops and outlet centers. Relatively high ceilings may bring safe shopping emotion to let any consumers to feel thoughts related to freedom, whereas lower ceilings may let consumers to feel dangerous to walk the locations in any shops. Hence it seems any shops ought not neglect whether their ceiling height is tall and the lamps ought avoid to locate in any low ceiling height locations in order to influence consumers number to be decreased.

- Can house facility management influence consumer individual purchase intention?

When one new property is built, whether the property consumers will consider how the new property is facilited to influence their purchase intention to the property will the new property's (FM) influence buyers in real estate markets' preferences choice and living interest. Any new property's internal characteristics of the house unit itsel , such as rooms available, when example, of external are location, accessibility to utilities services and facilities will have possible to influence the property buyer's final property purchase decision, so it seems that even the property price is cheap, it is not represent the property buyer will choose to buy the property, if he/she feels the property's facility mangement is poorer to compare other similar kinds of properties. So, it can help real estate analysts better explain and predict the behavior of decision makers in real estate markets. Property consumers will search for property information, concerns the property's quality, price distinctiveness, ability, facility mangement, service of the property's external environment to decide whether the property is high value to choose to buy to compare other kinds of properties.

However, the external environmental forces, such as limited resources, e.g. time or financial will influence whose property consumption choice and living the property's satisfaction feeling (represent) a feedback machanism from post-property purchase reflection used to inform subsequent decisions. The process of the property buyer's leaving experience will serve to influence the extent to which the property consumer how to consider future next time property purchases decision and new information methods. Hence, when one property consumer chooses to buy a house, it refers house features ar house internal attributes , such as quality of building, the design as well as internal and external design, which are important factors for a property consumer when he/she needs to select and purchases one house.

The other (FM) factors which can influence the property consumers' needs, include living space as features, such as the size of kitchen, bathroom, bedroom, living bath and other rooms available in the house. The environment of housing area is also important factor, e.g. the condition of the neighbourhood, attractiveness of the area, quality of neighbouring houses, type of neighbouring houses, type of neighbouring houses, density of housing, wooded area or free coverage, slope of the attractive views, open space, non-residential uses in the areas vacant sites, traffic noise, level of owner-occupation in neighbourhoos, level of education in neighbourhood level of income in neighbourhood, security from crime, quality of schools, religious of neighbourhood, transportation , shopping center, sport entertainment can be supplied to close to the house area. All these human related issue of the property's location will also influence the property buyer's living location selection. Hence, above (FM) influence property consumer purchase behavior, it is based on the relationship behavior. The consumer's house purchase intention and house features, living space, environment and distance to recreation center, supermarket, library etc. public facilities variable (FM) factors.

In conclusion, the house internal space facility management and external environment facility management factors will influence property consumer individual house purchase intention.

- The effects of in-store shelf design facility management factor influences consumer behavior

Can every store retailer's shelf design influence supermarket and large retail stores shoppers' behaviors when they visit the stores? However, currently many stores tend to build on traditional and repetitive design for their store shelf layout, it brings results in outdated store layouts.

Another important store shelf layout design aspect, retailer should consider carefully is the allocation of products on shelves. So, it seems that efficienct shelf space allocation management does not only minimize the economic threats of empty product shelves, it can also lead to higher consumer satisfaction, a better customer relationship.

Why does supermarket shelves design is important? Any retail tore will sell product category within a shelf. They can use the same nominal category , e.g. negular crisps next to light crisps, same food prouct shelf. Anyway, a goal-based shelf display can contain several product, that determine a common consumer goal, e.g. fair trade. Hence, these two categorical product structuring methods are also described in terms of how to put product, or food on shelf benefit and attribute -based product categories.

These shelf design food or product storing method will have more influence consumers to choose to buy the supermarket or retail store food or products more easily , due to products, or food put on their shelf very convenient and systematic to attract consumers' shopping consideration to the supemarket or retail store.

- Music (FM) environment influence consumer consumption desire

Is it possible that shop music (FM) environment can raise consumer purchase desire? In one shop or supermarket, it can provide soft music (FM) equipment to let consumers can listen soft music or songs in the supermarket or retail shop when the are staying to spend more time shopping and whether soft music facility can be expected to raise customer individual value-added options to the music facility shop in the supermarket ot retail shop. Can the music facilities prolong consumers to stay in the store? It is possible that tempo soft music can influence consumers to stay longer time in restaurants and supermarkets and retail shops. It is possible that the different types of music (FM) in any supemarket, restaurant, retail shop owning music listening facility shopping environment. It will have possible to influence consumers to prolong staying in their shops. For example, one wine selling retail shop has classical music (FM) listening equipment to let consumers to listen when they enter the wine shop, it is possible to cause consumers to choose to buy more expensive wine products. Some researchers indicate when the wine shop owns classical music facility to let all consumers can list classical music when they walk in the wine ship, it can evoke the wine consumers to choose to buy purchasing higher prices wine products in the long term classical music listening environment. Otherwise, in a fitness sport center, musical fir and excite or popular music (FM) environment can attract fitness sport players' emotion to play and kind of fitness sport facility longer time. Also, in one supermarket, the soft music facilities listening environment can persuade or attract food consumers to spend more time in the mall consuming food or beverage also purchase othe products more easily, due to they will listen soft music to be influenced to choose to prolong staying time in the supermarket. It seems that it has relationship between retail shop's music facility environment and consumer's emotion will be influenced by these different kinds of soft music or songs to raise consumption desire in the supermarket, if some consumers like to proplong to stay longer consuming time in the owning music facility environment's retail shop.

In fact, some researchers indicate the owning background music facility selling environment's ship , it can affect consumer decision making, memory, concentration consumption desire. So, classical , jazz soft music facility ought be installed in restaurants, retail shops, restaurants' environment. Otherwise, popular , exciting, noise, pop music facilty ought be installed in fitness sport centers, theme park entertainment parks business places in order to influence fitness sport players or theme park entertainers to prolong playing or entertaining time to feel real sport or entertainment theme park playing machine facility's entertainment enjoyable feeling as well as attracting restaurant or supermarket or retail shop's consumers to proplong their staying time to make consumption decisions. Hence, it seems that music facility environment can raise consumers' consumption desire in possible.

● University bookstore atmospheric factors how to influence student's purchase book behavior?

Any university bookstore how to do international control and structuring of book internal environment to raise students' purchase book desires in university itself school's bookstore, it will be one popular question to any universities. Hence, whether the university bookstore internal (FM) factors include: lighting, music, colors, scents, temperature, layout and general cleanliness as well as university external factors include: the university bookstore shape/ size, windows, university parking facility for students availability and location,which can play an influential role of the university bookstore image in order to influence the university itself students to choose to buy books from themselves bookstore or university outside bookstores.

Whether the university student needs to spend how long individual learning time and how mcuh learning nervous to spend time to choose any kinds of book in the univeristy bookstore or outside bookstores, this issue , he/she will consider. Because he/she does want to expect spend much time and nervous to choose to buy books in any bookstore. If the universitt's bookstore physical location and internal (FM) desing image can let its target student customers to feel it's all book products are stored in any attractive internal book shelves places, e.g. the cheapest and the most expensive different subjects of text books are stored in one system method to bring the positive image of value snd quality in order to let university target student customers can find their books' choice location to spend less time to search any books to read in the unviersity bookstore easily.

However, due to learning time is shortage to every university student of the universty's book shelves can display all text books in the attractive right locations in the university bookstore as well as the university's bookstore ought has an adequate space to let university students to walk to anywhere and find any subjects of text books and compare their book sale prices in the bookstore's any shelves' locations easily when they walk to the subject of book shelf location, then they can make accurate decision either to buy the right kind of subject book or not buy it to read in the short time. They will ferl their book choice purchase decision making process won't influence their learning time in themselves univeristy. Then, the university students will be influenced by themselve university's bookstore's attractive external university facilites in the univeristy's any teaching places and the university's bookstore internal attractive environment facility image which can influence the students to make final choices to buy their liking books to read from their university's itself bookstore. Hence, the university's bookstore internal and external building environment (FM) design factors will influence its students whether choose to buy from themselves bookstore or another outside general bookstore.

- How and why does retail atmospheric environment influence consumers behavior in retail shop?

Any shop's internal facility management design can influence atmospheric environment to influence consumer individual shopping desire, e.g. colour, lighting, music, crowding, design and layout factors, which internal shop (FM) environment can influence the first time shopping visiting client ' cognitive process how to feel the shop store image. Such as if the store's (FM) environment can bring enjoyable and fun and happy image to let them to feel shopping's enjoyment.

In conclusion, when consumers will like to stay longer time in the store. Due to the store's internal (FM) atmospheric environment can attract them to stay longer time in the store. Then, the customer's shopping value will raise and it can bring purchasing intention and shopping satisfaction. How can (FM) influence retail atmospheric physical (FM) environment ? Can (FM) bring indirect relationship to influence how the consumer individual causes positive or negative purchase intention when he/she has influence to proplong staying desire in the store, when the shop has good (FM) , it will bring long time to make consumption chance in the shop.

FIVE

HOW AMAZON LEARNS CONSUMER BEHAVIOR

Face reading technology and video camera recording consumer behavior predictive differences

- Recommendation of face reading technology is for confectionery food manufacturers at factory or office experiment and ethnographic consumer behavior video camera recording method is for product manufacturers at home
- Abstract

The impact of emotions on judges, evaluations and decisions have long been important to psychology and consumer behavior on consumption. I shall examine how distinct perspectives shape the processes of appraisal that lead to emotional experience and how different consumers might define happiness distinctly. I examine emotions that vary by positive, negative and mixed. I also suggest new ways to distinguish among emotions and to assess how new ways to consumers to aim to be discovered by better understanding how consumers manage their experience of emotion to achieve their own affective goals. In my report, I shall indicate three aspects to research. The first aspect, I indicate how one sample technology to detect consumer emotion to predict facial reaction, such as Noldus Face Reader technology is used orange juice, sweets and chocolates confectionery foods or drinks to detect young consumers' emotion whether who like or dislike to eat or drink different brands of confectionery products from whose facial reaction for factory or shop experiments. Besides, how to use video cameras to record consumer individual behavior at home to predict why who choose to buy your product to help manufacturer, as you to predict why your clients choose to buy your products or choose not to buy products to use.

● Main Problem Being Addressed of face reading and video camera technology limits

Technologies that detect consumers' emotions can help companies to reduce the amount of money waste on unsuccessful product launches by stopping products before they are launched. Methods can be accurately measured consumers' feelings and emotion for a food or beverage product irrespective of consumer's ability to accurately articulate those feelings are needed in order to generate more accurate food and beverage product testing results. These methods will be based on the measurement of human physiology-most likely facial expressions, but they reveal intentionally hidden or subconscious emotions. In addition, the method may be able to decide emotions: Such as happiness, sadness, surprise, fear, anger feeling when one youth person eats a food or drinks beverage product. The first aspect main problem concerns how face reading technology can be measured to predict consumer acceptance level of confectionery foods or soft drinks from their face expression in the short time more absolutely. However, this face reading technology can't be used to predict any consumer's individual enjoyable acceptance satisfactory level when who uses any manufacturer's products in the short time.So face reading technology can not be used to predict any consumer's emotion to reflect to use any product more easily.

Thus, I shall recommend how to use video camera recording ethnographic research method to find what factors to influence the consumer who decides to buy the product to use and evaluate whose satisfactory level to use the product at home. I concern how to use video camera to predict consumer individual behavioral process to find why who choose to buy the kind of product to evaluate the most absolute emotion response to find whether who satisfies or doesn't satisfy to use the product. Also how to use face reading technology to measure different level sugar elements to add the confectionery foods to detect the consumer's emotion whether who likes or does not like to eat the kind of confectionery food.

● Summary of ethnographic research
of facial reading technology and video camera technology

To detect consumer's emotion like or not like to eat the
confectionery foods, e.g. soft orange juice, sweet and
chocolates. The food manufacturer may attempt to use face reading technology to predict different level sugar elements to add its confectionery eating products to see consumer's different face impression to evaluate whether what sugar elements , e.g. how much weights are the suitable level to add to the kind of confectionery food. To detect buyer's emotion whether who enjoy or does not enjoy to use the manufacturer's product and to find what factor(s)can influence the consumer to choose to buy the product. The home product manufacturer may use digital cameras and computer recording method to record the volunteer daily routines filmed at home. It aims to detect consumer's individual using behavior to research whether what psychological factors are to influence who to choose to buy themanufacturer's product to use. Otherwise, Ethnographic research concerns how to use video camera to record consumers' behavior daily about one weeks. It aims to predict what factors case who to buy the kind of product. Hence, Confectionery manufacturers can use face reading technology to predict consumer emotion of satisfactory level to eat sweats, ice creams, chocolates, biscuits etc. sugar add confectionery. Home product manufacturers can use video camera technology to

predict consumer emotion of satisfactory level to use products at home e.g. clothing, radios, televisions, furniture, sleeping beds etc. home daily useful products.

- Comparative Benefits / Advantages

Face reading technology can help only confectionery eating food manufacturers to measure sugar element whether how much sugar weights are the most suitable to young people taste acceptable level more absolutely. Digital camera and computer recording technology can predict whether what factors can influence the consumer to choose to buy your competitor's similar product or your products and measure whose satisfactory level to let manufacturer to judge how to manufacture whose products of features are more suitable to be acceptable or attractive to consumers' taste.

If the confectionery eating food manufacturer could not detect consumers' emotion to know whether what level of sugar ingradient is the most suitable level to cause who are like or dislike to eat or drink confectionery foods from whose face expression absolutely. It will be serious loss to invest time and money to manufacture this foods and consumers will feel their foods or soft drinks is not health to eat to cause illness possibly. Traditional sensory and consumption tests predict consumer acceptance of new food products rather poorly, as are evidenced by the high their failure rates in the market. These tests typical reflect conscious processes whereas consumer acceptance may also be based on unconscious processes. For example, I feel functional (MFR) isn't an allowable technology space primarily due to consumer concern of manipulation. Miller (2012) indicated that " functional MRI mind reading technology is where something is wholly subjective and private, and it can't be predict consumer emotion to tell from what who're doing or looking at, what whose mental state is." Hence, It has a distinction between that kind of mind reading and what is brain reading, which essentially involves using brain scans to figure out what the factors can influence on consumer's mind in different situations to decide buy or not buy the food product. So, any consumer emotion researcher needs to wait a few seconds to see what consumers will do next. The technology is still limited, such as individual differences: Different consumers' brains code information sight differently, so consumer emotion researcher needs to learn how a specific individual codes consumers' emotion mental states. How to produce the most acceptable sugar level to manufacture any confectionery eating food or drink for children, it can keep consumers who will choose to buy other brands of confectionery eating food or drink more easily. This is the most important factor to influence your children taste choice to feel your brand confectionery eating food or drink is the best taste to compare other brand competitors. So, sugar ingradient (element) of the acceptable level is the most important research from face reading technology experiment in shop or factory.

The Netherlands (2014) indicated "Arnade had been carring to investigate consumers (man age 22 years) were recruited at the kaunas University of Technology. They were asked to rate the sample and then are characterized by Face reader program (Naldus Information Technology) Wageningen. The measurements are showed significant differences between facial expressions by the different samples of tested sugar element confectionery products and reflected liking ratings well. The positive correlations of facial expression happy and negative correlations of sad expression are predicted. It suggested that these may be the most valuable descriptors for explaining the quality of sweets and chocolates. It can be concluded that Noldus face reader technology is sufficiently accurate for differentiating between sugar confectionery products and can deliver additional information to conventional acceptance tests. " Otherwise, reasons for likes or dislikes of different foods or drinks are typically difficult to articulate, but may determine much of our food or drinks choice. Certain foods or drinks can be more active than other foods or drinks because for some reason who make consumers feel good when their express positive emotion. Arnade (2014) examined "consumers' facial reaction by the flavor of orange juice drinks using face reader technology measurement showed significant differences between facial expressions by the different samples. The explicit measurement reflected the liking ratings well. Especially expressions happy with liking and were good indicators for liked and liked samples respectively, 20 minimize artefacts, caused by the face reader software as emotion, they used liquid samples (juice) which need less processing in the mouth than solid samples." The aim of this work was to examine whether facial expressions measured with the Noldus face reader technology are a sufficiently accurate measure for differentiating between various types of sugar element confectionery including sweets, chocolates and juice drinks or soft drinks which need sugar element to add in the manufacturing processing and to investigate whether facial reactions are able to explain such these confectionery foods or drinks liking ratings.

The impact of emotions on judge , evaluations and decisions has long been important to psychology and consumer behavior on consumption. It seems face reading technology can predict whether the consumer likes or dislikes these confectionery foods, chocolates, sweets or juice, soft drinks liking ratings to measure whether sugar element is excess or less from young consumers' face expression, such as enjoying or not enjoying of feeling, smile or no smile response. Hence, face measuring technology can be more difficult to detect consumers 'emotion for product manufacturer. Because consumers need to spend more time to attempt to use their new innovative products.

● Recommendation Ethnographic consumer behavior research is for video camera recording to product manufacturers at home

Otherwise, it seems product manufacturers can't use face reading technology to detect consumers' emotion in the short time immediately. The products include any kind of products, e.g. high technological products, such as space mining of resources machines, satellite navigation system ,cars , machines etc. as well as home useful technological electronic products, such as mobile phones, washing machines, televisions, laptops as well as daily products, such as shirts, shoes, furniture, toys, tooth pastes etc.

These essential home product and high technologic product manufacturers who need to continue to innovate their old style products to follow consumers' taste to invent new style products to be accepted to their fresh taste.

It seems that manufacturers need to spend a long time to touch consumers' feeling whether whose old style technological products which are still accepted to them to use or not. Hence, it implies that a consumer decides to buy these high technological innovation products, whose choice isn't performed to show who must accept to use these high technological innovation productsfor long time, whose emotion is not sure whether who feels satisfactory to consume to use this product for a long time. When he/she uses this technological product for a long time, it is possible that who will feel it was not valuable to buy it before. Hence, video camera can used to record the consumer's behavior record whose image and to analyze whose facial expressions and bodily gestures at home about one week.

- How to use video camera recording to predict consumer's emotion .

How to use automated facial expression analysis for emotion and behavior prediction. The expression of emotion is achieved through combinations of verbal and nonverbal information produced from various sources of the body and the brains. Nonverbal information encompasses any message that is not expressed in words, including gestures, postures to be performed from individual behavior for individual daily life. Though people often don't invest much thought to the nonverbal aspect of communication to be performed to manage emotional experiences. Computers enable researchers to process to gather data in a short amount of time to predict facial expression consumers. The new methodological for social scientists may be a valid analysis to automated facial expression from consumer's daily behavior at home experiement for several days investigation more absolutely. Among the various models of nonverbal communication, we focus on facial expression which are captured by small digital cameras and later analyzed with computer software.

As Webb et. al. (2000) pointed out, "people are low-fidelity observational instruments recording and interpretation may be erratic over time, as the observer learns and responds to the research phenomena he or she observes. It means that we can observe consumer behavior to predict why who buy the product from whose daily life behavior performance. Recent studies applied automated feature extraction and classification to extract macro features . Such as the head and hand position and angle from video features taken during an experiment where a theft took place. It also implied that computer models obtained up to 71 percent correct classification of innocent or guilty participants based on the macro features extracted from the video camera. Furthermore, in an overview of detection research." Meservy et al.(2008) noted that "the accuracy of humans coding behavioral indicators only falls around 50 percent, but that computers trained to a automatically extract and identify relevant behavioral cues detect deception with significantly higher accuracy. Furthermore, computers operate without the other methods(e.g. physiological measures such as polygraph machines or lie detectors) and the lost of extensively trained human interviewers."

Ambady and Rosenthal (1992) showed that "another advantage of why automated facial detection technology coupled with computational models is that once the system secures the parameters for a model, prediction of behavior (vs simple detection and classification) can be made using only a small sample. This is a computational recording of what social psychologists, a way people sample a short except from social behavior to draw inferences of about states, traits and other personally relevant characteristics .For instance, based on an observation of a three minute video clip of a conflict between a married couple."

Carrere and Gottman(1999) also indicated "video cameras were able to predict the outcome of that marriage after six years. Using machine learning coupled with computer vision allows computers to cause this human cognitive process; models are trained on a short sample of facial features and those features automatically predict future behaviors. Computers were used in place of human coders to detect vocal behaviors (e.g. time spent speaking, influence over conversation partners, variation in pitch and volume and behavior mirroring) during a negotiation task. Their results imply that the speech features extracted during the first five minutes of negotiation are highly predictive of future outcomes." The researchers also noted that using computers to code speech features offers advantages such as high test-retest reliability and real time feedback. As a cost-effective and relatively accurate method to detect, track and create models for behavior classification and prediction, automatic facial expression analysis has the potential to be applied to multiple disciplines. Capturing behavioral data from participants may be a more accurate representation of how and what they feel, and a better alternative to self-report questionnaires that interrupt participants' affective cognitive processes and are subject to bias .Our model goes beyond to predict the future behavior within a given task (e.g. a virtual car accident or an error in performance). This opens up the possibility of such models becoming a common methodology in social scientific and behavioral research.

Installing video camera recording at sample consumers to carry on investigating their feeling to use their product to collect the more truly acceptable or not acceptable feeling to use the product reason, such as: video camera recording method is data synchronization and time series statistics calculation. In the next phase of analysis, video recording are recording with data collected from experimental tasks such as surveys or simple motor tasks. This is done to map the extracted facial geometry information to behavioral output data. In the experiments three to five second intervals of facial expressions were taken one to two seconds before each instance of the behavior to be predicted and used as the input data. After data synchronization we also computed a series of time-domain statistics on coordinates in each interval to use as additional inputs to our classifiers. For example one sample investigating. The input data for this study consisted of videotapes of forty one participants watching films that elicited the emotions of either amusement or sadness, along with measures of their cardiovascular activity responding. It should be noted that the recorded expressions were expressions, unlike the photographs of deliberately posed faces often used in prior facial expression research. However, I suggest these entertainment product or home product manufacturers who can use video cameras to record whose buyers' behavior to detect whose emotion to aim to design which kind of colors, styles, sizes and how to change whose old products' features to attract the more consumers' fresh demand taste .

Ethnographic research is interpretative research which seeks an understanding from the perspectives of the value systems of those being researched. Ethnographic search is one different method to learn about buyer individual behavior to compare with enquiring questionnaires to participants to fill to answer questions to gather data to carry on the sale and post purchase evaluation cycle to evaluate whether what are their product criteria or weaknesses which need to improve to raise their sale competition in their market.

Palmer (2012) reported " one sport shoe company's ethnographic research in action was provided by a product commissioned by the footwear brand Dr Martens. It aims to research how to understand young people's buying behavior. It wanted to understand how youth people used brands in their every lives. Why for example, did some brands , such as Nike trainers or baseball caps become popular in youth culture? The researchers identified groups of young people around the world who responded to Dr Marten's target market. In return for a payment, volunteers were followed for several days and their daily routines filmed with a handheld digital camera. In total, 180 hours of captured film was edited to just one hour of highlights showing the key drivers of youth culture which are relevant to the Dr Martens brand. It seems that young people preferred fashions that allowed them to customize an item of clothing and in some way take ownership of it. The research drew the conclusion that iconic fashion items for young people had to have a distinctive label or style that made their wearers stand out as part of a tribe." Hence, ethnographic research seems to help this company to know why the young clients choose to buy those brands sport shoes, it is possible that the these brands sport shoes' color or design can be accepted more to them to buy Dr Marten brand's sport shoes when they wear different style of clothing. Hence, it uses digital cameras to observe the worldwide choice of paying target youth volunteers whose daily individual behaviors at homes to get the more actual evidence to evaluate what factors influence youth clients choose to buy these brands of sport shoes. It seems this sport shoe company can take several hours of filming to yield just a few moments of true insights to participant's true attitudes and behavior.

Ethnography is one of many approaches that can be found within Social research. Ethnography was a descriptive account of a commonly or culture. Ethnography usually involves the researcher participating in people's daily lives for an extended period of time, watching what happens, listening to what is said, and/or asking questions through informal and formal interviews collecting documents. In more detailed terms, ethnographic work usually has most of the following features: People actions are studied in every contexts rather than under conditions created by the researcher, in experimental or high structured interview situations as well as data are gathered for a range of sources including documentary evidence of various kinds, but participant observation and/or relatively informal conversations are main ones as well as data collected is for the most past relatively unstructured in two senses and it doesn't involve following through detailed research design at the start and the categories that are used for interpreting what people say or are not built into the data collection process through the use of observation schedules or questionnaires to analyze.

Generally, fairly small scale perhaps a style setting or group of people. This is a facilitate in depth study and analysis of data involves interpretation of the meaning, functions and consequences of human actions and low are implicated in local and perhaps also wider contexts what are produced for the most part are verbal descriptions, explaining and theories and statistical analysis play a subordinate role at most. How ethnography can learn more about buyer behavior to help product manufacturers to detect consumers' emotion. It means collection of data to pursue an answers to these questions more effectively and to test those against evidence. Hence, video camera recording to consumer's individual useful behavior at whose home. It isn't set up for research purposes (such as experiments or formal interviews).

The methodological model for social research is physical science conceived in terms of the logic of the experiment. However, ethnography was sometimes dismissed as quite inappropriate to social science on the grounds that data and findings it produces are subjective. Hence, ethnographic research is the role to learn more about buyer behavior through marketers may have been listening more to consumers (e.g. through qualitative research), efforts have almost always been directed at controlling consumers ranges of products or services predetermined by producers have been pushed through with littler real involvement of consumers in the process at a time in which consumers are ever more aware of what is being done to marketers. To seeing consumer's daily life behavior can predict why who choose to buy your or your competitor's product. Then, the product manufacturer can judge what the reasons are caused to attract the consumer chooses to buy the product to use. Hence, the data analysis procedure will include these steps as below:

- First step, Facial expression videos camera record activity ; input data from given tasks will be carrying on researching at the same time.
- Second step, the feature extraction will be caused
- Third step, the chi-square feature selection will be caused
- Fourth step, the machine learning training will be caused
- The final step, the results of behavioral prediction and data classification will be output at the same time.

- Why ethnographic research can be predicted consumer's behavioral performance to detect emotion by video recording camera at home ?

Ethnographic field research involved the study of groups and people as go about every day lives. There has two distinct activities. First the ethnographer enter into a social setting and gets to know the people and observes all the approach. But second the ethnographer writes down regular systematic ways what who observes and learns when participating in the quality rounds of life of others. Thus, the researcher creates an accumulating written records of these observations and experiences. Two interconnected activities comprise the care of ethnographic search: participation in some initially familiar social world and the production of written accounts of that world by drawing upon such participation. Hence, ethnographers are committed to get close to the activities and everyday people. Getting close minimally requires physical and social proximity to the daily rounds of people lives and activities, the field researcher must be able to take up positions in order observe and understand whom.

Consumer behavior refers to the behavior that consumers display in searching for purchasing , using , evaluating and disposing of products and services that who expect will satisfy their needs and it's behaviors that are directly involved in the action of obtaining, consuming and spending products or services, including the decision processes that precede and follow these actions. It seems ethnographic research can helps the marketer to understand how consumer think, feel and select from alternative like products, brands and the like and how the consumers' buying behaviors are influenced by their environment, the reference group, family and salespersons.

Consumer buying behavior includes that: Attitude itself is a learning experience and can lead to a change in attitude before buyers enter the buying process. Thus, attitude don't automatically guarantee all types of behavior. Attitudes based on behavioral learning follow beliefs, behaviors and effect sequence. A consumer who is high involved with a product or service category and who perceives a high level of product or service differentiation between alternatives with follow the cognitive hierarchy (belief affect behavior). From the ethnographic research marketers perspective the sequence of attitude formation is from a communication point of views from a strategic point of view, such as it has proved useful in specifying the different elements that work to influence buyers' evaluations of attitude, product or services may be composed of attributes or qualities, some of which may be more important than others to particular people. So consumer's individual decision is to act on whose attitudes is affected by other factors, such as whether it is felt other factors, such as whether it is felt that buying a product or service would be met with approval by friends and family.

According to this approach, ethnographic research marketers must concentrate an assessing the characteristics of the environment, such as the physical surroundings and product or service placement, that influence members of that target market. Such as point of purchase (such as selling the sport shoe brand's some sample of design style shoes) are particularly useful in predicting to find reasons why individual consumer choose to buy these styles. Hence, I recommend ethnographic research marketers can focus on measuring consumers' effective emotion response to products or services and develop offering that elicit appropriate subjective reactions and employ effective symbolism to predict how the different brand products to be designed which kind of style, to be used what kinds of colors and what kinds of materials to be produced.

To decide which is the most acceptance to satisfy consumers' taste. Such as the above sport shoe brand company case showed that it attempted to use ethnographic method to research whether what the external or internal factors are influenced to the footwear brand Dr martens' other consumers to choose the Nike or Baseball brands sport shoes to buy. It discovered that what youth people whose daily wearing clothing colors, designs and materials external factors which can influence them to choose to buy which kinds of design styles, colors and materials made of sport shoes to buy. It seems famous brands of sport shoes and cheaper price and durability internal factors are not the important factors to influence them to choose to buy these brands. Otherwise, the youth people whose wearing clothing colors, design styles and material made external factors can influence their feeling to choose the most adaptable style of sport shoes to be accepted to adapt to accept to their wearing clothing fashion. Thus, it seems that ethnographic research is one good method to detect consumers emotion whether the individual consumer's choice is influenced by the product's internal factors more or external environment external factors more to influence every individual consumer to feel positive or negative emotion to make final decision to buy any product to use possibly. If the product manufacturer can use this ethnographic research method to attempt to find whether what external or internal factors can influence potential consumers' fashion acceptance level to choose to buy any new innovative products to predict their emotion before the new peoduct manufacturer decides to manufacture its products to sell in this competitive market. I believe that its predicting market success chance will be increased.

constructive consumer choice process

- How constructive consumer choice process measures which attribute factor(s) can influence consumer chooses to buy any product or food in psychological view.
- Main Problem Being Addressed

The second aspect problem is judged whether constructive consumer choice is an important process to influence any consumer to choose to buy any products. If it is a real essential choice process, how product manufacturers can reduce their negative emotion is caused to choose not buy their products during this constructive process. The second aspect main problem is researched about consumer will choose to make final decision to buy the best choice of product from among brands of products . Hence, the constructive consumer choice process is a real essential choice process to any consumer generally, when individual consumer needs to compare different brands of products to choose to buy any product.

How product manufacturers can predict whose choice method to decide to prefer to make final decision to buy any products in the short days or the short time in the constructive consumer process. If manufacturers can know overall consumers' choice method, manufacturers will not design the not suitable style of products to manufacture to sell and who can know what the overall consumers' negative emotion is influenced who decide not to buy their products from their design style in order to manufacture more suitable style of product design . I shall recommend how manufacturers can predict consumer emotion in the constructive consumer choice process in psychological view.

My research is concerned knowledge opinion about how to predict consumer emotion whether what attribute factor(s)
are the most influence to the consumer to choose to buy the
manufacturer's product in whose process of choice. If manufacturer can early know whether what the most attractive attribute factor(s) are the most influence to the consumer to decide to buy whose product, so who can concentrate on manufacturing the different kinds of products to get the most influence attribute factor to attract consumers to choose to buy whose products. Hence, the manufacturer can know what reasons can cause the consumers who do not choose to buy its products during constructive consumer choice process generally , who can know how to improve its product's design method to concentrate on producing the most acceptable satisfactory level to sell to whose consumers in .Also I believe that the manufacturer can raise sale numbers if who know what bad factors to cause whose consumers choose not to buy whose products during the constructive consumer choice process. It can increase chance to change its product innovative strategy to raise confidence to judge what attributed factors are the important influence to cause consumers who either do not choose to buy or choose to buy its innovative products.

The attributable factor of any product may include some or all these factors. For example: Safety, durability, reasonable price, fashion, pretty design, loyalty, etc. different factors whether which attributed factor can cause the consumer feels positive emotion to prefer to choose to buy the manufacturer's innovative products. I shall recommend how to predict consumers' positive emotion to the manufacturer's products in the consumer's constructive choice process. However, the benefits to manufacturers if who can predict what attribute factors have much influence consumers to make final decision in the constructive consumer choice process. It includes as below:

- Concentrate on manufacturing the new products to predict which attribute factors are the importance existed to influence consumers' whose final decision to choose to buy the manufacturer's any kind of products in order to raise chance to increase sale numbers.
- To let consumers have more confidence to choose to buy the manufacturer's any products to use for long time.
- Avoiding to spend excess money and resources and time to concentrating on manufacturing the new product which own much of not important attribute factors to influence consumers to choose not to buy the manufacturer's products .
- Market review of constructive consumer process research limit

I feel that constructive consumer choice process can only be predicted to find whether what attributable factors can influence the consumer to choose to buy the manufacturer's product from shopping retail market only, but it can't not predicted from online shopping.

Because consumer needs to spend more time to compare different similar brands of product to find what the attributable factor(s) own(s) to the brand of product to attract who to make the final buying decision. If the consumer choose to buy the product, usually, who won't spend more time to gather the similar products' information to decide to which kind of product and who will buy the product from internet immediately. Otherwise, if the consumer choose leave home to walk to different shops to choose to buy the kind of product, who have more time to spend to different shops to compare the different brand products to make final buying decision. Hence , constructive consumer choice process will only occur at visiting shops' consumption to any individual or group consumption.

- Related Background of constructive consumer process

May constructive consumer choice process is a psychological factor to influence consumers' emotion to make final decision to buy either kind of emotion product or rational product in consumption market generally. How can product manufacturers detect consumers' emotion to judge whether their products are belonged to be more kind of emotion product or rational product during they decide to sell different kind of products or foods to consumers?

Constructive consumer choice is an important process to influence any consumers to choose to buy any products. I shall give my idea to indicate how product manufacturers can predict whether their products are belonged to be either more kind of emotional product or more kind of rational product at different suitation. It aims to reduce their negative emotion is caused to choose not buy their products from their constructive consumer choice process.

Consumer decision making trends technological change and information explosion nowadays. Generally, consumers need to compare different brands of products from their characteristics , such as quality, fashion, design style, colors, prices, functions etc. factors to decide which is the most valuable choice to buy among of these different kinds of similar products from global consumption channel, such as electronic internet shopping channel or traditional retail shopping channel of two kinds of sale methods. Due to consumers can get any kinds of products' the most updated information from internet, television , magazines etc. advertisement channel at home conveniently. Thus, it causes nowadays consumers will concern to use a variety of strategic contingent on their consumption to demand to choose to buy what is the most valuable product considerately.

After consumers spend much time to make constructive choice, who will make final decision to choose to buy which kind of product is the most valuable from their positive emotion. In general, before any consumer chooses to make decision to buy any product, whose option is in a choice it will be assumed to have a utility or subjective value feeling to the product that it depends only on the option. Finally, it is assumed that the consumer has ability of skill in a computation that enables the calculation of which option will maximize whose received value and selects accordingly.

Why are preferences constructive logic buying decision in constructive consumer choice is important? One reason individuals may construct preferences is that who lacks the cognitive resources to generate well preferences for many situations. A second important reason is that consumers often multiple goals to be given decision problem. It implies preferences constructive choice will influence any consumer to change whose emotion to prefer to buy the product among of the same kind of target products. However, the fact that a choice is contingent need not simply that the processing was constructive , that is developed on the spot. A food or soft drink can be either a rational product or emotional product. For example, a consumer may have a well established, but contingent, preference for have chocolate on a cold day and a cold soft drink on a warm day, such a preference is not constructive to influence the consumer's emotion to spend long time to compare other similar foods or drinks to make the final decision to choose to buy the chocolate or a cold soft drink among of the other similar kind of target foods or drinks in supermarket. In this situation, it seems that the chocolate and soft drink is emotional product. A major purpose , therefore is to provide a conceptual framework for understanding constructive consumer choice how to influence consumers' emotion to make final consumption decision in the rational environment only. This framework then allows to accomplish the two major goals:

(i) Reviewing consumer decision research with the framework serving as a organizing device and (ii) Using this review to gaps in my knowledge that suggest new research directions to predict consumer's individual emotion of purchasing behavior. In general, in consumer view point, consumer product motive can provide two kinds of motives . One kind is emotional product motive which persuades the consumer on the basic of whose emotion, the buyer doesn't try to reason out or typically analysis the need for purchase. Another kind is rational product motive which arises on the basic of logical analysis and proper evaluation, the buyer makes rational decision after chief evaluation of the purpose, alternatives available, cost benefit and such valid reasons.

How to predict consumer decision tasks and decision strategies? In some cases, the two options may be simply to either accept or reject an alternative. The attributes may vary in consumers' potential consequences, the product desirability to the consumer and the consumer's acceptance to make off less of one attribute for more of another. For example, a consumer may fairly certain about the values of some of the attributes. (e.g. reliability, safety factors) to the product to influence the consumer's buying decisions. For example, a consumer considers the cars to decide that safety was the most important attribute, processed only that attribute with the best value on that attribute limited effectively requires selective attention to information or a consumer might engage in attribute processing by examining the price of each of the cars. Including that car (B) was the most expensive, car (A) was the least expensive, and that (C) had a very good price. However, the consumer could process in an alternative based fashion by examining the reliability, price, safety of car (A) in order to form a overall valuation of the car. In compensatory strategy, a good value on one attribute can't make up for a poor value on another. If a consumer decide to choose the safest car, then car(D) will be chosen regardless of as high price and regardless of the high ratings for car (B) on reliability or car (E) for fashion.

- Consumer decision strategies

First step, the amount of information processed. For example, an automobile choice is as implied by most rational choice models to consider each of the available cars or it may only a consideration of a limited set of information. (e.g. repeating what one choice last time). Second step, different amount, information can be processed for each attribute or alternative (selecting processing) or same amount of information can be processed each attribute or alternative. Third step, the pattern of processing (whether by alternative (brand) or by attribute. Final step, the consumer will select to buy the product, based on whether the strategy is compensatory or non compensatory.

In addition, aspects of the environment the capture involuntary attention may set in motion and consumer behavioral responses. (e.g. in a loud environment is as a threat to cause the consumer's negative emotion to decide to buy the product). It implies quiet environment has more positive influence to consumer's individual emotion. For many consumer choice, there is little emotion involvement or need to justify. The choice goals and the extent to which different strategies accomplish these goals in different task environment. For example, proposed measured of cognitive effort and accuracy. With respect to cognitive effort, any decision strategy can be decomposed into more elementary information processes, such as reading on item of information, comparing two items of information, eliminating items of information and so on for a general decision to analyze information processing for each individual consumer when who need to choose to buy any products. For another example, a consumer can conceptualize to read the value for each attribute weight, comparing the weight just read with the largest weight found previously until the most important attributable has been found and then reading the values for the options on that attribute and comparing the until the largest value is found. It weight adding strategy could be thought as reading weights and values, multiplying the two ,moving on to the next weight and value and multiplying them, adding the product.

Consumer sometimes face emotion choice. Such choices arise when there are choice conflicts between goals that are very important to the individual. (e.g. one can't attain all goals given the set of available options and must give up something on one important goal to attain more of another important goal). Examples of such emotion consumer choices include trading off the safety of an automobile against environmental concerns (if larger vehicles fare better in crashes but worse in gas mileage) or trading health risks due to the presence of insects in one's house versus health risks from having chemicals sprayed in one's yard. Such choice can easily lead to negative emotion, since the trade-offs required represent threats to the attainment of importance or valued goals. The degree of emotion often depends on the values of the options. (e.g. the degree of conflict and which specific attributes are involved in the conflict). However, the negative emotion is caused by the consumer's choice process, it is not only caused by external environment, e.g. noise influence. Choice processes under negative emotion may therefore be affected by accuracy and effort concerns as modified by emotion minimization concerns. In particular, two general copying strategies may apply in consumer emotion situations: problem focuses copying (direct actions aimed at improving the person environment relationship to influence the consumer's emotion), and emotion focused copying (indirect actions aimed at minimizing emotion through changes in the amount or content of thought about the situation). Hence, manufacture will expect that increased negative emotion due to the choice situation will lead to more extensive processing. New products were evaluated more favorably when their attributes were moderate only when consumers had limited knowledge about the product category.

Consumers had more extensive knowledge about the category , their evaluations were influenced by associations to specific attributes based on their final choice level. Thus, knowing what the consumer's the most need of attributes of the product is very important in whose construct choice process. The affective tests consumer emotion's prediction weakness. The primary purpose of affective tests is to assess the personal response (preference or acceptance) of current or potential customers to a product idea or a specific product characteristics. Qualitative affective tests are those (e.g. interviews and focus groups) that measure subjective response of a sample of consumers to the sample kinds of products by having those consumers talk about their feelings in an interview or small group setting. A highly trained interviewer/ moderator is required because of the high level of interaction between the interviewer/ moderator and the consumers. Types of qualitative affective tests include focus groups, focus panels, mini-group and one-on-one interviews. However, qualitative affective tests will have these problems, such as with focus groups, individual answer can get lost in the group conversation. In addition, individual can reject from expressing opinions contrary to the group because of perceived peer pressure or group think. Panels which are focus group that meet repeated suffer from the same problems as focus groups. With one-on-one interview fasters might substantially temper a negative assessment of a product in order to not to appear honest answer or because they like the interviewer and don't want to hurt their feelings.

● Internet questionnaires recommendation

I recommend any individual company can send internet questionnaires to individual to detect what attribute factors can influence individual consumer's emotion to make the final consumption decision to choose to buy its innovative new products by email before their new products will be manufactured. Thus, the manufacturer can predict whether what attribute factor can be the most potential influence to individual's emotion to choose to buy whose new products generally. For example, one car manufacturer can send email questionnaires to individual consumer to invite who to fill its questionnaires in its website, these questionnaire questions can indicate as below:

(a) What attribute factor(s) can influence you to choose to buy our company's new design style sport car products?. reliability .new fashion .fast speed .brand .popular. reasonable price . durability, .safety .more functions . unique design style

(b) Which factor do you feel which is the most important to influence you to make the final buying decision to choose to buy our company's new design style sport car products ?

In general, this company's all sport cars which are rational products. It means any consumer will prefer to spend time to compare its any style of sport cars to other brands of sport cars to make final decision to choose to buy which brand of sport car. For example, if one consumer feels safety attribute factor is the most important to influence who chooses to buy any sport cars. Then, he/she will demand to attempt to drive to detect this car company's any style of sport cars to test whether which can satisfy to whose safe demand. Even, if who feel other brands' style of sport cars can satisfy whose safe demand, he/she will be possible to attempt to drive to detect other brands of similar style sports cars to compare to this brand of sport car to make final purchase decision.

Owing to there are many brands of sport cars which are provided to individual consumer to compare to choose to make final decision to buy in any country. It seems that any consumer will prefer to spend time to make logical and rational analysis to compare them and who won't be influenced by whose emotion to decide to buy any brands of sport cars in the short time easily. Thus sport cars is belonged to rational product more then emotional product.

As this reason, so I recommend this sport car company needs to prepare email questionnaires to enquire its potential individual consumer to attempt to let who to give feedback to predict whether what attribute factors can influence whose emotion to choose to buy its any kind style sport cars as well as whether what attribute factor will be the most importance to compare the other attribute factors to make final cause to influence final decision to choose to buy its any sport cars to avoid the worst attribute factor is caused. Following the car company gathers different feedback to predict whether what attribute factors are as well as what the worst factor is from these sample potential consumer's idea of its email questionnaire. Then, it can predict the result from consumers' idea to make final decision whether which are the least attractive

attribute factors which will influenced any individual consumer to decide not to buy its any style of sport cars.
It aims to predict whether what are the least attractive attribute factors to cause bad emotion to the consumer to choose not to buy the kind of sport car generally. Such as, not reliable engines, old fashion , slow speed, unpopular brand, not reasonable price, not durability, not safety, less functions or not unique design style of whether which are the least attractive attribute factors. Hence, it can predict whether which attribute factors will be the attractive influence to cause its any potential consumer to choose to buy its any new innovative sport cars in order to concentrate on manufacturing any new innovative style sport cars to design which must own the most attractive attribute factors before it decides to manufacture its new style of sport cars. In conclusion, it seems that constructive consumer choice is an important process to influence any consumer to choose to buy any products. I recommend any company ought attempt to prepare questionnaires to investigate whether which the most attractive attribute factors are and which the least attractive attribute factors are influenced to each potential consumer will choose to buy or not buy to its launch innovative new products by email questionnaire channel. In general, youth people will feel ease to use online to shopping to compare to old people. I shall indicate online car brands comparison Constructive consumer choice processes

Table 1 An example of a consumer decision task

car reliability price safety speed

A worst best good very poor

B best worst worst good

C poor very good average average

D average poor best worst

E worse very good good best

Attributes are scored on seven point scales ranging from best to worst, with indicating the most desirable value for the attribute and worst indicating the least desirable value.

How to evaluate online sale method is more acceptable to sell the product.

- Explaining what situation makes the individual consumer doesn't accept to use internet technology sale channel to buy the product as well as it why internet will cause negative purchase emotion to any consumer to choose to buy any manufacturer's products .
    - Abstract

The third aspect solution, I shall explain why the electronic commerce sale channel in technology acceptance model, it is possible that why it can influence the consumer's positive emotion to be changed to be negative emotion to choose not to buy the manufacturer's product . Moreover, I shall teach manufacturer whether how to judge it ought or does not ought choose this technology model to sell its products from internet channel.

- Main Problem Being Addressed

The third aspect main problem is researched why internet sale will have what bad factors to influence consumers to cause negative emotion to decide not to buy manufacturers' products from online shopping. I shall recommend how to predict their products whether which are suitable to sell from internet and how to improve their sale methods to increase consumer's positive emotion to accept to buy their products from internet. The final discussion is judged in what situation it will cause individual consumer doesn't like to enter the manufacturer's website to choose to buy the manufacturer's products.

I shall also indicate why the manufacturer will cause negative emotion to whose consumers if who chose online sale channel. I aim to teach manufacturer how to know whether whose products ought or not ought to be chose to sell from online sale channel as well as how to reduce to cause bad influence to consumers' emotion from whose websites to avoid online sale failure chance. I shall use internet surveys to gather information to detect whether what factors influence the consumer choose prefer to buy or not to prefer buy the manufacturer's products from internet as well as how manufacturers can predict consumer's emotion in the constructive consumer choice process before who choose online shopping. Hence, if the manufacturer could predict whether what weaknesses are existed to reduce whose website attraction to whose consumers' attention. It will avoid whose online sale failure. The benefits to manufacturer include who can predict what weaknesses of whose website are, then who can attempt to revise which aspects of whose website weaknesses in order to raise whose consumers' positive emotion when who uses internet to enter the sale website to find any kinds of products to buy them. If the manufacturer's website can raise attraction ability to increase many customers to see whose website. Then, whose customer numbers will be increased possibly. Online sale influence research can only apply to manufacturers who sell their products from their website sale channel.

- Related Background of internet sale channel

Nowadays, many young people like to choose to use internet to buy any manufacturer's products. Although internet is popular to accept to young to use to buy any products, but it will have chance to cause negative emotion to individual consumers from positive emotion due to they enter any manufacturer's website to find some bad points to influence their feeling to be bad. Finally, the consumers will not choose to buy the manufacturer's products due to the manufacturer does not know what the bad points are existed to whose website. Thus, I believe that internet won't be accepted to be the best sale channel to adopt to use to sell to any manufacturers' products effectively, even internet sale channel will cause some consumers negative emotion to influence who choose not to buy the manufacturer's products if the product's manufacturer chooses internet to help who to advertise whose this product to sell from internet sale channel.

Previous research has linked the experience of loneliness with materialism, suggesting that when consumers attach too great an importance to possessions, they may reduce the importance of their social relationships, leading to isolation and feelings of loneliness. Thus materialism may arises a way to cope with loneliness, which suggests that to decrease materialism, one may want to first focus on building social relationships and reducing loneliness rather than focusing first upon reduced consumption.

Hung & Mukhopadhyay (2012) examined the influence of actor versus observes perspectives on the emotional experience. "They find that "actors tend to focus move on the situation at hand and experience more emotion, such as excitement, sadness when who recall or anticipate emotional experiences. Their previous research has linked experiences of loneliness with materialism, suggesting that when consumers attach to great an importance of their social relationship, leading to isolation and feelings loneliness. This may unfortunately, lead to downward, thus it focus on building social relationship and reducing loneliness rather than focusing first upon reduced consumption." It seems social environment can influence the consumer's social emotion to choose to consume the product. The meaning of happiness that is most relevant to influence choices, such select those with a present focus will prefer products that offer calm. Thus, it seems excited consumers will choose exciting products and calm consumers will choose relaxing products. It implies that who will prefer to choose to buy the kind of product from online shopping if the consumer is a excited person to accept new technology shopping model and enjoyed to loneliness to sit down to use whose laptop to choose to buy any online products at home quiet environment. Otherwise, if consumers don't like loneliness, who will like to leave their homes to go to retail shops to buy any manufacturers' new innovate products with their friends or families and who will feel more happy and enjoyable in this non technological shopping model. Thus, it implies the enjoyable quiet environment, loneliness, technology excited consumers will choose to buy products from online sale model more. Otherwise, the enjoyable noise environment, social relationship, calm consumers will choose to buy products from traditional retail shops sale channel. Thus, consumers' emotion will be influenced to feel enjoyable or non-enjoyable to buy the product from the online shopping model or traditional visiting retail shops model .It seems that noise or quiet shopping environment will influence individual consumer's emotion to make final decision to buy the product. If the consumer enjoys to choose to buy any brands of products in the quiet environment at home lonely, the online shopping technological model will be more chance to be accepted to make final decision to this consumer habitually. Otherwise, if the consumer enjoys to choose to buy any brands of products in the noise environment, social relationship with friends, the visiting retail shops model will be more chance to be accepted to make final decision to this consumer habitually.

What is this meaning to this consumer in these two different situation? I feel that the consumer will prefer to choose to buy the kind of product from online shopping if who is a excited person, so who can accept to use internet more than visiting retail shops , due to who enjoys to loneliness to sit down to use whose laptop to choose to buy any online products at home quiet environment. Otherwise, if the consumer does not like loneliness, who will like to leave whose home to visit retail shops to choose to buy any brands of products with whose friends or families in the noise shopping center environment, due to who will feel more happy and enjoyable to buy any products in the noise and social relationship with friends or family outside environment. It means that the product manufacturer needs to understand whether whose products can be more accepted to sell to its potential consumers from either online sale model or visiting retail shops traditional sale model as well as how to design its product styles to match its potential consumers to build positive emotion whether this product is suitable to sell from online sale channel. In general, the perceived case of use can influence perceived usefulness of the product, then to influence consumer's attitude to choose to buy the product. Hence, attitude can influence the consumer's commonly. I feel that the consumer will choose to visit retail shops to test the product's functions or attempt to touch the product or see the product's actual image in the retail shops, even who needs the salespeople to teach who how to use the product when feel the product is difficult to learn to use. Specially, it is a new innovative technological product, when it will be promoted to market to sell in the first time. Due to the consumer did not know this new product existed before, who needs the salespeople talk to whom to explain how to use this new technological innovative product to listen carefully. So, who will choose to visit retail shops to decide to buy this product with whose friends or families more than online shopping. Otherwise, if the consumer feels the product is ease to use and who like loneliness, who will accept to use internet to make final decision to choose online to buy the product in the quiet home environment more than traditional visiting retail shops model. It seems the external environment and the consumer's personality can influence the consumer's emotion to make final decision to choose to buy any brand of product. For example, the consumer feels the product is ease to learn to use or difficult to learn to use. It will influence the consumer choose to buy either from online or retail shops.

- How can internet cause positive emotion to consumers?

Online shopping lacks emotion physically experienced (e.g. examined, tried on, and used), it is difficultly for shoppers with little computer expertise, there are some general uncertainties associated in homes hopping of all kinds (e.g. concerns about product return, credit card security, loss of privacy, merchant legitimacy.) Each consumer's confidence might play an important role in predicting intentions to purchase. The factors influence whose confidence which may include, such as consumer's lower perceived risk, product appearance, image size and product movement were manipulated in context of simulated appeal web sites. Both manipulations in the computer medicated environment were expected to create virtual experiences affecting mood, perceived risk and purchase intent product image size is a significant factor. Product presentations using movement attract attention and generate good mood in on-line shoppers, even soft music listening in quiet home environment can influence consumer's emotion to cause online shopping intention. The benefits of online shopping in relation to traditional stores hopping are one of the driving forces in the adoption. Perceived usefulness has been used to explain consumer acceptance of online shopping. Perceived usefulness refers to the degree to which a person believes that using a particular system (e.g. an online shopping site) would enhance his or her job performance. Risk perception of online shopping can be risked into two predominant types behavioral risk and environment risk. Behavioral risk arises from online retailers who have a chance to behave in an opportunistic manner by taking advantage of the government's inability to monitor all transactions adequately.

It includes product risks, psychology risks and seller performance risks. Environment risk is caused by the unpredictable nature of the purchasing medium-internet, which is beyond the control of online retailer and consumer. It includes financial risks and privacy risks. Perceived risk can be affected or moderated by a variety of factors, including consumer demographics, internet experience, product characteristics and attributes of a web site etc.

The perceived product risk varies with the age and internet experience of consumers. As consumers get older, their accumulated experience and knowledge make their stopping more targeted of certain brands and make them more confident, which can reduce product risk and the need for conducting pre-product information searches. It is possible that in comparison to make consumers female consumers perceived the likelihood and consequences of negative outcomes as a result of purchasing online to be greater and their concerns regarding these verity of the consequences of privacy loss during online shopping were stronger. The effect of perceived risk may be subject to product characteristics. The risk is generally higher for high involvement products that require the problem solving behavior and have some degree of personal importance than for low involvement products. Hence, online retailers of low involvement products may have greater success in keeping buyers than those of high involvement products, if the former can provide on appealing shopping experience. Other attributes of products do matter to perceived risk . For example, the risk was perceived lower for product for categories associated with higher expenditure levels, more satisfying characteristics and feeling and touching before purchase. Consumer attitude is directly affected by users' belief about a system, which consist of perceived usefulness and once of use to use online to shopping in technology acceptance model to each individual consumer. In the technological acceptance model aspect view, it is possible that the consumer's perception of technology of safety and cost is important to influence who to choose to buy the product as well as self efficiency has been found to affect technology usage also through its effects on the emotional state of the user buy, for example, the manufacturer can reduce the consumer whose computer anxiety and it can increase behavioral control to its consumer more easily when its consumers enter it's product website to feel it is more safe to buy its products to compare to its online competitors' websites. Due to the characteristics of online retail context to innovative products, consumers are subjected to more influences in the virtual store where who are able to interact with an adaptive environment as a consequence on adaptive and interactive scenario is more appealing for consumers, with benefits for the decision making process. Thus, internet will influence consumers whose emotion to choose another online shopping model to any innovative products sale channel. Enjoyment can be considered the degree to which consumer perceives a certain technology as pleasant. It implies that richer technology leads to higher enjoyment for achieving a stronger influence on consumers' attitudes toward online retailers.

I shall recommend any one innovative product manufacturer ought send questionnaires by to any individual consumer by email to

enquire about such as below:
(i) Do you feel this kind of innovative product is either easy or difficult more to learn to use ? It aims to predict their emotion to give feedback to let who to know whether consumers' emotion will be felt more easy or more difficult to use this product from these sample population. Then , this manufacturer can judge whether it ought to sell this kind of innovative product from either traditional retail shops or online shopping model.
(ii) Do you feel you like to buy this product in either quiet environment or noise environment more? It aims to predict their positive emotion response to judge whether who accept to buy this kinds of innovative product in the quiet environment or noise environment more to decide to make visiting retail stores channel or online sale online to sell this product.
(iii) Do you like to use internet advertisement or magazine advertisement channel to find this kind of product? It aims to predict internet online sale model or retail stores sale channel which is more acceptable to sell the manufacturer's products to attract to influence many customers to make final decision to buy its products more popular and acceptable.
(iv) Do you need salespeople to talk to you to give truly products information to assist you to buy my brand of any products? .absolutely need .absolutely not need .may be need. may not be need. It aims to judge whether the online sale is more important sale channel or not to compare with retail shops sale channel. After it gathers these statistic information from these sample potential Consumers' email questionnaires, the manufacturer can analyze whether this kind of innovate product is more acceptable from online sale model or traditional retail shopping model in its country, even global sale. Thus, it can decide either to increase to open more retail shops or decrease retail shops numbers or concentrating on selling its products from online sale channel more sale methods.

Summary

Consumer emotion prediction can have many methods. However,

I feel that these three methods are the most useful. Firstly, video camera recording technology can predict why the consumer chooses to buy the kind of product as well as face reading technology can measure whether what weights of the sugar ingredients to manufacture the weight of sweets, chocolate, soft drinks of the most good taste foods. Secondly, the manufacturer can concentrate on manufacturing whose new product which can own the most attractive attributable factor to attract which customers to choose to buy to reduce the invent lose risk. Thirdly, website sale channel must not be suitable to any manufacturers to choose to sell which products. If who can know whether their products are suitable to sell from internet or retail stores sale channel more. It can reduce the risk to loss their customers in long time. However, if you feel your product or food ought to sell from online channel. I recommend you ought need to do marketing research to evaluate whether which sale channel is the most suitable to research to sell your products or foods to persuade your clients to choose to buy. Otherwise, if your online sale channel is not suitable to sell to cause bad emotion to your clients. Thus, I believe it will reduce your client numbers due to you sell your products in the wrong sale channel.

References

Ambady, N. and Rosenthal, R.(1992)' Thin Silces Of Behavior As Predictors Of Interpersonal Consequences: A meta- analysis, psychological Bulletin, 2: 256-74

Arnade, E. (2014) Journal Of Consumer Research, Make a face: Implict and explict measurement of facial expression by orange juices using face reading technology. Food quality and preference, vol.32, p.161-172. Retrieved: http://hdl.handle.net/10919/54538.

Carrere, S. and Gottman, J. (1999) ' predicting divorce amongnewlyweds from the first three minutes of a marital conflice discussion', family processes 38:293-301.

Hung & Mukhopadhyay.(June 2012), Emotion And Consumer Behavior, , vol. 40 no.5 (June 2012), 39-50.

Meservy, T.O. jnsen, M.L. Kruse, W.J., Burgoo, J.K. and Nunamaker Jr., J.F. (2008) ' Automatic extraction of deceptive behavioral cues from video', in H.Chen, E. Reid, J. Sinai, A. Silke and B. Ganor (eds) Terrorism Informatics (pp. 495-516), New York: Springer.

Miller, K. (2012), Consumer behavior, Washington, USA. Retrieved: http://www.amazon.com

Palmer (2012), Consumer behavior and credit card payment, Journal of management market resarch.

Webb et. al (2000), The impact of perceived corporate social responsibility on consumer behavior, Journal of business research 59(1): pp. 46-53 Jan. 2006.

SIX

THE RELATIONSHIP BETWEEN CONSUMER BEHAVIOR AND ONLINE SHOPPING

Human Behavioral network job brings social economic benefits

What does human network job mean ? Why may human network job be popular? Why human network job behavior may influence economy ?

Nowadays internet is popular to use. We can apply internet to find data , search any new things, even earn money. Why does internet may become huma network job source. For example, e-publish may be one kind of new human network job. Any authors may apply internet

channel to help them to sell electronic or paper books from e-publisher web store. They may apply facebook, you tub etc. any

online
channel to promote themselves new books to let new readers to know whether when they may buy themselves favourable new topic books to read
from electronic publisher web store.

Thus, future electronic publisher industry may help any authors to build internet network platform to help them to sell and promote ot advertise their any one new electronic or paper book topic to let global any one reader to choose to buy their any new topic books from electronic publisher web store easily and conveniently. However, it implies that electronic network platform author may be one kind of future new human network job in our societies.

How electronic network platform author job may bring economy benefit in macro economy view? A person can have few friends, contacts and still be very influential if these few
friends and contacts are themselves highly influential, e.g. one author must not need to know any one reader in global society. When they like to choose any electronic books from electronic internet network platform. They may become the author's any one topic book buyer, when they feel the author's any one topic book is fun and attract they make decision to buth the strange author whose the topic book from electronic book publisher's platform web store conventiently in short time. Although, they are strangers, they do not know themselves , but the reader can understand what it way that made Google from writing platofrm to create new creative mind and typing network job method to replace traditional hand writing book method for global authors. It will be one kind of new human network writing job.

Hence, global any one reader can apply an innovative search engine , such as google.com to find whether whom author personal new topic books are value to read from internet.
Then, the electroniuc publisher's web store may be new book store platform sale network to help the author to sell many electronic or paper books from electronic network platform
in short time. So, internet may be future new network plaform to

help global any one author to create network writing job absolutely. Furthermore, internet may be popular social media
to help any one author to build goold relationship between his/her readers. It is one kind of new network, human network job. New authors do not need to buy many paper books to prepare to put in any one book shop warehouse. Their every book can print on demand to reduce out of book stock in any one book shop. They may choose to sell either electronic books or paper books both from any one book publisher web store. So, electronic network platform may be one kind of good writing channel to help human authors to create income and it can also help authors to bring new creative mind and new topic fun content books to let readers to know and buy to read from electronic publisher network platform.

Why does human behavior may be one kind of new human network job to bring global economic advantages. ALthough, it may be free income or without inocme, but the person does the network behavior, his/her behavior may be bring advantages to influence many other people's health. For this case, when a worker in a coffee shop in an airport gets a vaccination aganinst the flu, it does not only helps him or her stay healthy, but also helps the many travellers who might otherwise have been inflected if that workers caught the flu. So, the externality , the result implies the vaccination of even a part of a community conveys benefits to the whole community. For example, governments pay special attention to the vaccinations of school children, teachers, health mothers, and the elderly, categories of people particularly susceptible not only to catching, but also to transmitting a disease.

It is not accidential that governments are heavily involved with vaccination . When there are externalities, free market, fail to persuade individual incentives with society's
their the worker's decision of whether to get a vaccine ends up attracting whether other people get sick. The workers might not fully take all these other people's potential suffering into account when making her or his vaccination decision.

As Stanford University does many suggestions, understand this and tries to help them make the right decisions and so providers free flu vaccines for its staff and students.
Small pockets of unvaccinated individuals can allow a disease to gain a spread more widely well-being. For example, parent weighing the costs and benefits of a vaccine for their child is not always thinking of the consequences of that vaccination to other people. THese are markets in which subsidizing or regulating behavior can make everyone better off. Because the reason for requiring that a child be vaccinated before enrolling in school is not just to protect that child, because each child's vaccination affects others via potential contagions.

Robots take our jobs behavioral and economy influences

Robot job behavior brings economy influences

If one day robots can replace human to do simple, even complex jobs. They will bring what influences to our global societial economy.The popular economic refrain declares that the
global middle class is dying and robots will soon take our jobs, e.g. shopping center customer service jobs, library service jobs, cinema ticket sale jobs, restaurant kitchen cooker jobs,
even, bus drivers, taxi drivers etc. public transport driving jobs, accountant, doctors etc. professional jobs. Whether it is beautiful or petty matter if our future societies have many human jobs can be replaced to do from robots. Businessman must may reduce to employ employees and reduce to pay salary or wage, when robots can be replaced to do their employees tasks. But, societies must bring unemployement rate rises , due to societies will have many people loss jobs when their employers choose to buy robots to serve their clients or do any office tasks or customer service or cleaning etc. tasks.

In micro economy view, employers may save money in long term, but in macro economy view, it will cause unemployment ratio rises , even crime rate rises when there are many people lose
jobs in societies. These models of doom, though, fail to account

for the hundreds of businesses riding the waves of change in their industries when robots may be invented to replace human to do many simple , even complex tasks in our future societies.

WE may image that one small factory needs to manufacture fishes canes to sell to supermarket, the small , cheaper stuff and higher margin parts of the fishes manufacture industry. Before, this factory needs to employe many human factory workers need to help every fresh customer makeing the perfect fishing gear, designed for performance, durability, and cost in order to achieve to manufacture every fish cane in whole fished processing manufacturing stages. Every worker needs to spend about 15 to twenty minutes to finish every fish cane , till to delivery to any supermarket to sell. If this fish canes manufacturing factory can apply manufacturing robots to help them to finish any one working tasks , every robot can only spend five minutes to finish whole fresh fish cane manufacturing process. Thus, every robot can

help this factory save 10 to 15 minutes time to finsh every fish cane manufacturing process. IN fact, time is money, because when every robot can help this factory to reduce 10 to 15 minutes time to compare human worker. Then, this factory can finish about 20 fish canes in one hour if it can use robot to help it to manufacture fish canes. Otherwise, if this factory still use human workers to help it to manufacture fish canes, then it can finsh about 3 to 4 fish canes in one hour. SO, the manufacturing efficiency ensures that robots must help this fish manufacturing factory to raise fish canes number more than human workers. So, in robotic behavioral economy view, manufacturing robots must help this fish canes manufacturing factory to raise fish canes manufacturing number and deliver increasing number to supermarkets to prepare to sell every day. Robots can help this fish canes manufacturing factory bring manufacturing time saving, rising manufacturing efficiency, improving performance and reducing wages expenditure long time advantages in micro economy view. However, manufacturing robots can also bring disadvanages to society, e.g. increasing unemployment ratio, increasing crime rate, this factory workers will lose jobs and income, they need earn social welfare from government and increasing government finance pressure in short time, even long time in macro economic view.

Stanford University graduate program in economics, Scott lecturer explained that "in demand and supply economic theory for robots supply and demand case, robots supply number increasing may influence human workers demand number decrease. It sometimes calls " the efficient frontier".

No specific human beings were mentioned in any of economics classes. As robots supply and demand in market case, They (robots) may be purely theoretical " agents" who reached to the most reasonable sale prices in order to persuade any one businessman buyer to make manufacturing robot buying decision whether robots can help him / her to bring how much saving time , saving money, saving cost, improving performance, efficiency economic benefit before he/she plans to reduce workers number when he/she decides to apply robots to replace human workers in his/her factory or office or any service department, e.g. cinema ticket sale service, shopping center customer service, shopping center cleaning , supermarket customer service etc. service or sale tasks. When robots can replace human to do any one of these tasks in any organizations. So, robots may be human worker agents who reached to prices the way robots would react to a software command. There was nothing that explained why some people thrived and others did n't or why truly brilliant, hardworking people could fail when much lazier folks succeeded." Having been admitted to the Stanford University graduate program in economics, Scott lecturer hoped to get his answers there.

How robots influence our future social changing? Using the right technology can be a boon to your business in this economy. For internet example, it is easier than ever to find well-matched customers all around the world, to stay in contact with them, and to more quickly design the products they want. If you focus solely on being cutting -edge, though you risk letting the technology take over what should be very robust relationships with your customers , employees, and colleagues. IN nowaddays society, technoligical advances and cutomation, personal relationships in business are more crucial than ever. I mean that robots can not replace human to serve clients to let them to feel more comfortable and passion more easily. For shoe shop case example, if the shoe shop apply one robot to serve its clients to replace human shoe salesperson to serve its shoe customers. Robots ensure that they can not persuade every shoe potential buyer to make shoe buying decision more easily when robots need to contact every shoe potential buyer. The reason is simple, because robots can not touch any one shoe buyer individual emotion very easier.

If the shoe buyer needs the robots to help him/her to choose any right shoe styles when he/she can not feel himself / herself can make the most right shoe style choice decision. The robots can not replace human shoe salesperson to make shoe style choice judgement more easily. They must need longer time to analyze whether which shoe style may be the most suitable to the shoe buyer. Otherwise, human shoe salesperson may attempt to make the most right shoe style choice decision to help any one shoe buyer to chooce the most right style shoe because he/she owns shoe style sale experience, shoe style knowledge, the most important reason is that they can feel every shoe customer individual emotion to touch whether he/she will feel comfortable or happy when they attempt to help every shoe customer to seek the most right shoe style in every shoe customer whole shoe searching processing. Othwerwise, serving robots are only one machine, they can not touch or feel every shoe customer individual emotion whether he/she feel comfortable or unhappy or happy when they need to contact them in whole shoe searching processing. Hence, I believe that some tasks robots can not repalce human staff to do very easily. Otherwise, robots may bring disadvanatges to let any one businessman to loss his/her customers, due to robots can not touch every customer emotion to compare human staff in service tasks more easily. Robots serving customer behaviors may cause money lose and customers number lose to the shop in micro economic view.

Intellectual human economic behaviors

What does intellectual human economic behaviors mean ? I believe that when we choose or decide to do intellectual behaviors, then our societies will be influenced to bring economic growth in consequence.I shall attempt to indicate pollution case to explain how and why eithet our intellectual or foolish behaviors may bring economic growth or recession in consequence as below:

On one hand, for air pollution social case aspect example, if we only consider to buy cars to drive for working aimr or holiday leisure aim. Then, our societies air will be polluted. Our health will be influenced to bad. Our car driving behaviors may cause global environment air pollution serously. In long tiem, global air pollution will bring our bodies health to be bad. Although, ourselves car driving behaviors may bring our driving travelling leisure enjoyment and comfortable feeling in short time, also we so not need to pay public transport fare often, but we need to compensate ourselves health economic intangible loss due to air pollution , when cars number increases, dirty air will cause ouselves health to become bad.

In the result, we will need to pay more medical expenditure when we are old age, due to ourselves bodies will become bad, due to we breathe global dirty air every day, due to ourselves cars pollute air in long time, e.g. 10 to 20 years, even 30 more without limited air pollution environment. So, driving cars behavior may be one kind of human foolish behavior and our foolish behavior may bring ourselves future long time medical expenditure absolutely.

One the other hand, water pollution social aspect, if we often keep much rubblish to pollute sea, oil exploration porcessing pollute ocean , ships gas pollute ocaen, then fishes will eat polluted food and drive dirty water, due to global ocean is polluted.

In fact, because human only to conside how to buy boats to carry on leisure enjoyment activities, or catch cruises to travel on the sea. Also, oil manufacturers only consider researching anywhere to find new oil exploration places to manufacture oil product, when their oil exploration processes pollute ocarn . Consequently, global fishes drink polluted warer or eat polluted food. They will have poison. SO, human will have high chance to eat poison polluted fishes, due to fishes are poison or are polluted.

So, human is doing foolish activities, we only hope to find oil exploration places to pollute ocean or we only spend money to buy ticket to catch ships to travel anywhere in global ocean. All of these human foolish behaviors will bring pollution to global ocean. On consequently, we will need to compensate to eat polluted or dirty or poision fishes, ourselves bodies health will be bad. In long time, we need have high chance to pay medical expenditure when we are old. So, pollution case may be one good example to explain how and why human foolish behavior may influence ourselves future need to compensate serious medical loss.

All of these human foolish behavior will bring pollution to global ocean. On consequently, we will need to compensate to eat polluted or dirty or poison fished , ourselves bodies health will be bad. In long time, we will have high chance to pay medical expenditure, when we are old. So, pollution case may be one good example to explain how and why human ourselves intellectual or foolish behaviors may influence future long time economic loss or economic growth or recession in micro and micro economic view.

On another water pollution aspect hand, if we often keep rubbish to sea, oil exploration processing pollutes ocean and ships‘ gas pollute ocean, then fishes will eat polluted food and drink dirty water, due to fishes will eat polluted food and drink dirty sea water because the global ocean is polluted seriously.

In fact, because human only consider how to buy boats to carry on any leisure water activities, or catches cruises to travel on the sea. Also, oil manufacturers only consider any where to find oil exploratin places to manufacture oil products from ocean, when their pol exploration processes can plooute ocean. Consequently, global fishes drink polluted water or eat direty food. They will have poison. So, human will have high chance to eat poison fishes.

Otherwise, such as pollutin case, it can infuence inflation or deflation. Consequently, the reason indicates supply and demand theory. If air pollution is serious, then we will consider health issue, global cars demand number may be influenced to reduce, when global cars number demand will reduce, global car prices and supply number will need to change to fall down in order to attract or persuade global car consumers choose to make car purchase decision.

Hence, global car manufacture number and car price will be influenced to reduce, due to global air pollution issue. Consequently, deflation will occur because when the country citizen usually does not spend much extra saving money to buy car expensive goods. Money value will be low. Otherwise, if global cair pollution is not serious, human considers to buy cars to enjoy driving leisure lives. So, global car demand is influenced to increase , also global car price will also influenced to increase.

Consequently, gobal human will choose to buy cars to drive. Due to we accept to spend extra saving to buy expensive car goods. Car sale price and supply may be influenced to rise up. Money value is influenced to reduce. Inflation may be influenced, due to global car consumers number increases, we would not have extra money to spend easily. Car expensive goods expenditure influences our spending habit to avoid to make car purchase decision more easily. So, human intellectual or foolish activities may bring inflation or deflation consequency in possible indirectly in macro economic view.

On conclusion, above pollution case explain that how and why human intellectual or foolish economic behaviors may bring inflation or deflation consequency as wll as economic growth or recession consequency as well as any goods demand and supply increasing or decreasing consequency. It implies that human behavior may have indirect relationship to influence any goods demand and supply number to either increase or decrease result as well as any goods price will be influenced to increase or decrease in micro and macro economic view.

The relationship between social change and human behavior

Why does economic changes may influence human individual behavioral change? I shall attempt to indicate shopping behavior and staying at home behavior to explain their case and effect relationsip as below:

Human behavior can be influenced by economic change or economic change can be influenced by human behavior? Why does recession may influence consumers reduce shopping desire? In social recession suitation, it is possible that many people lose jobs suddenly, due to businessmen lose many customers. They need to make decision to reduce employees number in order to continue to keep businesses. Consequently, many firms (organizations) their employees may lose jobs. When they have much time, due to lose jobs, they will feel to avoid to spend too much time and money to go to shopping often. Many losing jobs people, they will often stay at homes.

So, they will reduce time to go to shopping, then non essential products won't their preferable choice purchase products. Hence, recession will change many losing jobs people their shopping or consumption desires to avoid to buy non essential products often . Usually when economic boom, many people have jobs to do because consumers number must increase when many people have jobs to do. Then, many people can accept to spend money to buy non essential products often. Many people feel spend time to go to shopping can satisfy their purchase of any kinds of new products useful psychology or desire. So, recession is one good example to explain it can influence many people do not like often to leave homes to go to shopping easily. Many people like to stay at homes, becaue they feel worry about spending too much shopping time when they leave homes. Their staying home time is one good negative shopping behavior example. So, economic change may influence human individual behavior changes , they have direct cause and efect relationship in behavioral economic view.

May human behavior influence economic change? Is it possible that human behavior may bring the country social economic change in macro economic or micro behavioral economic view ? I shall indicate publishing industry example. Do you feel that if there are many students feel learning is very important when they read many books or many of students feel interesting to read or they have reading new books in habit, then it is possible that the country will have many students like to spend time to go to any book shops to choose the books, they feel that they can help they learn new knowledge. Then the country will increase students number, they often spend time to visit any one book shop every week. Their visiting book shops behavior which may become their habits. So, the country will increase students number, they often spend time to visit book shops. Also, it implies that visiting book shops behaviors may be their behavioral habits.

So, when the country has many students often spend time to visit book shops , their visiting book shops behaviors may help any one book shop to raise books sale chance. So, the country's student individual often visiting book shop behaviors, their habitual visiting book shops behaviors must may assist help any one book shop to increase books sale number absolutely.

Consequently, any one book shop , its books sale bumber must be influenced to increase to increase because the country will have many students like or feel need visit book shops habit in order to choose any suitable books to buy to read at home in order to raise themselves learning effort. When the country has many bok shops often have many students visit their book shops, then their books sale number may be influenced to increase. It explain why student individual visiting book shop behavior may help any one book shop sale number increases also.

How human productive behavior may influence economic development

May any country which citizen behavior assist themselves country development? It is one cause and effect economic question. I mean that if the country itself citicen can not concentrate mind or energy to choose to do one kind of industry in order to let themselves country can bring the most benefit, then whether the counry itself economy can bring the most serious economic benefit.

I shall attempt to indicate these countries themselves indistry choice to explain whether these countries themselves citizen productive behavior may help themselves countries to achieve the largest economic benefits. I shall indicate as below:

New Zealand farmer individual wine productive behavior

For New Zealand country example, this country concerns itself effort is foucs on farming agricultural aspect. So, this country has many farmers concentrate on farming agricultural aspect. May New Zealanders choose to spend time to produce different kinds of wines, e.g. wine or red grape wine is for the people are eating meat, or they are eating dinner.

When these New Zealanders their behaviors choose to do farming or agriculture to grow and produce different kinds of taste of white or red grape wine drinking products job. Themselves grape agriculture behavior will influence these New Zealanders themselves, they can learn how to improve different kinds of grape wine drinking products in order to achieve every kinds of white or read grape wines taste improving aim during their white or red grape producing process.

Why can New Zealander every individual white or read grape wine producers improve their white or read grape wine taste more easily? In behavioral economic view, it can explain that why any one New Zealander white or read grape wine producer can be encouraged or excited or persuaded to concentrate nervous and energy and effort to learn how to improve their white or red grape wine products easily.

In fact, New Zealand is one agricultural food export country. It has good natural environment resource , e.g. land, seed to provide any one farmer to produce themselves any kinds of agricultrual food products, e.g. fruit, or wine food products. Because New Zealanders know themselves country has enough natural resource . So, in common, many New Zealanders choose to attempt to do farming agricultural jobs in order to export themselves any kinds of fruit or meat or wine products to overseas or sell to domestic in order to earn profit.

So, when these New Zealand farmers number has been increasing every year. This country farmers will feel themsleves competition between this New Zealand farmers themselves are serious due to they may feel New Zealanders choose to do agriculture businesses in order to export themselves different kinds of farming food to overseas or sell to local to earn profit.

Hence, when many New Zealand farmers feel that farmers number has been increasing every year. They will feel themselves competition is serious. They must need to spend much time and nervous and effort to research what method is the best how to produce the best taste of white or red grape wine products in order to let local or overseas wine buyers to choose to buy his/her producing white or read grpae products to drink.

Hence, in competition psychological view, may influence many New Zealand white or reaad wine producers had been beginning to change their learning behavior on researching what method is the best in order to produce the best quality of taste red or white wine products to sell in order to attract overseas or local white or read grape wine drinkers to choose to buy his/her wine products. Their behavior will focus on learning how to raising or improving white or read grape wine taste method more than only focus on producing a large number white or red grape wine products. They believe wine quality is more important to compare wine producing number. So, New Zealand wine producers themselves wine producers behaviors have been changing on concentrating on researching wine quality method aspect more then wine producing number aspect in behavioral economic view.

America high technological productive behavior

For America example, US is one high technological country, it owns many high technological knowledge talent inventors, e.g. computer science inventors. Hence, US must attract many diferent countries owning high technological computer inventors choose to go to US to develop their computer science profession career. Also, it seems that when many computer science inventors or professions choose to go to US to develop themselves computer science new career. In behavioral economic view, due to their leaving themselves countries choice, which may bring influence themselve country job behaviors need to be changed. They must need to adapt US new live. Because they will forgive their past computer science job. These computer science professionals need to spend time to adapt US new lives. They " past computer science job behaviors" will need to be changed to their new US any computer employer's new computer science job model.

Because their traditional computer science jobs needed to be forgot in their themselves countries. They will feel their old computer science job knowledge and behavior needed to change in order to let their US any one new of computer company employer feels satisfactory to accept their new working behavior in any one US computer organization.

So, on the other hand, many US computer company employer will feel that they must need time to accept any one new overseas computer science professions their working behaviors, their working attitude daily, because these foreign comouter science professional, their past computer working behaviors and working attitude must be different to US domestic computer science professions.

In behavioral economic view, these overseas computer science professions, their working behaviors and attitude must be needed to change in order to adapt any one US new computer company itself domestic or local computer science professional stafs themselves daily working behaviors and attitude because these overseas and local computer science professionals must need to team work together.

In behavioral economic view, it is only one way that foreign computer science professionals must need to change themselves past country traditiona daily working behaviors and attitude in order to cooperate with these US local computer science professionals in teams more easily.

Consequently, if these foreign compute science professionals can change their past working behaviors and attitude to let any one US local computer science professional feels to cooperate with them easily in short time. Then, the US computer company itself whole computer professional teams themselves efficiencies will be influenced to raised or improved by the changing past working attitude and working behaviors of these foreign computer science professionals. So, in behavioral economic view, only if US any one computer company hopes itself computer teams themselves efficiency can be raised or improved when it decides to employ foreign computer science professionals and US domestic computer science professionals. They need to work in teams together. They must need to let these foreign computer science professionals to know how to change their working behaviors and attitude to let their domestic computer science professionals feel easy to work together. Then, the US computer company itself whole team efficiency must be rasied or improved easily in short time.

- China share market investing behavior

For China share market example, economic development depends on financial market. Because if many Chinese have interest to invest to carry on shares buying and selling activities in orde to learn how to earn shares interest and share profit when the China shareholder can make decision to sell himself/herself shares in the the high price, then he/she can earn money when he/she can sell the China company's shares in the high sale share price position.

If China has many Chinese like to spend time to carry on investing shares activities. Themselves shares buying and selling behaviors will influence China has many companies can increase fund from many Chinese shareholders in order to have enough money to expand or develop themselves businesses in China in long term.

Consequently, when China can have many Chinese like to attempt to carry on buying and selling shares investing behaviors in China share market. Themselves buying and selling shares behaviors can help many Chinese companies have effort to increase enough money or capital in order to continue to do their businesses in long term absolutely. So, it explains why when many Chinese become shareholders , they can assist China will have many companies continue to develop their businesses if many Chinese like to carry on shares buying and selling investing behaviors in long time in China financial investment market nowadays in behavioral economic view.

Why has any individual country have many people invest share behavior which can influence the country's macro consumption desire?

I shall apply shares market buying and selling investment behavior to explaiin why shares investment behavior which may impact the country's overal consumption desire as below:

In behavioral economic view, I assume that when the coutry has many people have interest to attempt to carry on shares buying and selling investment behavior, then their frequent shares buying and selling behaviors which may bring negactive consumption desire or shopping desire of these shares investors their consumer behavior.

The reason is simple, when the country has many share buyers number suddenly been increasing rapidly. Consequently, these large group share investors must need to spend much time to research any kinds of company shares variations, whether when their share prices will rise up of fall down in order to achieve buying the company's shares in the lowest price and selling the company's shares in the highest price level in order to earn profit.

Basic on this reason, they must need to spend much extra time to research share prices changing behavior every day, e.g. one working person will wait to leave his/her job, after he/she can spend time to gather data to research the day's share price changing behavior after dinner. So, the working person's right time may be his/her share price market research behavior. Before he/she may spend his/her night time to go to shopping after dinner, but nowadays, he/she will fogive to do his/her shopping behavior before dinner or after dinner at hight sometime. He/she will make decision to spend much night time to turn on computer to click on share market website to research his/her share purchase choice to investigate whether his/her share price whether it rises up or falls down at the moment in order to make his/her share buying or selling decision at ever night

time.
I mean the when the country has many people are share investors, their shares investment behavioral spenging time which will influence many shops lose customers at might often because the country will have many people feel need to spend night time to turn on computer or watch television to investigate share price variation. So, the country will have many people / share investors choose to stay at home in order to carry on share price variation investigation behavior, they need to listen share market update news from radios or watch the share market update news from computer or TV at home every night. Consequenly, they must reduce times to leave themselves homes at night. So, their shopping behavior also will be reduced. Because these share investors feel need to spend time to investigate share price variation news at homes which can bring economic benefits (high opportunity benefits) when they choose to forgive to leave homes to go to shopping times (opportunity cost) every night.
On conclusion, it seems that when the country has many people are share investors, then their share price investigating behavior may bring negative shopping emotion at night. Consequently, the country's any one shop may lose many customers from this share investor consumer group in behavioral economic view. Hence, when the country's share investors number had been increasing rapidly, it will influence any shops lose many customers from this share investing customer group at night frequenly in short time, even long time in behavioral economic view, because their shopping desires or shopping emotion will be brought negative feeling when they make decisions to spend much time to listen radios or watch TV or computers share price update nes at night. Hence, share market will bring negative impact to influence consumer shopping desire or negative shopping emotion in behavioral economic view.

Can technology influence human shopping behavioral change?
Nowadays, technological development has reached mature stage, whether technological mature stage may bring positive or negative

shopping emotion influence to global consumers. I shall aplly internet inventin or ecommerce shopping channel tool to explain whether internet technology can bring postive or negative influence to global consumer behavior in behavioral economic view.

Internet is a good technological tool, it brings e-commerce business chance. In fact, commonly, global has have many businessmen choose to use internet channel to carry on their products transactions between global online-buyers and their electronic websites. So, global many shoppers had begun to feel online shopping is more convenient to compare visiting shops shopping. Their shopping behaviors have been changed from internet technological tool. Global has many shoppers choose to buy any products from any overseas or local businessmen their web stores. They only need to spend time to find any businessmen their webstores to choose the most suitable products to pay visa to buy from their webstores. at homes. So, in general, global had have may shoppers had changed their shopping behaviors from visiting shops to visiting webstores at homes often.

So, it seems that internet technological tool had influenced global many shops disappear, but internet webstores will be replaced their actual shops on streets. Some of businessmen either they choose webstores to replace shops or choose websotes and shops both or still keep shops only. Hence, internet tool influences global businessmen have three kinds of products sale channels to let globa local and overseas consumers to choose how to buy their products.

However, in fact, many of global shoppers, youngers and olders had begun to accept to buy any products from webstores. They feel to spend time to leave homes to visit shops , their shopping behaviors will be wasted time to not essential part to their daily lives. Hence, since internet technological invention, it had changed many consumers their traditional visiting shops shopping habit to change to buying products from webstores channel.

However, on the one hand, internet creates webstores ecommerce shopping channel to let global many consumers do not need to leave homes to go to shopping. It brings negative visiting shops shopping

emotion to global general consumers nowadays. But on the other hand, it also brings positive visiting internet webstores shopping emotion to global general consumer nowadays. So, it seems that global many consumers feel that they often do not need to spend much time to go out shopping. Many global consumers feel convenient and enjoy to choose any products to buy from different internet webstores, when the online buyer chooses the most suitable product, he she only needs to pay visa card to buy the product from the online seller's webstore conveniently at home.
Hence, online shopping can bring economic benefit to online buyers, e.g. avoiding walking time or spending transport fare to visit the shop to go to shopping, shortening or reducing shopping time to do another important matter.
On conclusion, global many consumers began feel online shopping can bring more economic benefits on shortening shopping time, avoiding transport fare spending aspect. So, online shopping will be popular shopping behavior for future long time. It may encourage global many shoppers can make rapid shopping decision in short time in order to carry on any products buying transaction to global any one online shopper in short time easily in behavioral economic view. So, global many businessmen had begun to build themselves one attraction webstore in order to persuade different countries consumers to choose to click themselves webstores from internet channel to buy any kinds of products in short time easily.
So, internet technology had changed consumers traditional shopping behaviors to build positive online shopping emotion as well as raise online sellers' any products sale chance easily in behavioral economic view.

Why and how human behavior may influence the country's economic growth or recession?
When one country has many people choose to do the same matter for one period, whether their behavior may influence the country's pvera; economic growth or recession . I shall attempt to indicate cases toexplain their relationship as below:
For flowing rubblish behavioral case example, do you feel that when

the country has many people often flow rubblish on the streets, instead of their flowing rubblish behavior may bring streets dirty? But, their flowing rubblish behavior may explain that this country has people may have enough money to buy food to ear, or enough cloths to wear, enough bottles of water to drink, even they may have enough money to buy new television, radio, refrigeraters , washing machines, desktops or laptops electronic home products from old to new to use in order to satisfy their living needs. So, when they flow old electronic home products, their flowing old home electronic products behaviors may seem that they have enough money to buy other new home electronic products to replace old home electronic products to use at homes.

However, it seems thaat this country ought have many people have jobs to do. So, many of them, they can easy to make purchase decison to flow any old home electronic products and buy any new home electronic products to use . Because this country has many people have jobs to do. So, they can often not use old home electonic products to become rubblishs to flow on streets after they had bought any kinds of new home electronic homes.

In fact, it also implies that this country's economy grows rapidly. So, many businesses can glow up rapdly. When they expanded their businesses, they must need to increase employees number in order to let they help themselves to raise productivity or serve their clients absolutely. So, when the country has many businesses can grow up, it seems that its economy must be better or it is improved to compare past. Due to many different kinds of home electronic products had been often bought to use by this country people in this period. So, this country's any streets can be observed that expensive electronic home products were flowed on streets anywhere. then, this country will have many electronic home products sellers can sell their home electronic products very easily. When this country has many people can find any kinds of jobs to do easily. So, due to unemploymen rate had been decreasing.

In behavioral economic view, as this many electronic home products rubblish country case, we can observe this country may have many people have jobs to do. So, consumption number has been increased long time. So, cheap food, or expensive home electronic products may be rubblish on any streets. This country's people , their flowing rubblish behaviors may be explained that many of people have enough jobs to do, so they have ability to buy any good taste food to eat or buy any kinds of expensive electronic home products to use. So, this country's economy may be improved for this long period. So, in behavioral economic view, when this country can have many electronic home products rubblishs are flowed on anywherer in streets frequently. It seems that this country will have many people have jobs to do, so it causes they often change old home electronic products or replaced them easily, when they have enough income to spend to buy any kinds of new home electronic products to use at homes easily. Moreover, their flowing old electronic home products behaviors also indicate that this country has many people their salaries may be increased in possible from their emplyers. When this country can have many different kinds of home electornic products are sold. It means that this country's electronic home products needs or demand had been increasing, due to many people have jobs to do and income increases to excite their living of needs also improve. Consequently, this country may seem have better economic improvement. We can observe from this country's electronic home products rubblish increasing income in theis period.

On conclusion, this country ought experience economic growth at this period. So, " flowing expensive electronic home rubblish increasing number " may seem that this country's economic growth is rapidly in this period, due to many people have jobs to do as well as salaries increase in this period.

Technology how impacts human behavior changing?

Technology how influences human behavior to bring changing? For example, online share purchase and sale transaction from smart phone brings share investor can do share buying or selling transation in any where and any time conveniently, non manual driving auto vehicle, bring car owner feels comfortable and spends free time to do other matter, e.g. reading, listening mucis in himself or herself car freely. electrical energy vehicle can help car owner to reduce air polluton and it can brings the drivers do not feel drive long time in any journeys in order to avoid air pollution for environmental protection responsible car drivers in our societies. Thus, they will drive long time in any journeys when they can drive electronic energy cars to replace oil energy cars.

However, online technology can also bring consumers can choose to stay at homes to buy any things from seller individual online webstore conveniently. Such as online technology can bring shoppers do not need to spend much time to visit shops to buy any things. They can choose any kinds of products from any online sellers individual online webstores conveniently at homes. Online technology excite busy consumers can make purchase decision easily as well as it can help online sellers sell any kinds of products from internet easily.

In behavioral economic view, technology can change human behavior to be improved, it can let human feels comfortable, more free time ro use, rapid making any decisions, such as apply smart phones to make share purchase or sale transaction decision, online shopping decision, even travelling any where decision in short time, when the traveller finds the most cheap hotel accommodation room price and air ticket price frm any travel agent online tourism webstore, then the potential travel customer can follow the online hotel accommodation price and air ticket price data to make decision when to buy the air ticket from the airline travel agent or make decision when to prebook which hotel accommodation room to go to the country to travel from online travel agent tourism webstores. So, technology can encourage global any country travelers to make anywhere to trvel rapidly. If the traveler can find the country's general hotel rooms and airline tickets prices had been decreasing more sightly. The traveler may make travel decision to choose the country to travel in short time, then he/she can prebook the country;s any hotel room and airline ticket to pay by visa fraom the country's any hotel and airline travel agent webstores., before one week, even one month or more easily. Hence, online technology can also encourage traveler individual frequent travel times to be increased, due to global travelers can find any hotel rooms and airline tickets prices from internet conveniently at homes. They do not need to spend time to visit any airline travel agent to enquire travel choice country's hotel rooms prices and airline ticket prices. They can compare global travel of countries choices ' all hotels rooms and airline agents air tickets prices to make prebook airline seat and hotel room decision before one week, one month even six months early.

On conclusion, online technology can encourage global travelers can make travelling any where and when traveling time desicions easily. It can excite tourism industry develops in long time. Also, such as electricity cars invention can encourage environment protection car owners do car purchase decision easily, because they can choose to drive electronic energy cars to replace oil energy cars in order to avoid air pollution occurs easily. So, electronic cars can increase electronic car purchasrs number, due to many of environmental protection attitude of car owners can choose to drive electricity cars to bring air cleans, even non -manual driving cars can encourage lazy driving and free time driving car owners to choose to buy non-manual (artificial intelligent) cars to drive , because they can spend much free time to read, listen music or do any matters in themselves cars, they do not need to drive cars, robotic (AI) auto driving machine is such one non-manual driver to help them to drive themselves cars confidently. So, non-manual driving cars can attract lazy and enjoying free time driving car owners to choose to buy to replace traditional manual cars to drive easily. Moreover, online share transaction can help any share investors to make share buying and selling decision in short time easily. When they can apply smart phones technological tool to carry on share buying and selling activities easily. They can observe any share rising or falling price suitation from smart phones in any where any any time easily. So, smart phone technology can help global any shareholders to make share purchase and sale transaction easily. So, technology can encourage human makes decision in short time rapidly.

How and why employees behaviors may influence economy development?

In behavioral economy view,I believe the country's any organizational employees behavior may bring indirect relationship to influence the country's long term economic development. I shall indicate past manufacture industry social development period to explain their relationship. For many countries' past business activities had belonged to manufacturing industry, such as US, UK past before 1980 year, it focused on steel manufacturing and steel manufacturing related machine products. So, US, Uk developed countries manufacturing industries may be past main country's economic income sources. I assume US , UK past had one million number different kinds of industries. They ought had about seven houndred thousand number organizational businesses were belonged to manufactured industry. They may include:

Steel manufacturing and steel related machine manufacturing, e.g. vehicle manufacturing, home appliances, e.g. washing machine, television, radio, refrigerate cooler, heater, air condition etc. different kinds of different kinds of steel -related manufacturing machine, they were manufactured from US, UK steel machine manufacturers. So, US, Uk the other three hundred thousand number industry may be general service industry, e.g. hotel service, restaurent, cinema, public transport service, tourism lesiure , wine bar, supermarket etc. different kinds of non-manufacturing industries business organizations were operated in UK, US past before 1980 year.

So, in UK, US developed countries industry development history, they ought have high percentage of businesses belonged to steel related manufacturing machine and steel products. Also, in the past before 1980 year, US, Uk business employers , they employed many workers are manufacturing workers. They needed to spend long time to work in factories. They were skillful workers, and they are trained to manufacturing cars, washing machine, television, heater, etc. even steel itself different kinds of steel related products to prepare to deliver to their shops to sell to US, Uk local or overseas clients.

So, I believe that past UK, US ought employ many employees, they belonged to skillful manufacturing workers, manufacture increasing steel machine or steel related machine number of products rapidly daily. So, if UK, US had had many of these manufacturing factories owned high skillful workers, then their manufacturing steel-related machine or steel both kinds of products number must be influenced to raise rapidly. Consequently, their steel machine manufacturing products would been exported to overseas or would been sold to local both markets , they may be influenced to raise sale number. They (these manufacturing workers) needed to be trained to know how to manufactur these different kinds of machine products in the efficient teams and they ought to be trained to raise their efficiencies in order to shorten time to manufacturing many kinds of steel related manufacturing machine or steel itself products rapidly. So , if their efficiencies and manufacturing performance was improved, these US, UK any one manufacturing worker and their teams ought achieve raising productivities significantly.

Hence, when past UK, US manufacturing industry development period, if these two countries' any manufacturing factories could have many manufacturing workers could be trained to be skillful and proficient manufacturing workers. Then, in past every day to these factories workers, they ought help their steel or steel related manufacturing employers to raise any kinds of machine or steel products number in every team. So, when past in the manufacturing industry development, US, UK could have many factories' manufacturing workers themselves steel or steel related machine products manufacturing skill could be trained to to improve to any kinds of these machine or steel manufacuring products quality as well as their products number could be influenced to raise by themselves skillful improvement significantly every day.

Then, what would be influenced to occur to past UK, US manufacturing industry period? In behavioral economic view, when these two manufacturing industry developed countries, such as UK, US , if they had many factories workers can be trained to improve their skill in order to achieve any kinds of steel or steel-related machine products quality could be improved as well as products manufacturing number could be also increased absolutely. In consequence, past UK and US both countries ought increase themselves any kinds of steel and steel related machine products number to be supplied to themselves local shops to let local clients to choose any one kind of machine manufacturing products to buy easily as well as they could also export to supply overseas any countries to buy their different kinds of steel or steel related machine products to let overseas steel or steel related manufacturing machine product buyers, they can have many of these different kinds of these steel or steel-related different kinds of manufacturing machine from UK and UK these both countries easily to compare other countries.

On conclusion, I believe that past US, and UK macro manufacturing industry income GDP would increase significantly. So, they would have good economic growth performance because when many of these manufacturing workers themselves manufacturing effort could be improved. So, it explained when employees manufacturing abilities can influence economic growth indirectly.

www.ingramcontent.com/pod-product-compliance
Ingram Content Group UK Ltd.
Pitfield, Milton Keynes, MK11 3LW, UK
UKHW041631190726
13854UKWH00006B/2430

9 798888 157244